access *to* *history*

War and Peace:
International Relations
1878–1941

ESSE

D0620392

30130 164720661

access to history

War and Peace: International Relations 1878–1941

THIRD EDITION

David G. Williamson

HODDER
EDUCATION
AN HACHETTE UK COMPANY

Study Guide authors: Angela Leonard (Edexcel) and Martin Jones (OCR)

The Publishers would like to thank the following for permission to reproduce copyright material:
Photo credits: © Bettmann/CORBIS, pages 26, 50, 63, 71, 75, 95, 177, 193; © BPK, page 39; © CORBIS, pages 64, 191; Hulton Archive/Getty Images, page 68; © Hulton-Deutsch Collection/CORBIS, pages 2, 113, 120, 149, 175; Mary Evans Picture Library, page 3; Popperfoto/Getty Images, page 136.
Acknowledgements: Cambridge University Press for an extract from *Nationalism in Europe* by T. Baycroft, 1998; *The Economist*, page 198; HarperCollins for an extract from *Modern Times* by P. Johnson, 1983; Little, Brown & Company for an extract from *The Search for Peace* by Douglas Hurd, 1997; Longman for an extract from *Europe 1880–1945* by J.M. Roberts, 1972; Penguin for an extract from *Europe Since Napoleon* by D. Thomson, 1966.

Every effort has been made to trace all copyright holders, but if any have been inadvertently overlooked the Publishers will be pleased to make the necessary arrangements at the first opportunity.

Hachette UK's policy is to use papers that are natural, renewable and recyclable products and made from wood grown in sustainable forests. The logging and manufacturing processes are expected to conform to the environmental regulations of the country of origin.

Orders: please contact Bookpoint Ltd, 130 Milton Park, Abingdon, Oxon OX14 4SB. Telephone: (44) 01235 827720. Fax: (44) 01235 400454. Lines are open 9.00–5.00, Monday to Saturday, with a 24-hour message answering service. Visit our website at www.hoddereducation.co.uk

© David G. Williamson 1994
First published in 1994 by
Hodder Education,
An Hachette UK Company
338 Euston Road
London NW1 3BH

Second Edition published in 2003.
This Third Edition published in 2009.

Impression number   5   4   3   2   1
Year   2013   2012   2011   2010   2009

All rights reserved. Apart from any use permitted under UK copyright law, no part of this publication may be reproduced or transmitted in any form or by any means, electronic or mechanical, including photocopying and recording, or held within any information storage and retrieval system, without permission in writing from the publisher or under licence from the Copyright Licensing Agency Limited. Further details of such licences (for reprographic reproduction) may be obtained from the Copyright Licensing Agency Limited, Saffron House, 6–10 Kirby Street, London EC1N 8TS.

Cover image: *The Trail of War*, 1919 (depicting destroyed Turkish aircraft) (oil on canvas), by Sydney Carline (1888–1929), © York Museums Trust (York Art Gallery), UK/The Bridgeman Art Library.
Typeset in 10/12pt Baskerville and produced by Gray Publishing, Tunbridge Wells
Printed in Malta

A catalogue record for this title is available from the British Library.

ISBN: 978 0340 990 148

Contents

Dedication   vii

Chapter 1 International Relations 1879–1941: An Introduction   1
1 The Ideological Background   1
2 The Great Powers 1879–1941   5

Chapter 2 Bismarck's Alliance System 1879–90   12
1 The Period of Adjustment 1871–8   12
2 Bismarck's Web of Alliances 1879–83   17
3 The Anglo-French Quarrel over Egypt and its Consequences   20
4 The Bulgarian Crisis and the Disintegration of the Three Emperors' Alliance   23
5 The Key Debate   27
Study Guide   29

Chapter 3 The Origins of the First World War   30
1 The 'New Course' in German Foreign Policy and its Consequences   31
2 Nationalism and Worldwide Imperial Rivalries   34
3 The Making of the Triple *Entente*   38
4 The Second Moroccan Crisis, 1911, and its Consequences   43
5 The Balkans and the Great Powers 1906–14   46
6 The Outbreak of the First World War 1914   50
7 The Key Debate   54
Study Guide   57

Chapter 4 The First World War 1914–18   59
1 The Military and Strategic Background of the War 1914–15   60
2 1916: The Deadlock Still Unbroken   67
3 1917: 'No Peace without Victory'   69
4 1918: The Final Year of the War   74
5 The Armistices of October and November 1918   76
6 The Key Debate   78
Study Guide   80

Chapter 5 The Peace Settlements 1919–23   81
1 Problems Faced by the Peacemakers   82
2 Aims and Principles of the Victorious Great Powers   83
3 The Organisation of the Paris Peace Conference   86
4 The Settlement with Germany   88
5 The Settlements with Austria, Hungary and Bulgaria   96
6 The Settlement with Turkey 1919–23   99
7 Enforcing the Treaty of Versailles 1920–3   102
8 The Key Debate   105
Study Guide   107

Chapter 6 Reconciliation and Disarmament 1924–30:
The Locarno Era   109
1 The Impact of the Dawes Plan   109
2 The Locarno Treaties   112
3 The 'Locarno Spirit' and Germany's Re-emergence as a Great Power   115
4 Russia and Eastern Europe During the Locarno Era   117
5 The Development of the League of Nations   119
6 Progress Made Towards Disarmament   128
7 The Key Debate   130
Study Guide   132

Chapter 7 The Democracies on the Defensive 1930–6   134
1 The Great Depression 1929–33   135
2 The Rise to Power of Hitler   137
3 The Reaction of the Great Powers to Nazi Germany 1933–5   141
4 The Abyssinian Crisis   146
5 The Remilitarisation of the Rhineland   148
6 The Spanish Civil War   150
7 The Rome–Berlin Axis and the Anti-Comintern Pact   152
8 The Key Debate   153
Study Guide   154

Chapter 8 The Countdown to War in Europe 1937–41   157
1 Hitler Considers his Options   158
2 The Arms Race: Britain, France and Germany 1936–9   159
3 Britain, France and Appeasement   162
4 The *Anschluss* and the Destruction of Czechoslovakia   164
5 The Anglo-French Guarantees and Attempts to Construct a Peace Front   169
6 The Race to Gain the Support of the USSR   171
7 The Outbreak of War   173
8 The Spreading Conflict, October 1940 to June 1941   176
9 The Key Debate   180
Study Guide   182

Chapter 9 The Countdown to War in Asia 1931–41   186
1 The Manchurian Crisis   186
2 The Outbreak of the Sino-Japanese War   190
3 Japan and the Anti-Comintern Pacts 1936–9   192
4 The Road to Pearl Harbor 1940–1   192
5 The Key Debate   195
Study Guide   196

Chapter 10 Interpreting International Relations 1878–1941   197
1 The Causes of the First World War   197
2 The Peace Treaties   198
3 The New Global Balance of Power   198
4 The Fragile Stabilisation 1924–9   199
5 The Road to War in Europe and Asia 1931–41   199

Glossary   204

Index   211

Dedication

Keith Randell (1943–2002)

The *Access to History* series was conceived and developed by Keith, who created a series to 'cater for students as they are, not as we might wish them to be'. He leaves a living legacy of a series that for over 20 years has provided a trusted, stimulating and well-loved accompaniment to post-16 study. Our aim with these new editions is to continue to offer students the best possible support for their studies.

To Antonia

1

International Relations 1879–1941: An Introduction

POINTS TO CONSIDER
The purpose of this introductory chapter is to help you to understand the overall pattern of events before studying the complexity of international relations during the period 1879–1941 in greater detail. It sets the scene by examining:

- The ideological background
- The Great Powers 1879–1941

Key dates

1879		Austro-German Alliance
1894		Franco-Russian Alliance
1904		Anglo-French *Entente*
1907		Anglo-Russian colonial agreement
1914	August	Outbreak of First World War
	October	Turkey declared war on Britain and France
1915		Treaty of London
1917		USA declared war on Germany
	October	Bolshevik revolution in Russia
1918		Defeat of the Central Powers
1919		Treaty of Versailles
1929–33		Great Depression
1933		Hitler appointed Chancellor of Germany
1939		British guarantee of Poland Nazi–Soviet Pact
	September 3	Britain and France declared war on Germany
1941		Germany attacked USSR Pearl Harbor attacked

1 | The Ideological Background

The late nineteenth and the early years of the twentieth century were a period of peace and growing **economic integration**, but at the same time public opinion was becoming more nationalist and imperialist. The emergence of the popular press, the cheap newspapers with a wide circulation, and the extension of the

Key term

Economic integration
Mutual dependence and the coming together of national economies.

franchise all ensured that public opinion increasingly influenced foreign policy. **Imperialism**, **nationalism** and **militarism** were the prevalent national ideologies in the two decades before 1914 and intensified the divisions and tensions between the Great Powers who, in the words of the historian F.S. Northedge, surveyed 'each other through their visors like medieval knights in the jousting field'.

Imperialism

European imperialism and the expansion of power into Africa and Asia in the final two decades of the nineteenth century were caused by several factors. Businessmen and industrialists put pressure on their governments to annex areas where they had important economic interests. Strategy also played a key role. Britain, for instance, occupied Egypt in order to safeguard the Suez Canal and the route to India. Increasingly the Great Powers, fully supported by public opinion, began to believe that they could only remain powerful as long as they had colonial empires which could provide trade, access to raw materials and opportunities for settlement.

Statesmen and political thinkers became affected by **Social Darwinism** and were convinced that international life was a struggle for survival where only the strongest nations would survive. The French economist Paul Lerroy-Beaulieu (1843–1916), for example, stressed that it was 'a matter for life and death' for France to become a 'great African nation or in a century or two she will be no more than a secondary European power, and will count in the world as much as Greece or Romania'.

Kaiser Wilhelm at a German army review in Berlin in 1912. Wilhelm (in the centre on horseback) is surrounded by imperial footguards whose uniforms hark back to King Frederick of Prussia (1740–86).

Key question
Why was imperialism such an influential ideology before 1914?

Imperialism
The policy of acquiring and controlling dependent territories carried out by a state.

Nationalism
A patriotic belief by a people in the virtues and power of their nation.

Militarism
Excessive emphasis on military ideals and strength. The supremacy of military values such as discipline, obedience and courage in a society.

Social Darwinism
The application of Darwin's theory of the survival of the fittest to international relations, justifying the absorption of smaller, weaker states by more powerful ones.

Key terms

Key question
In what ways did nationalism change its character by the end of the nineteenth century?

Nationalism

Imperialism went hand in hand with nationalism. Earlier in the nineteenth century in Italy and Germany nationalism had been essentially a **liberal ideology** aimed at achieving national unification and establishing a constitutional government. The main aim of nationalists was to unite their countries. Once this was achieved the emphasis of nationalism gradually shifted to asserting the power of a nation on the global stage. To unify their countries and overcome class or regional differences, governments frequently exploited nationalism by pursuing a policy that later historians have called **social imperialism**.

Key question
What was militarism?

Militarism

The nationalist and imperialist rivalries of the Great Powers inevitably encouraged militarism. The armed forces were the key instruments, not only in defence, but also in carving out empires and projecting national strength. In Germany, particularly, the army enjoyed huge prestige and was independent of parliamentary control, while in Britain public opinion played a key role in forcing the government to accelerate the construction of modern battleships, the **Dreadnoughts** in 1908 (see page 40). In both Germany and Britain **pressure groups** were formed to force the government to accelerate the build-up of the armed forces. The acceptance of military values by large sections of people in all the great European states undoubtedly contributed to the mood which made war possible and to the enthusiasm with which the outbreak of war in 1914 was greeted in every belligerent state.

Key terms

Liberal ideology
Belief in constitutional government and individual and economic freedom.

Social imperialism
A policy aimed at uniting all social classes behind plans for creating and expanding an empire.

Dreadnought
A battleship of 17,900 tons compared to the conventional size of 16,000, its speed was 21 knots rather than 16, and it was much better armed than its predecessors.

Pressure group
An association formed to promote a particular interest by influencing government policy.

HMS *Dreadnought* – the ship that gave its name to the new style of battleship – leaves Portsmouth escorted by a tug in 1906.

Fascism and National Socialism

Extreme nationalism, imperialism and militarism were all major components of **Fascism** and **National Socialism**, but in Italy and France extreme nationalist groups were already attempting to fuse these ideologies with **socialism** to create a more socially united and therefore stronger national state. One French nationalist, Charles Maurras (1868–1952), wrote in 1899 that there existed 'a form of socialism which when stripped of its democratic and cosmopolitan accretions [additions] would fit with nationalism just as a well-made glove fits a beautiful hand'.

It was the impact and consequences of the First World War that enabled Fascism and Nazism to become mass movements. In Italy, economic crises, a sense of being cheated at the Paris Peace conference in 1919 of its just rewards as a member of the victorious coalition (see page 98), and above all the fear of a Bolshevik revolution, created the context in which Benito Mussolini, the leader of the Italian Fascist Party, gained power in 1922 (see page 126). In Germany it took another 10 years and the impact of the Great Depression (see page 135) before Hitler (see page 137) and German National Socialism could come to power.

Key question
Why did Fascism and National Socialism develop into major political movements after the First World War?

Key terms

Fascism
The Fascist Party was formed in Italy by Mussolini in 1919.

National Socialism
German National Socialism had many similarities with Fascism, but its driving force was race, and in particular anti-Semitism.

Socialism
A belief that the community as a whole rather than individuals should control the economy.

Key date

Great Depression: 1929–33

Summary diagram: The ideological background

Imperialism caused by:
- Economic factors
- Emigration
- Strategic reasons
- National prestige
- Social Darwinism

Militarism defined by:
- Political influence of the armed forces
- Popularity of armed forces in the nation
- Increasing militarisation of the populations

Reinforces nationalism
Makes it more competitive and aggressive

Combination with socialism
Produced National Socialism and Fascism

2 | The Great Powers 1879–1941

The 'have-not powers'

By 1914, Italy, Germany and Japan had managed to acquire only modest empires. All three saw themselves as 'have-not powers', which determined their foreign policy right up to 1941.

Germany

In reality Germany was far from being a 'have-not power'. Its economy was the strongest in Europe, its population growth was outstripping Britain and France and it had the most formidable army, which had defeated France in 1870–1. Yet, looking at the British and French Empires, it perceived itself to be excluded from global power and feared that ultimately it might be strangled by the great imperial powers. Consequently, one of the main themes of German foreign policy from 1890 to 1914 was *Weltpolitik*, which aimed at forcing Britain to hand over some of its colonies to Germany.

When faced with the British blockade in the First World War and the loss of its few possessions in Africa and Asia, Germany sought compensation in Europe and particularly Russia by creating a German-dominated *Mitteleuropa*, which would compensate for its lack of a colonial empire. By November 1918 German troops controlled almost as much of western Russia as Hitler did in the summer of 1942.

This prize was snatched away by defeat on the Western Front in 1918. The Treaty of Versailles stripped Germany of all its wartime gains, global investments and colonies and in the eyes of the German people confirmed its status as a have-not nation, even though its potential strength remained unimpaired. The collapse of Austria-Hungary, the creation of a weak Polish state and Russia's loss of the western Ukraine left Germany in a potentially strong position.

The key question was, how would Germany exploit its latent strength? Would Germany use it, as its foreign minister Gustav Stresemann (see page 111) did between 1924 and 1929, to co-operate with Britain and France in the peaceful reconstruction of a Europe which Germany through its natural strength would come to dominate, or would it use force? Once Hitler was swept into power by the Great Depression, it became increasingly clear which option Germany was going to take. Hitler was determined to colonise western Russia and thereby create *Lebensraum* for the German people and finally free Germany from its dependence on the Western Powers.

Italy

Italy had been unified in the same decade as Germany, and liked to see itself as a Great Power in the traditions of Ancient Rome. In reality, Italy was one of the weakest of the European powers both economically and militarily. In 1896 its attempt to annex Abyssinia ended with a humiliating defeat at Adowa.

Key question
With what justification did German nationalists and imperialists consider Germany to be a 'have-not' power?

Key dates
Outbreak of First World War: August 1914

Treaty of Versailles: 1919

Hitler appointed Chancellor of Germany: 1933

Key terms
Weltpolitik
Literally 'world policy' or a policy that attempted to make Germany a global power.

Mitteleuropa
A German-controlled central Europe.

Lebensraum
Literally 'living space' which Hitler hoped to acquire in Russia for German settlement.

Key question
Why was Italian policy essentially opportunist?

Italian foreign policy right up to 1940 was essentially opportunistic and aimed at securing influence and territory in the Mediterranean. Italy could gain most when Europe was divided into rival alliances, which attempted to outbid each other for its favours. Thus, in May 1915 Italy was bribed by the Treaty of London with promises of territory in North Africa and along the Dalmatian coast to join Britain and France rather than the **Central Powers**.

Key date
Treaty of London: 1915

Although Italy emerged from the war strengthened by the collapse of Austria-Hungary, the failure of the Allies to honour the promises made at the Treaty of London left it embittered, and even more determined to assert its power in the Mediterranean and northern Africa. Indeed, what was called the **'mutilated victory'** of 1918 was one of the causes of Fascism's growing popularity and Mussolini's coming to power in 1922.

In the 1930s Mussolini initially hoped to benefit from Hitler's seizure of power to extract concessions from Britain and France, but their failure to agree to the Italian occupation of Abyssinia gave Mussolini little option but to gravitate towards Nazi Germany. In May 1939 he signed the Pact of Steel with Germany, but did not declare war on Britain and France until June 1940, when he was convinced that with the fall of France Hitler had already won the war.

Key terms

Central Powers
The wartime alliance of Germany, Austria, Turkey and Bulgaria.

'Mutilated victory'
A victory which was scarred by the refusal of the Allies to give Italy what had been promised.

Japan

In 1914, Japan was a formidable regional power with a population of some 46 million. Japan had initially, in 1858, been compelled to grant the Western nations considerable economic privileges and rights when it opened up its ports to trade with the West, but thanks to a policy of rapid modernisation Japan had managed to avoid becoming dependent on any one European power. By 1899 Japan had not only regained its economic freedom, but also embarked on a period of territorial expansion that ended with defeat in 1945.

Key question
Did Japan remain purely a 'regional power' throughout the period 1900–41?

Lacking the strength to operate in isolation and foreseeing confrontation with Russia in Manchuria, Japan negotiated an alliance with Britain which enabled it to defeat Russia in 1905 and strengthen its position in Korea and southern Manchuria (see page 37). Driven on by the intense nationalism of its army officers and the various patriotic societies, both of which were to exercise a powerful influence on foreign policy up to 1945, the Japanese government attempted to exploit the mounting chaos in China caused by the overthrow in 1912 of the Chinese imperial government by internal revolution. For the next 30 years the main aim of Japanese foreign policy was directed towards exploiting the ever-deepening chaos in China in order to build up its own economically self-sufficient empire, the **Greater Asia Co-Prosperity Sphere**. In 1941 this was to bring Japan into direct conflict with the USA.

Key term

Greater Asia Co-Prosperity Sphere
A bloc of territory dominated and exploited by Japan which embraced Manchuria, China and parts of South-east Asia. Japan's aim was to create a self-sufficient bloc free of the Western Powers and under its own control.

The 'haves'

France

France had been defeated by **Prussia** in 1871, and both economically and in terms of population size it had been overtaken by Germany and Britain. France's industrial base was small and its coal deposits were a fraction of those of Britain and Germany. France had nevertheless managed to rebuild and re-equip its army and compensate for the relative smallness of population by building up a large North African empire, which would provide men in time of war.

However, the key to France's survival as an independent power lay in its ability to forge a strong alliance system to contain Germany. The crucial move in this direction was the alliance with Russia in 1894. Worried about the ultimate effectiveness of the Russian Alliance, the French tried to underpin it by bringing years of Anglo-French friction and rivalry to an end through the negotiation of the 1904 colonial agreement and **entente** with London. Germany's and Austria's isolation in Europe by 1914 is striking evidence of the success of French policy in breaking out of the isolation in which Bismarck had initially so successfully confined it for almost 20 years after its defeat.

With British and later US help, France was able to defeat the Central Powers in 1918, but it was a **pyrrhic victory**. France emerged in 1919 as an exhausted power. It had failed to weaken Germany permanently through the Treaty of Versailles, and largely, as a result of the Depression, its attempts to integrate Germany peacefully into Europe also came to nothing (see page 116). With the Nazi seizure of power and Italy's realignment with Germany after 1936, France increasingly became dependent on Britain, and in September 1939 went to war with Germany as Britain's junior partner. France was defeated by Germany in a brief campaign in June 1940.

Great Britain

A Chinese statesman had observed to the British Prime Minister, Lord Salisbury (1830–1903), in the 1890s that Britain and China 'were two empires on the decline'. Although Britain was enormously wealthy in 1914, the fundamental basis of its power was being eroded. Britain had built up its wealth on the basis of domination of the world's trade, underpinned by control of the seas. By 1900 this had been dangerously weakened. France, Russia, Germany and even Italy were all capable of playing a global role and moving into areas such as China, where previously Britain had enjoyed a virtual **trade monopoly**.

Economically, Britain was being overtaken by Germany and the USA and absolute control of the seas was threatened by the construction of the German fleet. Through its sheer size, the British Empire became an unwieldy and vulnerable giant.

Key question
To what extent did French power decline during the period 1871–1941?

Key dates

Franco-Russian Alliance: 1894

Anglo-French *Entente*: 1904

Defeat of the Central Powers: 1918

Britain and France declared war on Germany: 3 September 1939

Key terms

Prussia
The largest federal state in Germany.

Entente
A friendly understanding between states, rather than a formal alliance.

Pyrrhic victory
A victory won at such a high cost that it damages the victor.

Key question
To what extent was Britain a giant with feet of clay during the period 1871–1941?

Key term

Trade monopoly
Exclusive control of trade.

Consequently, Britain attempted to defuse challenges to its position by a policy of compromise and **appeasement**, which enabled the successful negotiations of the Anglo-French and Anglo-Russian colonial agreements of 1904 and 1907.

Britain was ready to appease Germany, too, but only at the cost of Germany abandoning its naval challenge. It was primarily this challenge that led to Britain entering the war in 1914.

Superficially, Britain emerged from the war in 1919 as a clear winner. All its war aims had been fulfilled, but the war had also gravely weakened the British Empire financially and encouraged the growth of nationalism in India, Ireland and Egypt. Britain's decline was masked by US isolationism and the weakness of the USSR and France. As before 1914, Britain tried to safeguard its position through avoiding entanglements and appeasing potential enemies. Only when it became clear that a settlement with Nazi Germany was impossible did Britain take the radical step of guaranteeing Poland. Ultimately Britain went to war in 1939, as in 1914, to stop the German domination of Europe. By the autumn of 1940 Britain had escaped immediate defeat by Nazi Germany, but to continue fighting, it had increasingly to become financially and militarily dependent on US aid.

The great powers of the future
Both Russia and the USA were seen in different ways as the great powers of the future.

Russia
By 1914 Russia had a population that was double the size of Germany's and an economy that was developing rapidly. Nevertheless, the effective deployment of this massive strength was always threatened by domestic instability, which had already boiled over into open revolt in 1905. By 1914 foreign observers were unanimous that Russia was sitting on 'the edge of a volcano'.

In 1917 that volcano erupted. After three years of **total war**, Russia was engulfed by revolution. With the victory of the **Red Army** in the Russian civil war in 1920, the European powers were confronted with **Bolshevism** in power in Russia. Briefly, with the Soviet invasion of Poland in 1920, it seemed as if the Red Army would drive deep into Europe, but it was defeated outside Warsaw and forced to retreat. The creation of a Polish state embracing much of the western Ukraine ensured that the **USSR** was cut off from central Europe until the partition of Poland with Nazi Germany in September 1939 (see page 172).

However, with the coming to power of the Nazis in 1933, the USSR joined the League of Nations, and in 1935 signed a pact with France. At this point it seemed as if the pre-1914 Franco-Russian Alliance had been restored, but Britain's and France's appeasement of Nazi Germany in 1938 during the Sudeten crisis (see page 167) and their deep distrust of Bolshevism ultimately

Key dates

Anglo-Russian colonial agreement: 1907

Bolshevik revolution in Russia: October 1917

British guarantee of Poland: 1939

Key terms

Appeasement
The conciliation of a potential enemy by making concessions. The term is particularly applied to Neville Chamberlain's policy towards Nazi Germany.

Total war
A war waged by a state in which the whole population is involved and every resource is used to further the war.

Key question
What prevented Russia from effectively deploying its potential strength in Europe from 1905 to 1941?

Key terms

Red Army
The Soviet army.

Bolshevism
The ideology of the Russian Communist (Bolshevik) Party. It was based on the theories of Karl Marx and Lenin, which predicted the overthrow of capitalism and the creation of socialism.

Key dates

USA declared war on Germany: April 1917

Nazi–Soviet Pact: 1939

Germany attacked USSR: 1941

Pearl Harbor attacked: 1941

Key question
What role did the USA play in world politics from 1900 to 1941?

Key terms

USSR
The Union of Soviet Socialist Republics. The new Bolshevik name for Russia.

Superpower
A state much larger in size and possessing much larger armed forces than most of the other powers.

Congress
The US parliament.

Great Depression
The world economic slump from 1929 to 1933.

persuaded Stalin to sign the Nazi–Soviet Pact with Hitler in August 1939. In the short term this agreement gave the USSR greater security and kept it out of the war. Stalin assumed that Britain, France and Germany would exhaust themselves fighting in western Europe. Instead France was defeated in June 1940 and the British were expelled from the Continent. In June 1941 Hitler invaded the USSR. His ultimate defeat in 1945 opened the way up to the USSR becoming a **superpower**.

United States of America

The USA for most of the nineteenth century had been shielded from any danger of Continental European intervention by Britain's undisputed supremacy of the seas. The USA had consequently been able to enjoy the benefits of neutrality and isolation in complete security. However, the formidable challenge to the Royal Navy launched by Germany did open up the disturbing prospect of a German naval presence in the Atlantic, and by 1914 the USA had taken the precaution of building up the third largest navy in the world.

Like Japan, the USA also became an imperial power. In the colonial war against Spain in 1898 US forces had seized Cuba and Puerto Rico in the Caribbean and the Philippines and Hawaii in the Far East. Although US public opinion was still isolationist, the USA's extensive financial and economic interests in both Europe and the Far East made it increasingly more difficult for it to keep out of world affairs. This was clearly seen in April 1917 when in response to Germany's determination to sink all neutral ships trading with Britain, of which the largest percentage were American, the USA declared war on Germany.

By 1919 the USA had already emerged as a potential superpower, but far from playing a world role it retreated into isolation when **Congress** effectively vetoed membership of the League of Nations (see page 95). Yet even then the USA could not turn its back on the European economy and between 1924 and 1929 played a key role in formulating the Dawes and Young Plans, which did much economically to stabilise post-war Europe. In the late 1920s there was even speculation that the USA would join the League of Nations.

However, the impact of the **Great Depression** drove the USA back into isolation. Despite the coming to power of Hitler, Congress was determined to keep the USA out of another world war. Although the USA was ready to supply Britain with money and war material in 1940, it was only the Japanese attack on the naval base at Pearl Harbor and Hitler's declaration of war on the USA that finally brought it into the Second World War.

The 'corpses'

In the First World War one German general described his country's two principal wartime allies, the Turkish Empire and Austria-Hungary, as 'rotting corpses'!

Austria-Hungary

Austria-Hungary consisted of two virtually independent states – Austria and Hungary – which shared a common crown and operated a joint foreign policy. The Hungarians strengthened the anti-Russian tendency of Austrian foreign policy as they feared the impact of Russia's sympathy for the Balkan **Slavs** on their own large Slav population. Austria-Hungary contained within its frontiers some 11 different nationalities which were to present the peacemakers of 1919 with insuperable problems when they came to draw up the frontiers of the new small states that replaced the Empire.

Austria's fate was perceived by contemporaries to be linked with the Ottoman Empire. Vienna feared that the Balkan states, which had virtually driven the Turks out of the Balkans by 1912, would eventually also destroy the Austrian Empire. Above all, the Empire felt itself threatened by the emergence of a strong independent Serbia, which it was convinced enjoyed the backing of Russia and was aiming to liberate the Serbs in the Austrian province of Bosnia. The empire's main defence against Russia remained the Austro-German Alliance of 1879. Through this alliance the German problem became linked with the Balkan, or eastern, question with potentially lethal consequences for the peace of Europe, as Berlin's support for Austria began to be regarded by France and Russia as a camouflage for German expansion into south-eastern Europe (see the map on page 47).

The Turkish Empire

In 1914 the Turkish Empire was in a more advanced stage of decay than Austria, but even before 1914 there had been hints of the remarkable revival of energy that was to galvanise the Turks under Mustapha Kemal (see page 101) into forcing the British and French in 1922–3 to renegotiate the punitive peace treaty of Sèvres (see pages 100–1).

In 1908 the **Young Turk Movement**, in a desperate attempt to prevent the disintegration of the Ottoman Empire, seized power and began the process of modernising Turkey. Turkey was then drawn increasingly into the German orbit. In 1913 the German government was invited to send a military mission to Constantinople to help modernise and re-equip the Turkish army, and in October 1914 Turkey declared war on Britain and France.

Turkey's defeat in 1918 led to the loss of its empire in the Middle East to Britain and France. In the Second World War Turkey remained neutral.

Key question
Why did Austria fear the nationalism of the Balkan states?

Key terms

Slavs
An ethnic group in central and eastern Europe, of which the Russians are the largest component.

Young Turk Movement
The name given to a reform movement in the Turkish Empire. Its members were originally exiles in western Europe.

Key question
To what extent was the Turkish Empire in decline?

Key dates

Austro-German Alliance: 1879

Turkey declared war on Britain and France: October 1914

Summary diagram: The Great Powers 1879–1941

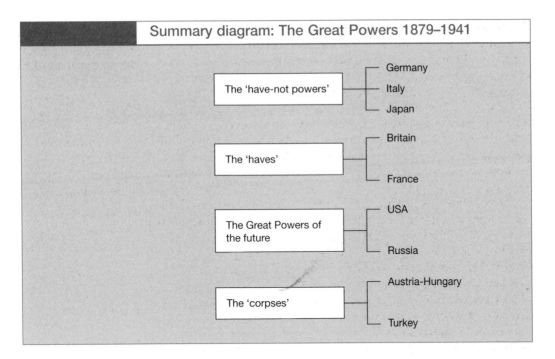

2 Bismarck's Alliance System 1879–90

POINTS TO CONSIDER

The defeat of France by Prussia in 1871 led to the creation of the German Empire and a major shift in the balance of power in Europe. This chapter analyses the consequences of these events under the following headings:

- The period of adjustment 1871–8
- Bismarck's web of alliances 1879–83
- The Anglo-French quarrel over Egypt and its consequences
- The Bulgarian crisis and the disintegration of the Three Emperors' Alliance

Key dates

1871	Treaty of Frankfurt: war ended between France and Germany
1873	League of the Three Emperors created
1878	Congress of Berlin
1879	Austro-German Alliance
1881	Three Emperors' Alliance
1882	Triple Alliance
	British forces landed in Egypt
1884–5	Foundations of the German colonial empire laid
1885	Bulgaria and Eastern Roumelia united
1887	Reinsurance Treaty
1890	Bismarck dismissed

1 | The Period of Adjustment 1871–8

The unification of Germany

The defeat of first Austria in 1866 and then France in 1871 by Prussia was to have a profound effect on international relations. Before 1867 Germany as a unified state had not existed. Instead there was a loose **confederation** of 39 German states, which was dominated by Prussia and Austria. Rivalry between these two states erupted into war in 1866 and led to the creation of the North German Confederation. Unlike the former German Confederation this was essentially a powerful new German state dominated by Prussia with the potential to change the balance of power in Europe. France was therefore determined to veto any

Key question
Why did Disraeli argue that the unification of Germany was a 'revolutionary' event?

Confederation
A grouping of states in which each state retains its sovereignty.

Key term

Central and eastern Europe in 1871.

Key date

Treaty of Frankfurt –
war ended between
France and Germany:
1871

move to complete German unification by Prussia and in 1870
declared war. French defeat in 1871 led to the creation of the
German Empire, whose birth, to the utter humiliation of France,
was proclaimed in the Hall of Mirrors in the Palace of Versailles
on 30 January. In May the war was ended with the Treaty of
Frankfurt by which France ceded the provinces of Alsace and
Lorraine to Germany and an indemnity was to be paid after
which the Prussian army of occupation would be withdrawn from
northern France.

Profile: Otto von Bismarck 1815–98

1815	Born in Schönhausen
1848	Made a reputation for himself as an ultra-reactionary supporting the Crown during the revolts of 1848–9
1851–8	Prussian ambassador at Frankfurt
1859–61	Prussian ambassador at St Petersburg and Paris
1862	Appointed Chief Minister of Prussia
1866	Established North German Confederation after the defeat of Austria
1871–90	Chancellor of the German Reich
1890	Dismissed by Kaiser Wilhelm II
1898	Died

Bismarck was born into an old, established, landed family in Prussia. He entered politics in 1847 and made a reputation for himself as an extreme **counter-revolutionary** when he supported the Prussian King during the revolutionary turmoil of the years 1848–9. As a reward he was appointed Prussian ambassador to the German Confederation in 1851. He rapidly became critical of Austria's attempt to dominate the Confederation and at every opportunity urged Prussia to seize the leadership of Germany. He became the Prime Minister of Prussia in 1862 and, after defeating both Austria and France, created the German *Reich* in 1871. Up to 1871 he was intent on challenging the existing order, but once Germany was unified he was anxious to avoid any further changes which might destroy what he had created.

Some historians see him as the single-handed saviour of the peace between 1871 and 1890. The American scholar William Langer, in his classic study *European Alliances and Alignments, 1871–90*, argues that 'no other statesman of [Bismarck's] standing had ever before shown the same great moderation and sound political sense of the possible and desirable', but this view is not shared by all historians. Bruce Waller, for instance, has pointed out that Langer's views on German foreign policy 'were strongly coloured by the effort to take a fair-minded view after the excesses of First World War propaganda'. He argues that Bismarck 'created and preserved tension' by encouraging rivalry in the colonies and the Balkans and even suggests that at times 'Bismarck's actions would have led to war had it not been for the good sense of other European statesmen'.

However, even if Bismarck's skills are exaggerated, unlike his successors in 1914 (see page 50), he did use the Austro-German Alliance of 1879 to moderate Austrian policy. Arguably it is hard to believe that war would have broken out in 1914 if Bismarck's policies had still been followed.

Key terms

Counter-revolutionary
Person who opposes a revolution and wants to reverse its results.

Reich
Empire.

Key figure

Benjamin Disraeli (1804–81)
Tory leader in the House of Commons for 20 years, British Prime Minister 1868 and 1874–80. He was an ardent imperialist who believed that patriotism and nationalism could overcome class divisions.

The creation of the German Empire marked a real shift in the balance of power in Europe. **Disraeli**, the leader of the Conservative Party in Britain, went so far as to argue in the House of Commons that:

> This war represents the German revolution, a greater political event than the French revolution of the last century … You have a new world, new influences at work, new and unknown objects and dangers with which to cope … The balance of power has been entirely destroyed …

The new Germany possessed the most formidable and experienced military force in Europe, based on a growing economic strength. It had abundant supplies of coal and iron ore in the Ruhr and Upper Silesia and, thanks to the growth of the railways, an integrated economy. Already by the early 1870s many of the great firms, such as Krupp and Thyssen, which were to become world leaders some 30 years later, were established.

Of course, economically the Germany of the 1870s was not yet as strong as the Germany of 1913, but even so its unique combination of military and economic strength had its own dangers. Sooner or later France would recover and would seek to reverse its defeat of 1871. If Germany used power unwisely and inspired fear, it would be all the easier for France to gain allies and encircle Germany with a hostile alliance. Count Otto von Bismarck, the German Chancellor, was all too aware of this danger. He sought therefore to isolate France and reassure Britain, Austria and Russia that Germany was a 'satiated' state.

The Balkans and the League of the Three Emperors

Key question
Why were the Balkans an area of potential international crisis?

For Bismarck there was also the danger that Germany might become involved in an Austro-Russian war over the future of the Balkans. The accelerating decline of the Turkish power opened up the prospect that Turkish rule in the Balkans might collapse. For both Russia and Austria, the Balkans were of great strategic importance. Russia could not allow a hostile power to control the western shores of the Black Sea and the straits of the Bosphorus and Dardanelles, which were the main access to the Mediterranean. Similarly, Austria did not want the emergence of an independent group of Balkan states which would block any future extension of its influence into the Balkans, and also attract the support of the Slavs within its own empire, particularly within Hungary. Britain too was concerned about the Russian threat to its position in both the Mediterranean and India, and did not want to see Russia fill the **vacuum of power** left by the decline of Turkey (see the map on page 47).

Key date
League of the Three Emperors created: 1873

Key term
Vacuum of power
Territories left undominated by another state after the withdrawal or collapse of the original ruling power.

Both Russia and Austria attempted to enlist Germany as a future ally, but initially Bismarck was able to avoid any unilateral commitment by proposing that the three powers form the League of the Three Emperors. In the event of a crisis they would only consult together with each other.

The Eastern crisis of 1875–8

The advantage for Germany of the League of the Three Emperors was that it isolated France and enabled Germany to avoid making a choice between Russia and Austria. It was in many ways the model for German foreign policy until Bismarck's dismissal in 1890. However, the eruption of the great Eastern crisis ultimately forced Bismarck to make a choice between Russia and Austria, even though he spent the next decade attempting to bring these powers together again.

The crisis began in July 1875 with a revolt against Turkish rule in Bosnia and Herzegovina. Within a year it had spread to Bulgaria, and Serbia and Montenegro declared war on Turkey. Briefly it looked as if the whole Turkish Empire in Europe would collapse, but contrary to expectation the Turks defeated the Serbs and stabilised the situation.

The Eastern crisis now entered a new and dangerous phase as the Russian government was not ready to sit back and tolerate Turkey re-establishing itself in the Balkans. Initially Russia did obtain Austrian consent to drive the Turks out of the Balkans, provided it did not set up a large pro-Russian Bulgaria and allowed Austria to occupy Bosnia and Herzegovina. Russian troops advanced on Constantinople. Turkey held out until January 1878, but was then forced to agree to a peace that, contrary to all assurances, set up a large and apparently pro-Russian Bulgaria. Inevitably this triggered a major international crisis which could have resulted in war between Russia and Austria which would be backed by Britain. It opened up the scenario that Bismarck dreaded: France would be able to offer assistance to one or other of the belligerents in return for a promise to revise the Treaty of Frankfurt.

Key question
What international problems did the Eastern crisis of 1875–8 cause?

The Berlin Congress

Faced with the Eastern crisis it is not surprising that Bismarck agreed to hosting, at Austria's suggestion, a congress at Berlin. Bismarck in his role as '**honest broker**' dominated the negotiations. Yet however hard he tried to be neutral, the very fact that he presided over a congress that stripped Russia of many of its gains from the Turkish war made the Russians bitterly resentful of Germany's 'false friendship'.

Under Bismarck's skilful chairmanship the congress managed to find at least temporary solutions to some of the intractable problems of the Balkans:

- Bulgaria was broken up into three parts. The largest of these sections was the core state of Bulgaria, which officially became a **self-governing principality** ultimately under Turkish control. The Russians were to control its administration for nine months until a new government could be formed. The second part, Eastern Roumelia, was to be placed under a Turkish governor, although a commission of European powers was to draw up a reform programme for him to introduce, while the rest of Bulgaria was returned to direct Turkish control.

Key question
What decisions were taken at the Berlin Congress?

Key terms

Honest broker
Impartial mediator.

Self-governing principality
A semi-independent state ruled by a prince.

Key date

Congress of Berlin: 1878

- The three Balkan states of Serbia, Montenegro and Romania gained complete independence but lost some of the land given to them by the Russians.
- Austria was given the right to occupy, but not annex, Bosnia and Herzegovina and to station troops in the Novi Pazar region between Serbia and Montenegro.
- Britain was permitted to occupy Cyprus, and France was encouraged eventually to move into Tunisia (see the map on page 47).

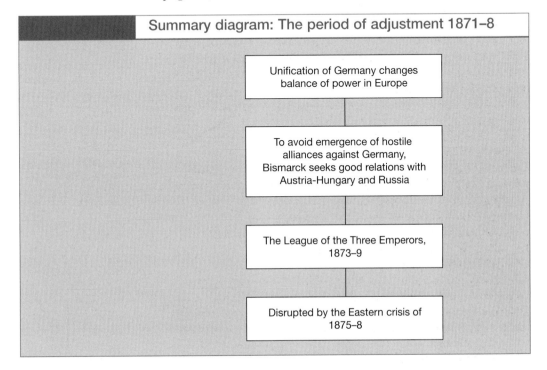

Summary diagram: The period of adjustment 1871–8

Unification of Germany changes balance of power in Europe

To avoid emergence of hostile alliances against Germany, Bismarck seeks good relations with Austria-Hungary and Russia

The League of the Three Emperors, 1873–9

Disrupted by the Eastern crisis of 1875–8

Key question
What was the significance of the Dual Alliance?

Key term

Tariffs
Taxes placed on imported goods to protect the home economy.

Key date

Austro-German Alliance: 1879

2 | Bismarck's Web of Alliances 1879–83

The Austro-German Dual Alliance 1879

A major consequence of the Berlin Congress was the deterioration in relations between Germany and Russia. In July 1879 the German government further antagonised the Russians by introducing grain **tariffs** to protect German agriculture by excluding cheap, imported Russian grain. This was a serious economic blow to Russia as nearly 75 per cent of its exports were grain, a large proportion of which went to Germany.

Bismarck would have preferred to renew the Three Emperors' League, but in the face of mounting Russian hostility this was, in the short term at any rate, impossible. Instead he began to consider a defensive alliance with Austria alone. During the Eastern crisis he had come to the conclusion that in the final analysis Germany could not tolerate the defeat of Austria by Russia as this would immeasurably strengthen Russia and directly threaten Germany's future security. Consequently on 7 October 1879 the Austro-German Dual Alliance was signed.

Its terms were:

- Should one power be attacked by Russia, the other would come to its rescue with 'the whole war strength' of its empire.
- If one of the two empires were attacked by any other power, its ally would adopt a neutral but friendly attitude.
- The treaty was in the first instance to last five years but could be renewed.
- It was secret, but in the event of Russian threats its gist would be leaked to the Tsar to deter him from taking any further action.

The Dual Alliance gave Germany considerable influence over Austrian foreign policy. Bismarck was to exploit this to ensure that Vienna did not provoke an unnecessary war with Russia. He also hoped that the mere existence of the treaty, even if its details were secret, would force Russia back into negotiations with Austria and Germany.

The Alliance of the Three Emperors

Bismarck's calculations proved correct. Although the **Pan Slav** nationalists urged Tsar Alexander II to ally with France and attack Austria, the Russian foreign office doubted whether France would be able to offer much assistance in the Balkans and managed to persuade the Tsar to agree to opening negotiations with Germany.

Talks began with Bismarck in January 1880. The Russians wanted an agreement that would recognise their gains in the Balkans and close the Straits of the Bosphorus and the Dardanelles to the British navy. Bismarck was not ready to sign a treaty with Russia unless Austria was also involved. At first Austria still pinned hopes on co-operation with Britain against Russia, but with the defeat of Disraeli in the general election of 1880, British foreign policy became markedly less hostile to Russia. Under German pressure, Vienna therefore agreed somewhat reluctantly to accept a new version of the Three Emperors' League. The Three Emperor's Alliance was signed with Russia on 18 June 1881. Its main terms were:

- Austria-Hungary and Germany agreed that the Straits should be closed to the warships of all nations. This stopped the threat of Britain sending its navy into the Black Sea and greatly strengthened Russia's position.
- Austria conceded the eventual reunification of Bulgaria, while Russia agreed that at some time in the future Austria would be able to annex Bosnia and Herzegovina.
- If a member of the League found itself at war with a fourth power, unless it was Turkey, the other two powers would remain neutral.
- There were to be no further changes in the Turkish Empire without the consent of the three empires.
- The treaty was in the first instance to last three years.

Key question
What was the aim of the Alliance of the Three Emperors?

Pan Slavs
Russian nationalists who believed that the Slavs in central and south-eastern Europe should be liberated by their fellow Slavs in Russia.

Key term

Three Emperors' Alliance: 1881

Key date

The treaty did not provide any long-term solution to Austro-Russian rivalry in the Balkans, but it did temporarily reduce the friction between Austria and Russia.

The Triple Alliance 1882

Despite the Three Emperors' Alliance, Russian policy in the Balkans remained unpredictable. The new Tsar Alexander III continued to receive advice from the Pan Slav leaders who were also beginning to establish contacts with Russian sympathisers in the French army and media.

Bismarck's response was to strengthen the Austro-German Dual Alliance. First he expanded it in 1882 into a Triple Alliance with Italy. Since Austria had controlled much of northern Italy, and in 1859 and again in 1866 had fought to prevent its unification, the Italian government had understandably seen Austria as a hostile power. It also had claims to the Italian-speaking Tyrol and Trieste, which were still controlled by Austria. However, the French occupation of Tunis in 1881, which the Italians regarded as their own sphere of interest, caused Italy to propose an alliance with Austria. Bismarck immediately suggested extending it into a Triple Alliance. The key clauses of the treaty were:

- Both the Central Powers were now committed to support Italy in the unlikely chance of an attack from France.
- Italy, in turn, would help them only if they were attacked by two other powers (say France and Russia).

Key question
How did Bismarck manage to strengthen Austria against Russia?

Key date
Triple Alliance: 1882

A French cartoonist's view of the Triple Alliance.

The real gain for Germany was that if war broke out with Russia, Austria would now no longer have to keep troops on its Italian frontier just in case Italy might be tempted to make a surprise attack to the rear.

Austria's position was then further strengthened by an alliance with Serbia in June 1882 and with Romania in 1883 which Germany joined and turned into a **defensive alliance** against Russia. Simultaneously, Bismarck also successfully strengthened the influence of the pro-German ministers in the Russian government by both refusing demands at home for further rises in tariffs, which would damage Russian trade, and encouraging German banks to finance Russian loans. As a result in 1884 the Tsar agreed to renew the Three Emperors' Treaty.

Key terms

Defensive alliance
An agreement between two states whereby each will come to the defence of the other if attacked.

Khedive
The title used by the governor and ruler of Egypt and the Sudan.

Summary diagram: Bismarck's web of alliances 1879–83	
Dual Alliance	Germany and Austria, 1879–1918
Alliance of the Three Emperors	Germany, Austria and Russia, 1881–5
Triple Alliance	Germany, Austria and Italy, 1882–1915

3 | The Anglo-French Quarrel over Egypt and its Consequences

Anglo-French involvement in Egypt

Ever since Napoleon's invasion of Egypt in 1798 the French had considered Egypt as an area of special interest to them. Egypt was a self-governing territory within the Turkish Empire which was ruled by the **Khedive**.

The Suez Canal, which was opened in 1869, was built by a French company. This at a stroke revolutionised, to quote the historian A.J.P. Taylor, 'the geography of world power', and it rapidly became a key link in Britain's communication with India. In 1875 Britain became the majority shareholder in the Suez Canal Company when it bought 40 per cent of the shares from the Khedive.

In April 1876, Egypt went bankrupt and could no longer pay the interest on the money lent by Europeans investors. Britain and France consequently agreed to take over joint control of Egypt's finances. For five years they co-operated amicably, but problems developed when they faced a nationalist uprising led by officers in the Egyptian army. This swept across Egypt and threatened the security of the canal itself. Initially, the French government was ready to send troops to occupy the zone together with the British, but at the last moment the French parliament vetoed the dispatch of French troops, and it was left to the British to restore order. The nationalist forces were subsequently defeated at Tel-el-Kebir in September 1882.

Key question
Why did the French resent the British occupation of Egypt?

Key date
British forces landed in Egypt: 1882

Unexpectedly, the British had now become the masters of Egypt, and despite repeated assurances that they would leave as soon as order had been restored, they did not do so until 1922. Indeed, it was not until 1956 that they finally quit the canal zone.

British action in 1882 infuriated the French and made any co-operation with Britain virtually impossible for more than 20 years. Illogically, the French felt humiliated and cheated by Britain's action even though it was their parliament which had vetoed any French participation in it. They saw the British apparently in permanent control of a key territory of the Turkish Empire, which they considered was their own special sphere of interest.

Key question
What were the consequences of the Anglo-French quarrel over Egypt?

Germany's exploitation of the Anglo-French quarrel

Bismarck had made no secret of the fact that he wished to encourage France to seek compensation for the loss of Alsace-Lorraine by building up a colonial empire in Africa. In 1880 he told the French ambassador: 'I want you to take your eyes from Metz and Strasbourg by helping you find satisfaction elsewhere.' This would both distract France from seeking revenge against

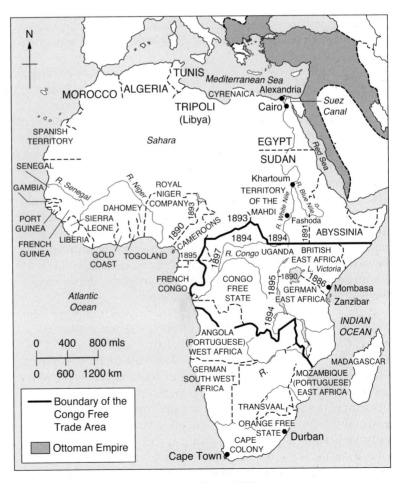

European colonies and interests in Africa 1897.

Germany and create tension with the other colonial powers, particularly Britain. At the same time, Bismarck could exploit Britain's isolation to squeeze concessions and satisfy the growing demand in Germany for colonies. He commented to the German ambassador in London that 'England can secure for herself the continuance of our active support for her political interests through sacrifices which she would hardly feel.'

In 1884 the German government, in order to protect German trading interests and forestall British claims, annexed territory in South West Africa, the Cameroons, Togoland and New Guinea. In the following year Germany and France were able to co-operate and override British objections to calling an international conference in Berlin to decide on the future of a huge belt of central African territory stretching from the Atlantic to the Indian Ocean. Relations improved dramatically, and the French Prime Minister, **Jules Ferry**, commented that France was no longer 'the Cinderella of European politics'.

The end of Franco-German co-operation

By early 1885 the cost of the French military campaign to colonise Indo-China was becoming increasingly unpopular with the French public. When the news came through that the French had been pushed out of Lang-Son, riots broke out in Paris, and the Ferry government fell.

Over the course of the summer the new government gradually reverted to a more anti-German policy. In October, the Prime Minister, Louis Freycinet (1828–1923), was forced to accept as Minister of War the **charismatic** and fiercely nationalistic General **Boulanger**, who believed that his mission was to prepare for war against Germany. He rapidly became a cult figure for the extreme nationalist **League of Patriots**, and for a time it seemed, much to the alarm of Bismarck, that he might even seize power and become a dictator. The German army was confident that it could again defeat the French, but it was doubtful whether France could now be dealt with in isolation. French attempts to establish closer relations with Russia were powerfully helped by the eruption of the Bulgarian crisis (see page 23), and in the autumn of 1886 for a brief period of time it looked as if a Franco-Russian Alliance directed against Germany might be possible.

Key date

Foundations of the German colonial empire laid: 1884–5

Key figure

Jules Ferry (1832–93) Prime Minister of France 1880–1 and 1883–5.

Key question
Why was Franco-German co-operation so short-lived?

Key terms

Charismatic Inspiring great enthusiasm and loyalty.

League of Patriots The French far-right league, founded by the nationalist poet Paul Déroulède in 1882.

Key figure

Georges Boulanger (1837–91) Entered French politics in 1884 and was an effective and charismatic War Minister. He appealed to those who wanted revenge against Germany. In 1889 it seemed as if he might stage a coup, but he lost his nerve and fled to Brussels.

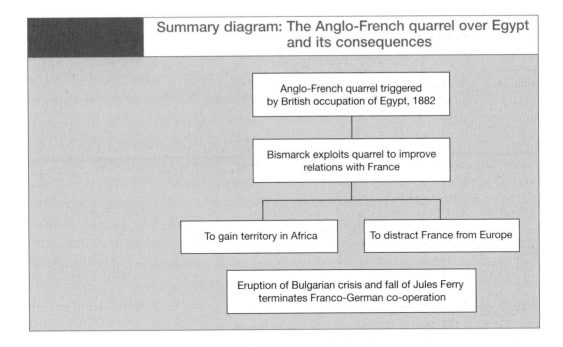

Summary diagram: The Anglo-French quarrel over Egypt and its consequences

Anglo-French quarrel triggered by British occupation of Egypt, 1882

Bismarck exploits quarrel to improve relations with France

To gain territory in Africa

To distract France from Europe

Eruption of Bulgarian crisis and fall of Jules Ferry terminates Franco-German co-operation

4 | The Bulgarian Crisis and the Disintegration of the Three Emperors' Alliance

Developments in Bulgaria 1879–87

At the Berlin Congress it was agreed that the Russians should administer **rump Bulgaria** for a transition period of nine months before handing the state over to an elected ruler, who would administer it as a self-governing territory within the Turkish Empire (see page 16). In April 1879 when Prince Alexander of Battenberg, the nephew of the Tsar, was elected Prince of Bulgaria, the Russians hoped at first that they would effectively be able to dominate the new government behind the scenes. However, tension rapidly began to develop between Alexander and his Russia advisors. In September 1883, he asserted his own independence by expelling two key Russian officials.

The Russians were now determined to remove Alexander, but in September 1885 his position appeared to be strengthened when a revolt broke out in Eastern Roumelia, which resulted in its unification with Bulgaria. The Russians accepted a compromise put forward by Britain whereby the two states would remain technically separated but under the same ruler. They were not, however, ready to tolerate Alexander as that ruler. In August 1886 the Russians had him kidnapped and forced him to abdicate. Even then the Bulgarian parliament stubbornly refused to accept the Russian candidate, General Ernroth, as its ruler and voted instead in July 1887 for Prince Ferdinand of Coburg, who was born in Vienna and had served in the Austrian army.

Key question
Why did the Russians want to remove Alexander?

Key term

Rump Bulgaria
What was left of Bulgaria after its partition at the Berlin Congress.

Key date

Bulgaria and Eastern Roumelia united: 1885

The international impact of the crisis

Alexander's kidnapping revived British and Austrian fears of Russia's intention of taking over Bulgaria. The Austrian Foreign Minister made it clear in November 1886 that 'even a temporary single-handed occupation of Bulgaria by foreign troops [meaning, of course, Russian], without the previous consent of Turkey and the other powers would be a violation of the treaties, which in our opinion is not admissible'. Meanwhile in Berlin the Russian ambassador told Bismarck that 'It is absolutely necessary that we should make Austria disappear from the map of Europe.'

The League of the Three Emperors was visibly falling apart. War between Russia and Austria now seemed possible and Austria and Britain both looked to Berlin to take the lead against Russia, but Bismarck was determined not to be pushed into confrontation especially at the very time that Boulanger was urging a war of revenge against Germany. He attempted to restrain both Austria and Russia, whom he described as 'two savage dogs'. Bismarck again made very clear to his Austrian allies that Germany would not be dragged into war against Russia. On the other hand, he was not prepared to stand back and see Austria defeated by Russia. To reconcile these two often conflicting objectives he pursued his traditional policy of strengthening Austria while at the same time attempting to reassure Russia of Germany's peaceful intentions.

Bismarck aimed to deter Russian expansion into the Balkans by encouraging Britain, Italy and Austria-Hungary to negotiate the First Mediterranean Agreement in February 1887. This provided for the maintenance of the **status quo** in the Mediterranean, including the Adriatic and Aegean seas. He hoped that the agreement would encourage these three powers to stand up to Russia and convince Tsar Alexander that only through negotiations with Berlin could a compromise over Bulgaria be arranged.

The Reinsurance Treaty, 18 June 1887

Any improvement in Germany's relations with Russia was dependent on the outcome of the struggle to influence the Tsar which was bitterly waged between the Pan Slavs and the traditionally pro-German officials of the Russian Foreign Office. In March 1887 Tsar Alexander III finally became impatient with the increasingly more outspoken attempts of the Pan Slavs to influence his foreign policy and rejected their demands for a break with Germany. He still refused, however, to follow the advice of his Foreign Minister, to renew the Three Emperors' Treaty of 1881, but he did agree to negotiate a secret three-year agreement with Germany, which was signed on 18 June 1887. Its terms were:

- Both empires were pledged to be neutral in a war fought against a third power unless Germany attacked France or Russia, Austria.

Key question
How did Bismarck keep peace between Austria and Russia?

Status quo
A Latin term to denote the state of affairs as it exists at the moment.

Key term

Key question
What was the role of the Reinsurance Treaty in Bismarck's alliance system?

Reinsurance Treaty: June 1887

Key date

- Germany recognised the rights 'historically acquired' by Russia in the Balkans, particularly in Bulgaria and Eastern Roumelia.
- Turkey was not to open the Straits to the navy of a power hostile to Russia – this essentially meant Britain. If the Straits were opened, Germany and Russia would regard it as a hostile act towards themselves.

In his attempt to reconcile Austria and Russia, Bismarck had effectively created two contradictory diplomatic systems. On the one hand the Reinsurance Treaty promised Russia German backing at the Straits and in Bulgaria, while the Mediterranean Agreement, the negotiation of which was encouraged by Bismarck, supported Austria by encouraging the territorial status quo.

Key question
What was the impact of the Bulgarian crisis on Franco-German relations?

The impact of the Bulgarian crisis on Franco-German relations

Bismarck's ultimate fear was that if an Austro-Russian war over Bulgaria broke out, Germany would face the threat of a war on two fronts. Throughout 1886 there was growing support in France for a war of revenge. In 1887 popular excitement in both Germany and France reached fever pitch when a French frontier official was arrested by German frontier guards. Tempers cooled, however, when it was discovered that he had in fact been invited across the frontier to discuss official business, and Bismarck intervened personally to order his release. In May relations with Germany began to improve when Boulanger, as a result of a change in government, resigned as War Minister.

While concentrating mainly on defusing the Bulgarian crisis, Bismarck was also able successfully to isolate France in western Europe. The Triple Alliance (see page 19) was renewed in February 1887 and an Italian–Spanish Agreement was signed aimed at preventing French colonial expansion in North Africa. By May 1887 France, as the historian William Langer observed, was 'completely hedged about'.

Key terms

Reichsbank
The national bank of Germany.

Bonds
Certificates issued by a government or large company promising to repay borrowed money at a fixed rate of interest by a specified date.

Key question
How did Bismarck seek to deter Russian aggression after the Bulgarian crisis?

The aftermath of the Bulgarian crisis

The Reinsurance Treaty did not immediately calm the tension in the Balkans. The election of Prince Ferdinand of Coburg to the Bulgarian throne in July 1887 was regarded by the Russians as an Austrian conspiracy. Once again the Pan Slavs whipped up a press campaign against Germany, which was accused of secretly supporting Austria. In the autumn the Russians carried out large-scale troop manoeuvres on Germany's eastern borders and, so it seemed, began to prepare to advance into Bulgaria. To stop this, Bismarck very effectively used financial pressure. In November 1887 the German government stopped the *Reichsbank* from accepting Russian **bonds** as **collateral security** for loans raised in Germany.

This financial pressure had very serious economic consequences for the Russians as Germany was the source of most of its foreign loans. Russia was plunged into financial chaos which effectively prevented it from occupying Bulgaria or risking war with Austria.

Key term

Collateral security
Bonds or property pledged as a guarantee for the repayment of a loan.

In December, Bismarck, again quite contrary to the spirit of the Reinsurance Treaty, further strengthened the position of Austria by persuading Britain and Italy to conclude with it a second Mediterranean Agreement aimed at keeping Russia out of Bulgaria and Turkey. These measures successfully deterred the Russians from invading Bulgaria, but they continued to do everything they could to undermine Ferdinand of Coburg. They also turned to France for the loans which the Germans were no longer ready to finance. Inevitably this strengthened Franco-Russian relations, but neither side was yet ready to conclude an alliance.

'Dropping the Pilot.' *Punch*'s view on Bismarck's departure.

Bismarck's dismissal

Bismarck dismissed: 1890

When William II came to the German throne in June 1888 (see page 32), and began to urge on Bismarck a British alliance, the Tsar rapidly became more appreciative of Bismarck's policy and offered to renew the Reinsurance Treaty permanently. Bismarck, however, was dismissed in March 1890 before negotiations could begin and his successor, convinced that it contradicted the Triple Alliance and would complicate Germany's relations with Britain, did not renew it. This effectively signalled the end of the Bismarckian alliance system.

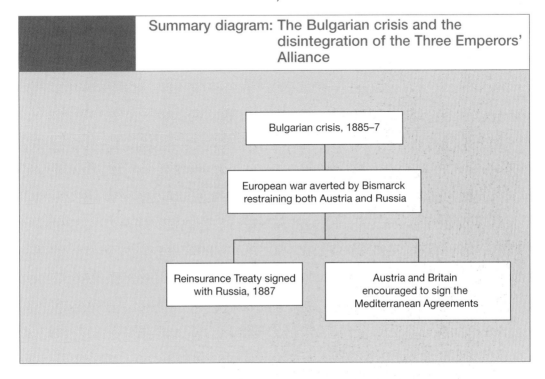

Summary diagram: The Bulgarian crisis and the disintegration of the Three Emperors' Alliance

5 | The Key Debate

Why was France not in the position to challenge Germany in 1871–90?

By the 1870s there were two major fault-lines in Europe: Franco-German tension resulting from France's defeat by Germany in 1871 and Austro-Russian rivalry caused by the decline of Turkish power in the Balkans.

Franco-German tension

Republic
A state ruled by a president rather than a monarch.

France rapidly restored its finances and rebuilt its armed forces after the defeat. Yet alone France was not capable of defeating Germany. As a **republic**, France was viewed with suspicion by both the emperors of Austria and Russia, and in 1882 it had quarrelled with Britain over Egypt. France was not therefore in a position to build up a hostile coalition against Germany. However, in a major war involving Germany, it would almost certainly be numbered among Germany's enemies. France would fight to prevent a German-dominated Europe. Nevertheless as long as Germany remained a 'satiated' power and did not threaten any other European state, France had little option but to accept the verdict of 1871.

The Balkans

It was the Balkans that were the real threat to peace. The accelerating decline in Turkish power left a vacuum, which neither Russia nor Austria could allow the other to fill. Here was a real clash that could have led to war in 1878 and again in 1885–7. It was an area of instability that could erupt into crisis at any time. At times it seemed as if Austria and Russia would agree on creating zones of influence in the Balkans, but their mutual distrust was too great. Essentially by 1890 there appeared to be no obvious solution in sight. Peace depended on a mixture of luck, mutual deterrence and restraint.

Key question
Why did peace in the Balkans depend on a mixture of luck, mutual deterrence and restraint?

The role of Germany

The key to containing these areas of conflict lay in Berlin. Given Germany's position at the centre of the European continent every crisis involving the European powers had potentially important consequences for its security. An aggressive Germany could fuse these tensions into an enormous explosion, which could trigger a major conflict. Bismarck above all feared that a major war over the Balkans would give France the chance to break out of isolation and revise the Treaty of Frankfurt. Germany was thus forced into pursuing out of self-preservation what amounted to a European rather than a German foreign policy.

Key question
Why was Germany forced into pursuing a 'European rather than a German foreign policy'?

Study Guide: A2 Question

In the style of Edexcel

'The pattern of alliances and agreements formed in
Europe in the years 1879–1907 was shaped primarily by
Germany's concerns about its security.' How far do you
agree with this opinion? (30 marks)

Exam tips

*The page references are intended to take you straight to the material
that will help you to answer the question.*

In order to answer this question you should reread Chapter 1,
pages 5–8, and read Chapter 3, pages 31–3, as well as the relevant
sections of Chapter 2 indicated below.

This question will require you to consider how far the changes in
international relations were influenced by Germany's concerns and
how far by the concerns of the other powers players involved –
Russia, Austria, Britain and France. You will also be expected to
assess how far German policy was essentially defensive throughout
the period. How far did the New Course (pages 31–2) depart from
the principles underpinning Bismarck's policy designed to protect
the gains of the Treaty of Frankfurt? How far do the policies of
Weltpolitik and the development of the naval arms race indicate a
change in the direction and objectives of German policy?

In dealing with the interests of the other powers, you should keep
in mind Austro-Russian rivalry over the Balkans and Anglo-French
imperial rivalry.

In the process of organising your information, you should consider
which factors were primarily responsible for shaping the following
developments:

- the Dual Alliance of 1879 (pages 17–18)
- the Alliance of the Three Emperors 1881 (pages 18–19)
- the Triple Alliance 1882 (pages 19–20)
- the Reinsurance Treaty 1887 (pages 24–5)
- the non-renewal of the Reinsurance Treaty in 1890 (page 31)
- the Franco-Russian Alliance 1894 (page 33)
- the Franco-British Agreement 1904 (pages 40–1)
- the formation of the Triple *Entente* 1907 (pages 38–43).

You could decide to deal with each in turn, but your answer may be
stronger if you instead decide which factors were significant in
shaping agreements, and organise your material around these
factors. For example, the formation of the Triple *Entente* of 1907 was
driven by very different concerns from those which shaped the Dual
Alliance of 1879.

In reaching your overall conclusion on both aspects of the
question, you should take account of imperialism as a key factor
which influenced German policy in the latter part of the period, and
the policies of Britain and France throughout it.

3 The Origins of the First World War

POINTS TO CONSIDER

In 1907 a German economist, Sartorius von Waltherhausen, observed that contemporary Europe was 'a terrible contradiction'. On the one hand, 'we see how the members of the various nations come together ever more frequently … how they try to understand each other, try to learn from each other, that the races of neighbouring countries are becoming more and more mixed by migration and marriage, that no great work of science, technology or art is born, which does not rapidly become the common property of Europe'. On the other hand, there was darker side: the arms race, 'the struggle for the domination of Africa', Anglo-German commercial rivalry and, of course, 'the endless troubles in the Balkan Peninsular'.

Within seven years Europe was plunged into a terrible and costly war. The empires of France, Russia and Britain on the one side, and Germany, Austria and Turkey on the other, fought a brutal war of attrition which was to last four years and cost, at a conservative estimate, some 12 million casualties. The war impoverished Germany, bled France white, and shattered the Austrian and Turkish empires. It also led to the triumph of Bolshevism in Russia and Fascism in Italy. By inflicting serious and long-term damage on the European economies, it also ultimately led to Hitler coming to power in 1933 in Germany.

Understandably, then, the causes of the First World War constitute one of the most hotly debated issues in modern history. They and the events leading up to the outbreak of the First World War are examined under the following headings:

- The 'New Course' in German foreign policy and its consequences
- Nationalism and worldwide imperial rivalries
- The making of the Triple *Entente*
- The Second Moroccan crisis, 1911, and its consequences
- The Balkans and the Great Powers 1906–1914
- The outbreak of the First World War 1914

Key dates

1890		Bismarck's dismissal
		Reinsurance Treaty lapsed
1894		Franco-Russian Alliance signed
1897		German naval construction started
1898		Fashoda crisis
1902		Anglo-Japanese Treaty
1904		Anglo-French *Entente*
1904–5		Russo-Japanese War
1906		First Moroccan crisis
		Anglo-French staff talks
1907		Anglo-Russian Agreement
1908		Bosnia and Herzegovina annexed by Austria
1911		Second Moroccan crisis
1912–13		First and Second Balkan Wars
1914	June 28	Sarajevo incident
	July 28	Austria declared war on Serbia
	July 30	Full Russian mobilisation ordered
	August 1	Germany declared war on Russia
	August 3	Germany declared war on France
	August 4	German troops invaded Belgium
		Britain declared war on Germany

1 | The 'New Course' in German Foreign Policy and its Consequences

The end of the Reinsurance Treaty

Key question
What were the reasons for the non-renewal of the Reinsurance Treaty?

Key dates
Bismarck's dismissal: 1890

Reinsurance Treaty lapsed: 1890

Once Bismarck was dismissed by Kaiser Wilhelm II (see page 27), German foreign office officials advised his successor, General Leo von Caprivi, not to renew the Reinsurance Treaty with Russia. They argued with some justification that it conflicted with the Dual Alliance of 1879 and the Mediterranean Agreements of 1887 (see pages 24 and 26). Instead they decided to work for a new alliance system or 'New Course', which would associate Britain with Germany's two allies, Italy and Austria, and so hold in check both Russia and France. It was felt that Germany was now strong enough to give up Bismarck's complicated system of checks and balances and should ally with states with which it had apparently a common interest.

Britain's refusal to join the Triple Alliance

Key question
Why was Britain unwilling to join the Triple Alliance?

The problem for the Germans was that, while the British government was ready to settle colonial disputes with them, as eventually it also did with France and Russia (see pages 41 and 42), it was not prepared to negotiate binding alliances. Berlin refused to believe this, and remained convinced that sooner or later French and Russian pressure on Britain's large and vulnerable empire would end in war and force Britain to turn to Germany for help. 'For us', as Caprivi remarked in 1893, 'the best

Profile: Kaiser Wilhelm II 1859–1941

1859	– Born
1888	– Ascended the throne
1890	– Dismissed Bismarck
1896	– Sent 'Kruger telegram'
1905	– Visited Tangier
1908	– *Daily Telegraph* affair
1914	– Gave Austria unconditional support against Serbia
1916	– Sidelined by Generals Hindenburg and Ludendorff
1918	– Abdicated
1919–41	– Lived in exile in Holland
1919	– Holland refused to hand him over as a 'war criminal' to the Allies
1941	– Died

Wilhelm was an unstable and neurotic figure, who suffered from rapid mood swings and may even have been mentally ill. His complex love–hate relationship with his English mother and Britain created considerable political problems in the years 1890–1914. When he came to the throne in 1888, he was determined to rule Germany himself. By 1897 he had greatly increased his own power at the expense of excluding genuinely independent-minded men from office. In 1908 he gave an interview to the *Daily Telegraph* which made him the laughing stock of Germany and effectively led to the end of his period of personal rule, although he still continued to intervene directly in military and foreign affairs until 1916. He was forced to abdicate in November 1918 and fled to Holland. He was wanted as a war criminal by the Allies in 1918, but the Dutch refused to hand him over. He died in 1941 in German-occupied Holland.

opening of the next great war is for the first shot to be fired from a British ship. Then we can be certain of expanding the Triple into a **Quadruple Alliance**.' Ultimately, however, this was wishful thinking, and the British were determined not to join the Triple Alliance, because, as Lord Salisbury, the British Prime Minister, observed, the 'liability of having to defend the German and Austrian frontiers against Russia is greater than that of having to defend the British Isles against France'.

Having failed to secure a British alliance, Germany now became increasingly more dependent on Austria as its key ally, and consequently the Austrians were in a position to put pressure on the Germans to back them against Russia when the next major Balkans crisis erupted. It also accelerated the negotiation of the Franco-Russian Dual Alliance.

Quadruple Alliance
An alliance of four powers.

Key term

Key question
What was the impact
of the Franco-Russian
Alliance on the
European balance of
power?

Key term

State visit
Ceremonial visit by
a head of state.

Key term

**Franco-Russian
Alliance signed: 1894**

Key date

France and Russia draw together

The Kaiser's **state visit** in July 1891 to London convinced the
Russians – wrongly of course – that Britain and Germany had
signed a secret alliance. Nikolay Giers, the Russian Foreign
Minister, therefore suggested to the French that the two states
should begin to negotiate an *entente*. Talks began almost
immediately, and the French fleet visited the Russian base of
Kronstadt as a symbolic act of friendship. Within a month the two
states had already agreed 'to take counsel together upon every
question of a nature to jeopardise the general peace'.

A year later this was backed up with a secret defensive military
agreement which was approved by both governments in January
1894. Its terms were as follows:

- Russia would assist France with 'all her available forces' if it was
  attacked by Germany or Italy supported by Germany.
- France would do the same for Russia if it was attacked by
  Germany or Austria backed by Germany.
- The treaty was to last as long as the Triple Alliance
  (see page 19).

The treaty marked the end of France's isolation in Europe and,
even though its precise terms were secret, fuelled German fears
that in any future war France and Russia would be allies.

The potentially dangerous situation in which Germany now
found itself was partly obscured by the shift of European rivalries
in the 1890s from Europe and the Balkans to Africa and China.
Outside Europe, Germany, France and Russia were able often to
co-operate at the cost of the British Empire. For a time Germany
still remained confident that Britain, whose huge and vulnerable
empire was coming under intense pressure, would be forced into
an agreement on Germany's terms with the Triple Alliance, but
this, as we have seen, was a miscalculation.

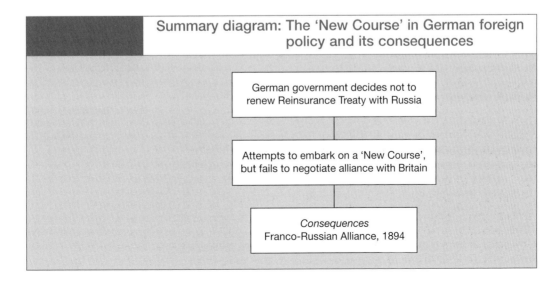

Summary diagram: The 'New Course' in German foreign
policy and its consequences

German government decides not to
renew Reinsurance Treaty with Russia

Attempts to embark on a 'New Course',
but fails to negotiate alliance with Britain

Consequences
Franco-Russian Alliance, 1894

2 | Nationalism and Worldwide Imperial Rivalries

The 1890s witnessed a renewed scramble for territory and influence in Africa and Asia by the Great Powers joined by Japan. However, contrary to expectations, imperial rivalries in Africa and China did not lead to the outbreak of a major war between the European powers, but they did encourage the growth of nationalism, imperialism and militarism in each European country (see pages 2–3).

The struggle for empire was at its most intense in the following regions:

- the Upper Nile
- South Africa
- China.

The Upper Nile and Fashoda crisis

The French, bitterly resentful of Britain's dominant position in Egypt, which it had acquired in 1882, intended to seize a wide strip of territory right across central Africa from the Indian Ocean to the Atlantic. Both Britain and France raced to control the territories of the Upper Nile. In September 1898 a small French force reached the Upper Nile first and hoisted the French flag at Fashoda, but was confronted a few days later by an army under General Kitchener (1850–1916), which had just defeated the Sudanese forces at Omdurman. An armed clash that could have led to war between Britain and France was avoided when Kitchener decided not use force to eject the French. Instead it was left to the two governments to find a diplomatic solution. France, deserted by both Russia and Germany, had little option but to concede totally to British demands in the Sudan.

Fashoda has been called by the historian J.V. Keiger, 'the worst crisis in Franco-British relations since **Waterloo**'. Yet, paradoxically, it also led to an improvement in Anglo-French affairs, as influential voices in Paris began to argue that France should cut its losses, write off Egypt and gain British backing for the annexation of Morocco.

South Africa
The Jameson raid and the Kaiser's response

Here the British faced similar threats to their colonial ambitions but this time from the Germans, whom they feared would try to extend their power eastwards from German South West Africa to the borders of the **Transvaal**. This would effectively block any northward British expansion. The economic significance of the Transvaal had been transformed by the discovery of gold there in 1886, and by 1894 its economy was dominated by Germans. German bankers controlled the Transvaal's National Bank and some 20 per cent of the foreign investment in the state came from Germany.

Key question
Why did imperial rivalries in Africa and China not lead to a major war?

Key term

Waterloo
In 1815 the British defeated Napoleon in the Battle of Waterloo.

Key question
How serious was the Fashoda crisis?

Key date

Fashoda crisis: 1898

Key term

Transvaal
This was an independent state, although by agreement with the British in 1884 it could not conclude treaties with foreign powers without their agreement.

Key question
Why did the Jameson raid damage Anglo-German relations?

Key terms

Boers
Descendants of
Dutch settlers who
had originally
colonised South
Africa.

Jameson raid
Armed intervention
in the Transvaal led
by the British
politician in Cape
Colony, Leander
Starr Jameson, over
the New Year
weekend of 1895–6.

The independence of the **Boers** was, however, threatened by the large number of British prospectors and adventurers who poured in. When Cecil Rhodes, the Prime Minister of Britain's Cape Colony, illegally launched a badly planned and unsuccessful attempt to overthrow the Boer government, the so-called **Jameson raid**, in 1895, the Germans could hardly remain indifferent to it. The Kaiser at first wanted to declare the Transvaal a German protectorate, send military aid to Paulus Kruger, the President of Transvaal, and then summon a congress in Berlin, which would redraw the map of South Africa, but in the end he was persuaded by his own diplomats that because of British sea power, these were just empty threats. Instead he sent a telegram to Kruger congratulating him on preserving the independence of his country against attack.

This caused intense resentment in Britain as it was perceived to be Germany meddling in the private affairs of the British Empire. Windows belonging to German-owned shops were smashed and for the first time popular anti-German feeling became widespread and intense.

The Boer War and the absence of a Continental League

Key question
Why were the
continental powers
unable to intervene on
the side of the Boers?

Four years later Kruger, who had rebuilt the Boer army and equipped it with modern German artillery, declared war on Britain believing that France, Germany and Russia would intervene and force Britain to make concessions. 'There could never be', as the historian A.J.P. Taylor observed, 'a more favourable opportunity, in theory, for the Continental Powers to exploit British difficulties.' Yet nothing happened both because British control of the seas made military intervention physically impossible and because neither France, Russia nor Germany could in the final analysis agree to co-operate. Britain was therefore able to defeat the Boers in a long, drawn-out war, which ended only in 1902.

China

Key question
Why did the Trans-
Siberian Railway
change the strategic
situation in China to
Britain's
disadvantage?

Key term

Ice-free port
A seaport that is
free of ice in the
winter, so that it can
be used throughout
the year.

As in Africa, Great Power rivalry in China was determined by a mixture of political, economic and strategic factors. Up to the 1890s Britain had been able to dominate China's foreign trade and, through its superior sea power, block any attempts by other powers to divide up the Chinese Empire; but the construction of the Trans-Siberian Railway by Russia, which commenced in 1891, completely changed the situation as Russia would now be able to deploy troops to back up its demands. Russia's main aim in China was to annex Manchuria and gain an **ice-free port** in Korea. In China, unlike Africa, Britain now faced the prospect of a challenge to its commercial position from a major military land power. Russia could usually rely on the backing of France and Germany in China, while Britain's only potential ally was Japan, which saw Russian expansion into Korea and Manchuria as a threat to its own security.

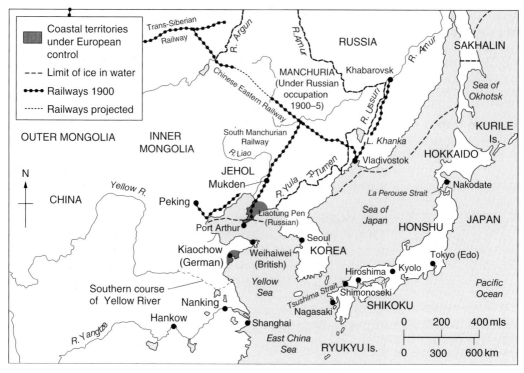

Map of northern China, Manchuria and Japan.

China and Japan: two contrasting histories

Both empires were in 1800 **isolationist** and hostile to Western contacts, but Japan adapted to Westernisation and emerged as an important regional power by 1900, while China seemed to be on the verge, like Africa, of being divided up between the Great Powers. A major step in opening up China to Western influence was the Treaty of Nanking of August 1842. The British forced the Chinese not only to import opium from India, but also to cede them the island of Hong Kong and to open up five coastal cities to foreign traders. Over the next 50 years further concessions were forced out of the Chinese.

Japan's isolation ended when the Americans sent a fleet in 1854 and persuaded its government to open up two ports for trade and the use of the US navy. In 1868 a political revolution took place in Japan, the so-called Meijii Restoration, which gave greater power to the Emperor. He then rapidly transformed Japan into a modern state.

Isolationist
Remaining aloof from international politics.

Key term

Key question
Why was the Anglo-Japanese Alliance signed?

Key dates

Anglo-Japanese Treaty signed: 1902

Russo-Japanese War: 1904–5

The Anglo-Japanese Treaty of 1902

To protect their interests, Japan and Britain negotiated a defensive alliance. Japan recognised Britain's interests in China, while Britain accepted that Japan was 'in a peculiar degree politically as well as commercially and industrially' interested in Korea. Both powers then went on to agree in January 1902 that if these interests were threatened, each power should be free to take the necessary action to protect them. In the event of war between Japan and another country, Britain would remain neutral unless a third power came to Russia's assistance. Similarly, if Britain were involved in a conflict in the Far East, Japan would only intervene if a third power declared war against Britain.

Key question
Why was the Russo-Japanese War fought in isolation?

The Russo-Japanese War 1904–5

When it became clear by 1904 that Russia would not withdraw troops from Manchuria and cede to Japan a dominant position in Korea, the Anglo-Japanese Treaty enabled Japan to launch a surprise attack on Port Arthur. The subsequent Russo-Japanese War was fought in isolation. Neither France, which had just signed a colonial agreement with Britain, 'the *Entente*' (see page 41), nor Germany wanted to fight Britain, and each feared that its involvement in a Far Eastern war would make it vulnerable to an attack in Europe. After the defeat of the Russian fleet at Tsushima and of the Russian army at Mukden, the Russians, paralysed by revolution at home, agreed to mediation by the US President in August 1905. By the terms of the Treaty of Portsmouth (New Hampshire), Russia ceased to be an immediate threat to either Britain or Japan in the Far East and withdrew from Korea and Manchuria.

Summary diagram: Nationalism and worldwide imperial rivalries		
	Africa	Anglo-French rivalry in Egypt and the Sudan comes to a head at Fashoda, 1898
		Anglo-German rivalry fuelled by German support for Kruger, 1896
		Yet neither France nor Germany able to organise a Continental League during the Boer War, 1899–1902
	China	Construction of Trans-Siberian Railway opens up Northern China to Russian influence
		This challenges Britain's monopoly of trade and Japan's influence in Manchuria and North Korea
	Russo–Japanese war	Japan and Britain sign a defensive alliance, 1902
		In 1905 this enables Japan to defeat Russia and halt Russian expansion in China

3 | The Making of the Triple *Entente*

At the end of the nineteenth century it was the British Empire that was under pressure and a war between Britain and Russia over China seemed imminent. Although Germany faced a potentially hostile Franco-Russian Alliance in Europe, in Africa and the Far East it was often able to co-operate with these two powers against Britain. By 1907, however, the international situation had undergone a sea change. It was Germany that was isolated and Britain had settled its most acute disagreements with both Russia and France. Anglo-German relations had sharply deteriorated to a point where war between these hitherto friendly powers was a distinct possibility. In any war between the Dual Alliance and the Triple Alliance, it was safe to predict that by 1907 Britain would join France and Russia. The main causes of this dramatic change, which some historians call a **diplomatic revolution**, are as follows:

Key question
To what extent did the Triple *Entente* mark a 'diplomatic revolution'?

- Growing Anglo-German commercial rivalry.
- The construction of the German fleet combined with an aggressive or clumsy *Weltpolitik*, which forced Britain into taking action to preserve its position as a Great Power.
- The Anglo-Japanese Alliance of 1902 made Britain independent of Germany in the Far East.
- The Franco-British Agreement of April 1904 at last marked the end of Anglo-French hostility over Egypt.
- Germany's violent reaction to French claims to Morocco in 1905 only cemented the Franco-British *Entente* even more.
- Russia's defeat by Japan in 1905 made Russia less of a threat to British interests in China and made possible the Anglo-Russian Agreement of 1907.

Key terms

Diplomatic revolution
A complete change in alliances and relations between states.

Second industrial revolution
The development of electrical, chemical and engineering industries beginning at the end of the nineteenth century.

Creditor nation
A state which lends or invests surplus capital abroad.

Anglo-German economic rivalry

Between 1900 and 1914 Germany became an economic giant. The German steel and iron industries, protected from foreign competition tariffs, could undercut rivals abroad by selling at some 40 per cent below the current price. Germany had also made startling progress in developing chemical, electrical and engineering industries which were in the forefront of the **second industrial revolution**. By 1910 Germany also possessed the second largest merchant fleet in the world (second only to Britain) and after Britain and France was the third largest **creditor nation**. German exports dominated the Middle Eastern, South American and South African markets and had largely displaced British goods there.

Inevitably the German 'economic miracle' was a challenge to Britain's long commercial and industrial supremacy and caused considerable anxiety and hostility. A popular book by E.E. Williams, *Made in Germany*, argued with considerable exaggeration that 'on all hands England's industrial supremacy is tottering to its fall, and this result is largely German work'. In retaliation against German imports there were growing demands

Key question
How great a role did economic rivalry play in the deterioration in Anglo-German relations?

Key term

Free trade
Trade between
nations unimpeded
by tariffs.

Key question
What role did Anglo-
German naval rivalry
play in the causes of
the First World War?

Key date
German naval
construction started:
1897

in Britain for the end of **free trade** and the introduction of tariffs. This in turn led to German fears that they were about to be shut out of British markets and to increased demands for the acquisition of a larger German colonial empire.

Anglo-German naval rivalry

It was above all the Anglo-German naval arms race that inflamed public opinion in both countries. The launching of the German naval programme in 1897 alarmed Britain, and led to an escalating arms race between the two states, which by 1912 – in the words of the Austrian Foreign Minister – had become the 'dominant element of the international situation'. The construction of the German navy struck at the core of British power: in order to preserve its empire, Britain had to retain control of the seas. As long as Germany continued to build up its navy, Britain would therefore ultimately be numbered among Germany's enemies.

The German government intended to build within 20 years a German fleet of 60 battleships, which was to be aimed against British naval bases in the North Sea. Admiral Tirpitz, the head of the German navy, was convinced that this would ultimately force

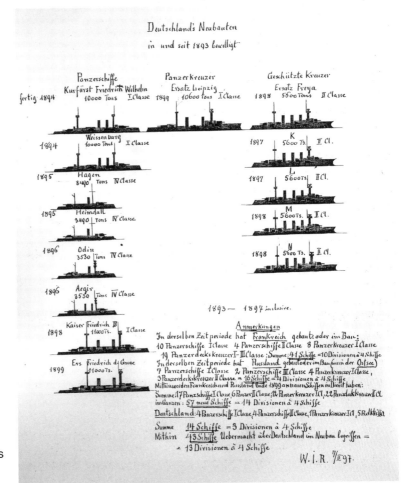

A naval chart drawn in 1897 by Kaiser Wilhelm. He heads the chart with 'Germany's new ships built in and since 1893'.

Profile: Alfred von Tirpitz 1849–1930

1849	– Born
1897–1916	– Minister of Marine
1924–8	– Nationalist Deputy in the **Reichstag**
1930	– Died

Tirpitz joined the Prussian navy in 1865, and as Minister of Marine became a leading advocate of building up a German fleet which could challenge the British in their own home waters. His intention was to create a fleet of 60 **capital ships** which would be able to force the British to make major colonial concessions. He hoped to build the fleet in stages, but this tactic failed once Britain responded by increasing the size of its own fleet. By 1914 Tirpitz realised that the German fleet was too weak to challenge the British and therefore agreed to the building of submarines. In 1916 he was dismissed. After the war he became a militant anti-Republican and supported plans for a right-wing dictatorship.

Reichstag
The German parliament.

Capital ship
A battleship – a ship with heavy armour and powerful guns.

Key terms

Britain to make major colonial concessions to Germany. This programme was also genuinely popular in Germany and appealed to the new German nationalism.

The British government responded to the challenge by modernising the Royal Navy and designing in 1906 the new Dreadnought battleship, which made every other ship afloat obsolete. This, however, only made it easier for the Germans to catch up as it inevitably reduced Britain's overwhelming lead. Thus, when in 1908 the Germans announced a supplementary programme consisting of four capital ships per year for the next four years, often hysterical demands in the British popular press and skilfully orchestrated campaigns by the Navy League pressure group pushed the British government into agreeing to build eight new battleships in 1909 and a further 10 over the next two years.

In 1909–10 and then again in 1912 attempts were made to find a formula which could defuse the dangerous tensions generated by the naval race, but each time there were insuperable objections to a settlement. Britain wanted to safeguard its naval supremacy by negotiating a **fixed ratio** for capital ships, while the Germans wanted a cast-iron assurance that Britain would remain neutral if Germany had to fight France and Russia. Britain could not afford to stand aside and see another defeat of France by Germany, which would lead to the German domination of the European continent.

Fixed ratio
A scheme whereby Germany would agree not to increase the number of ships beyond a certain percentage of the British fleet.

Key term

Theophile Delcassé (1852–1923)
French Foreign Minister 1898–1905. He was forced to resign by the Germans in 1905, but during 1911–13 he was Naval Minister and 1914–15 again Foreign Minister.

Key figure

The making of the Anglo-French *Entente*

After their humiliation at Fashoda, the French were determined to occupy Morocco (see page 34). Once it was clear that the Germans would not help them, **Delcassé**, the French Foreign Minister, began to look to London. Britain had initially been

Key question
Why was the Anglo-French *Entente* agreement negotiated?

Key terms

Protectorate
A territory that is controlled and protected by another state.

Anglo-French colonial *entente*
An understanding reached by Britain and France on colonial issues. Sometimes called the *Entente cordiale* because it led to the restoration of good Anglo-French relations.

Condominium
Joint control of a territory by two states.

Key date

Anglo-French *Entente*: 1904

hostile to the prospect of a French **protectorate** in Morocco, as it might threaten the great British naval base in Gibraltar, but by 1902 Morocco was on the verge of civil war and the restoration of order by the French seemed the better option. The looming war in the Far East between Japan and Russia also played an important part in pushing the states into agreement as both feared what the historian John Lowe has called the 'nightmare scenario of Britain and France having to fight each other as the "seconds" of their allies' (see page 37).

Ultimately, of course, the French hoped to associate Britain with the Franco-Russian Dual Alliance, while the British government hoped that an **Anglo-French colonial *entente*** would lead to a similar agreement with Russia. The agreement was signed on 8 April 1904 and settled Anglo-French colonial problems in three main areas:

- The French exchanged their fishing rights around Newfoundland for territorial compensation in west Africa.
- Siam (present-day Thailand) was divided into two zones of influence and a **condominium** was set up in the New Hebrides.
- France agreed not to block British plans for financial reform in Egypt, provided Britain recognised France's right to maintain law and order in Morocco. Secret clauses then made provision for the establishment of a protectorate at some future date by France over Morocco and by Britain over Egypt.

While it improved Anglo-French relations, it is important to grasp that this agreement was not an alliance since neither country was committed to come to the help of the other in the event of war. Arguably, together with the Japanese Alliance, it made Britain even more independent of continental entanglements and it was only Germany's violent reaction to its provisions for the French control of Morocco that turned the agreement into a virtual Franco-British Alliance against Germany.

The German reaction: the First Moroccan crisis 1905–6

Key question
What did the Germans hope to achieve by triggering the First Moroccan crisis?

The German Chancellor, Count Bernhard von Bülow (1849–1929), decided to challenge the right to control Morocco which had been given to France by the Anglo-French Agreement. Optimistically, he believed that he could destroy both the Dual Alliance and the *Entente cordiale*, and that a new Russo-German Alliance would emerge, which would effectively isolate France.

In early 1905 the French government, ignoring all warnings from Berlin, began to reform the Moroccan administration. The Kaiser interrupted his Mediterranean cruise to land at Tangier and greeted the Sultan of Morocco as an independent ruler. The Germans then demanded a conference on the future of Morocco and the resignation of Delcassé. At first it seemed that Berlin really would win a significant success. The French cabinet agreed to a conference and forced Delcassé to resign. Then, in July, the

Kaiser and Nicholas II of Russia met at Björkö and signed a defensive alliance to co-operate against any power in Europe.

Yet all these successes were purely temporary and by April 1906 Germany had suffered a crushing defeat. The Russian government never ratified the Björkö Agreement and let it lapse, and France was significantly strengthened when the British government came down firmly on the side of the French.

When the conference opened at Algeçiras in January 1906, Germany secured the backing of only Austria and Morocco. The other nine states agreed that France had a special interest in Morocco. Together with the Spanish, the French were therefore entrusted with the supervision of the Moroccan police, while France was also given control of the state bank. However, the Germans did win the concession that all the powers should enjoy equal economic rights within Morocco.

The Moroccan incident was, as the historian A.J.P. Taylor has stressed, 'a true crisis, a turning point in European history'. For the first time since 1870 a Franco-German war seemed a real possibility. There were no armies or fleets mobilised, but the senior official in the German foreign ministry, Friedrich von Holstein, and the German military high command were certainly ready to risk war, as Russia was weak and the French army was inadequately equipped. In December 1905 the **Schlieffen Plan** was perfected for a **two-front war**, while the British and French military staffs also began seriously to discuss what action should be taken if Germany invaded France.

The Anglo-Russian *Entente* 1907

The Anglo-Russian *Entente* of 1907, like the Anglo-French Agreement, was not initially aimed at Germany. The British had long wished to negotiate a compromise with Russia that would take the pressure off Afghanistan and northern India. On the Russian side, the Anglo-French *Entente* and Japan's victory in the Far East made an agreement with Britain increasingly necessary. It had little option but to improve its relations with London if it was to maintain its alliance with France.

The Anglo-Russian Agreement was signed in August 1907. Like the Anglo-French Agreement it was concerned only with colonial matters:

- The Russians gave up all claims to Afghanistan and recognised British interests in Tibet.
- Persia (present-day Iran) was divided into zones of influence: the north went to Russia, the south to Britain, with a neutral zone in between.
- Both empires recognised Chinese sovereignty over Tibet.

Germany on the defensive

The **Triple *Entente*** was not a formal alliance system, but it did mark a shift in the balance of power in Europe. No longer could the Germans assume that an Anglo-Russian war would break out that would enable them to force Britain – or Russia – into

---

Key term

Schlieffen Plan
It envisaged a two-front war against France and Russia. France was to be defeated within a month by a flanking movement through Belgium, Holland and Luxembourg and then the mass of the German army would move eastwards to deal with Russia. The plan was later revised to omit Holland.

Key dates

First Moroccan crisis: 1906

Anglo-French staff talks: 1906

Anglo-Russian Agreement: 1907

Key question
Why did Britain and Russia sign the colonial agreement of 1907?

Key term

Two-front war
A war in which fighting takes place on two geographically separate fronts.

Key question
To what extent did the Triple *Entente* push Germany to the defensive?

Key term

Triple *Entente*
The name often applied to the co-operation of Britain, France and Russia 1907–17.

becoming a subordinate ally. The *ententes* did not, however, completely remove all friction between their members. Anglo-Russian friction continued, for instance, in Persia. Nor did they necessarily mean that Germany would be isolated and encircled. There were still influential voices in France arguing for a settlement with Germany. In 1909 the French and Germans even signed an agreement for economic co-operation in Morocco.

Yet by the end of 1910 Franco-German relations were again rapidly worsening, as local French officials in Morocco were breaking the Algeçiras Agreement by steadily increasing their power in administrative, economic and financial affairs. In Germany the new Foreign Secretary, von Kiderlen-Wächter, was also determined to pursue a more decisive and aggressive foreign policy.

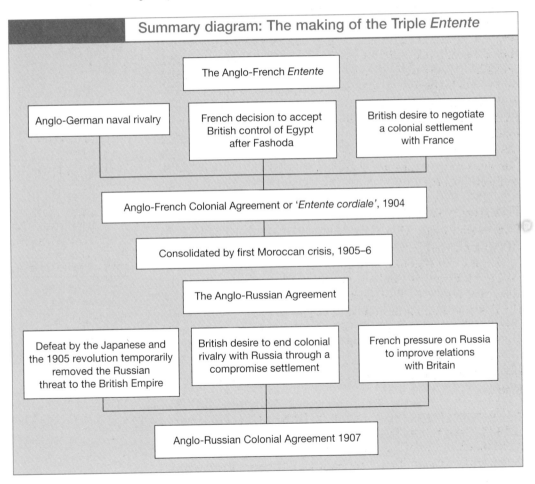

Summary diagram: The making of the Triple *Entente*

The Anglo-French *Entente*

Anglo-German naval rivalry

French decision to accept British control of Egypt after Fashoda

British desire to negotiate a colonial settlement with France

Anglo-French Colonial Agreement or '*Entente cordiale*', 1904

Consolidated by first Moroccan crisis, 1905–6

The Anglo-Russian Agreement

Defeat by the Japanese and the 1905 revolution temporarily removed the Russian threat to the British Empire

British desire to end colonial rivalry with Russia through a compromise settlement

French pressure on Russia to improve relations with Britain

Anglo-Russian Colonial Agreement 1907

Key question
What were the causes and consequences of the Second Moroccan crisis?

4 | The Second Moroccan Crisis, 1911, and its Consequences

Kiderlen-Wächter's opportunity to reassert Germany's rights in Morocco came when in May 1911 French troops intervened in Fez after riots against the Sultan of Morocco had broken out. It soon became clear that France, contrary to the agreement of 1906, was going to occupy the whole country. The German government immediately insisted on territorial compensation from territory in the French Congo, and sent on 1 July the *Panther*, a gunboat, to the south Moroccan port of Agadir. The hope was, as Kiderlen-Wächter expressed it, that 'By seizing a [territorial] pawn, the Imperial government will be placed in a position to give the Moroccan affair a turn which should cause the earlier setbacks of 1905 to pass into oblivion.'

Initially, the French government was ready to negotiate with the Germans as the Russians, still resenting the lack of French help during the Bosnian crisis (see page 48), made it clear that they could offer the French no military assistance at all. But then on 21 July Britain intervened decisively. The Chancellor of the Exchequer, David Lloyd George (see page 85), voiced his government's policy when he stated that Britain could not 'be treated where her interests were vitally affected as if she were of no account'.

The British were anxious to prevent a German diplomatic success which they feared would destroy the *Entente*, but they were also signalling to the French that Britain must not be ignored in any new Moroccan agreement. In fact, the warning was seen as an ultimatum against Germany and it made a Franco-German compromise much more difficult to achieve. In the end, through secret negotiations, the French reached an agreement with the Germans in November 1911, which allowed France to establish a protectorate over Morocco, provided that Germany was given a small part of the French Congo and its economic interests in Morocco were respected. Essentially this was another diplomatic defeat for the Germans as they failed to extract any major concessions from the French.

The acceleration of the arms race

The Second Moroccan crisis had very serious consequences for the peace of Europe. It heightened tension between Germany and Britain and France, which fuelled the arms race and made Germany increasingly desperate for a diplomatic victory. The German government, pushed by the army, public opinion and a highly effective pressure group called the *Wehrverein*, increased the size of the army by about 29,000 men in 1912 and then a year later a further increase of 117,000 men and 119 officers and non-commissioned officers was approved. In Britain, the Navy League (see page 40) and the **National Service League** subjected their own government to similar pressures.

The French meanwhile compensated for their smaller population by extending the period of conscription from two to three years and by modernising their artillery and equipment. Russia had to rebuild its armed forces after the disaster of the Russo-Japanese War. By the financial year 1913–14 Russia was spending over 800 million roubles on rearmament. By June 1914 the peacetime strength of the Russian army was on target to reach almost two million men, which was three times as large as Germany's.

Key terms

Wehrverein
Literally 'Defence League'. This pressure group was founded in Germany in 1912 to press for an increase in the size of the army.

National Service League
A British pressure group founded in February 1902 to alert the country to the inability of the army to fight a major war and to propose the solution of national service.

Key date

Second Moroccan crisis: 1911

Key question
What impact did the Second Moroccan crisis have on the arms race?

The Strengthening of the Triple *Entente*

Key question
To what extent did Poincaré strengthen the Triple *Entente*?

When Raymond Poincaré became French Prime Minister in 1912 he was determined as a consequence of the Second Moroccan crisis to strengthen the Triple *Entente*:

- A Franco-Russian naval convention was signed in July 1912 in which both navies agreed to work out joint tactics in the event of war.
- The French and Russian military chiefs of staff also met and decided that should war break out with Germany both armies would immediately attack.
- At the same time talks between the British and French naval staff also took place about the part each navy would play in the event of war with Germany in the Mediterranean and the English Channel.

In November the French and British governments exchanged letters defining the *Entente*. In essence they stated that the naval and military agreements between the two countries did not constitute a proper alliance, but if either state were attacked by a third power, they would immediately meet to discuss whether they would take any joint measures. This was as far as the British cabinet was willing to go.

By the end of 1912 both the Dual Alliance and the Anglo-French *Entente* had been greatly strengthened. Germany, facing isolation, was consequently all the more determined to cling to its alliance with Austria. It was this that was to make the Balkan crises of 1908–14 so dangerous.

Profile: Raymond Poincaré 1860–1934

1860	–	Born in Lorraine
1893–95	–	Education Minister
1906–7	–	Finance Minister
1912	–	Prime Minister
1913–20	–	President
1922–4	–	Prime Minister
1926–9	–	Headed National Union government
1934	–	Died

Poincaré trained as a lawyer and entered parliament in 1887. He was a popular right-wing patriot, and as Prime Minister and then President did all he could to strengthen France's relations with Russia and Britain. When he became Prime Minister again in 1922 he took charge of foreign policy and pursued a strong line against Germany, which led to the occupation of the Ruhr. He fell from power in January 1924, but was back again as leader of the National Union government from 1926 to 1929 which managed to stabilise France's finances.

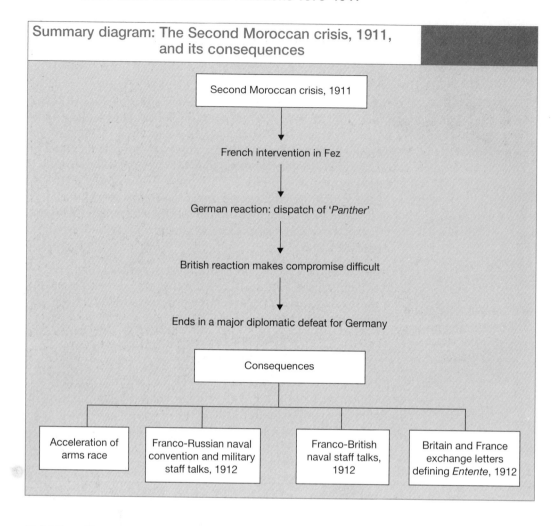

Summary diagram: The Second Moroccan crisis, 1911, and its consequences

Second Moroccan crisis, 1911

↓

French intervention in Fez

↓

German reaction: dispatch of 'Panther'

↓

British reaction makes compromise difficult

↓

Ends in a major diplomatic defeat for Germany

Consequences

| Acceleration of arms race | Franco-Russian naval convention and military staff talks, 1912 | Franco-British naval staff talks, 1912 | Britain and France exchange letters defining Entente, 1912 |

5 | The Balkans and the Great Powers 1906–14

Key question
Why were the Balkans a major crisis point during the years 1906–14?

Between 1890 and 1905 the Balkans remained relatively quiet. Britain was no longer concerned by the Russian threat to the Straits as it could now protect its interests in the eastern Mediterranean from bases in Egypt. As Russia wished to concentrate on the Far East, it signed with Austria in May 1897 an agreement whereby both states would do as little as possible to disturb the existing situation in the Balkans and Near East. In 1905, weakened by defeat in the Far East and the subsequent turmoil at home, the Russian government hoped to maintain this agreement, but its very weakness upset the balance of power in the Balkans and tempted Austria to take advantage of it to defend its interests against an increasingly aggressive Serbia.

In 1903 the pro-Austrian Serbian King, Alexander Obrenovich (1876–1903), had been assassinated by Serbian nationalists and replaced by Peter (1844–1921), of the rival Karageorgevich dynasty. Peter followed a fiercely anti-Austrian and strongly nationalist policy, which he hoped would attract Russian support. Ultimately his aim was to free the South Slavs, who increasingly

The growth of Balkan independence 1822–1913.

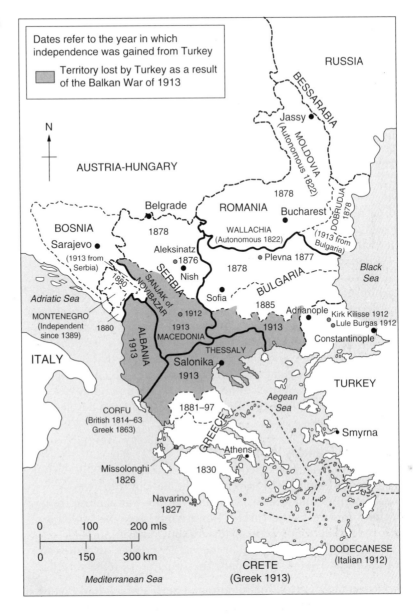

Dates refer to the year in which independence was gained from Turkey

Territory lost by Turkey as a result of the Balkan War of 1913

N

RUSSIA

AUSTRIA-HUNGARY

BESSARABIA

Jassy

MOLDOVIA (Autonomous 1822)

Belgrade

ROMANIA

Bucharest

1878

DOBRUDJA 1878

BOSNIA

1878

WALLACHIA (Autonomous 1822)

(1913 from Bulgaria)

Sarajevo

(1913 from Serbia)

Aleksinatz
●1876
Nish

SERBIA

SANJAK of NOVIBAZAR

1880

Plevna 1877

1878

BULGARIA

Black Sea

Adriatic Sea

MONTENEGRO (Independent since 1389)

1880

Sofia

Sofia

1885

Adrianople Kirk Kilisse 1912
●Lule Burgas 1912

● 1912

1913 MACEDONIA

ALBANIA 1913

THESSALY

1913

Constantinople

ITALY

Salonika
1913

TURKEY

Aegean Sea

CORFU (British 1814–63 Greek 1863)

1881–97

GREECE

Smyrna

Missolonghi 1826

Athens

1830

Navarino 1827

0   100   200 mls

0   150   300 km

DODECANESE (Italian 1912)

CRETE (Greek 1913)

Mediterranean Sea

resented being part of the Austro-Hungarian Empire. Austria's main aim in the Balkans was now at all costs to weaken Serbia.

The Bosnian crisis 1908–09

Key question
Why did the Bosnian crisis *not* start a major war?

Key date

Bosnia and Herzegovina annexed by Austria: 1908

In 1908 a group of army officers seized power in Turkey. This temporarily revived Austro-Russian co-operation as both powers feared that this would lead to the strengthening of the Turkish Empire. In September 1908 the Russian and Austrian Foreign Ministers approved an agreement whereby Russian warships would be able to pass through the Straits, while this right would still be denied to the other powers. In exchange, Austria would be able formally to annex Bosnia and Herzegovina, which it had in fact administered since 1878 (see page 17). The Russian Foreign Minister claimed that any Austrian move would have to be confirmed later by a European conference, but this was never put down on paper, a fact that explains much of what was to follow.

The Austrians went ahead and annexed Bosnia and Herzegovina in October, while the Russians found little international support for their plans at the Straits. The annexation, however, met with a storm of complaint throughout Europe. In Russia and Serbia, which eventually hoped to make these provinces part of a Greater Serb state, there were demonstrations calling for war against Austria. Facing strong criticism in the Russian press, Isvolsky, the Russian Foreign Minister, demanded the calling of the European conference, to which he insisted the Austrians had in principle agreed. The Austrian government immediately vetoed this proposal as it feared a repetition of what had happened at Algeçiras where Germany and Austria had been heavily outvoted (see page 42).

What made the crisis so dangerous was that Austria, which had the unconditional backing of Germany, was ready to fight Serbia even if supported by Russia. However, the Russians received no backing from the French, who were busy negotiating an economic agreement covering Morocco (see page 43) with Germany, and had no option but to accept the annexation.

The dangerous consequences of this crisis were that it did long-term and serious damage to Russia's relations with Germany and Austria and made co-operation in the Balkans much more difficult, whilst at the same time bringing Russia and Serbia together.

The First Balkan War 1912

In 1912 the Italians invaded Libya, which was legally still part of the Turkish Empire. This prompted the Balkan states to overcome their internal rivalries, and declare war against Turkey. Within three weeks the Turkish Empire in Europe had collapsed, and Bulgarian troops were advancing on Constantinople.

The sheer speed and scale of the victory created an acute crisis for the Great Powers. What made the situation so tense was that:

- Austria faced a greatly strengthened Serbia which had occupied part of Albania. Austria, however, was determined to make Albania an independent state so as to deny Serbia access to the Adriatic. At first Russia supported Serbian claims and Austria began to concentrate troops near the Russian frontier.
- Russia was equally determined to stop Constantinople falling to Bulgaria as the Straits were becoming increasingly vital for its economic development. Between 1903 and 1912 a growing percentage of Russian exports, particularly of grain, which was the main export, were passing through them.
- The crisis also threatened to activate 'the alliance system'. Behind Austria stood Germany and behind Russia stood France. Although neither wanted war in the Balkans, both powers made clear that they would stand by their ally if it was attacked.

> **Key question**
> Why did the First Balkan War threaten the peace of Europe?

- The German declaration on 2 December 1912, promising help to Austria if attacked by a 'third party', was answered by a statement from London stressing that Britain would not remain neutral in a major conflict.
- Partly in response to this, on 8 December 1912 the Kaiser called a conference of his service chiefs. Von Moltke, Chief of the General Staff (see page 61), argued for 'War – the sooner, the better', but on Tirpitz's insistence it was decided to wait until the Kiel Canal had been widened to take modern battleships.

The immediate danger to Russia passed when Bulgaria failed to take Constantinople and the Balkan states signed an armistice with Turkey on 3 December. The Great Powers then agreed to call a peace conference in London to settle the territorial problem in the Balkans. By the Treaty of London of 30 May 1913 the Turks gave up all their territory in the Balkans except for a small zone around the Dardanelles and Bosphorus, which satisfied Russia, while Austria's demand that an independent Albania be set up was also agreed.

Key question
Why was Austria the 'clear loser' in the Second Balkan War?

Key date
First and Second Balkan Wars: 1912–13

The Second Balkan War

At the end of June 1913 the Second Balkan War broke out when Bulgaria, which felt cheated of its just share of territory, attacked Serbia. The Greeks, the Romanians and the Turks all supported Serbia and within a month Bulgaria was defeated. The subsequent Treaty of Bucharest increased the territories of Serbia, Greece and Romania, while Turkey, through the Treaty of Constantinople, regained some of the territory it had lost to Bulgaria.

The clear loser in the Second Balkan War was Austria, even though it was not a belligerent, because Serbia had now emerged stronger, and was in a position to resist pressure from Vienna.

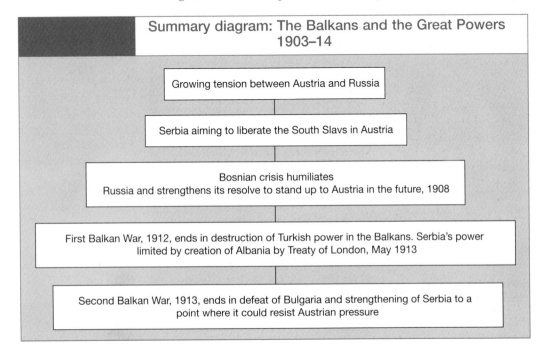

Summary diagram: The Balkans and the Great Powers 1903–14

Growing tension between Austria and Russia

Serbia aiming to liberate the South Slavs in Austria

Bosnian crisis humiliates Russia and strengthens its resolve to stand up to Austria in the future, 1908

First Balkan War, 1912, ends in destruction of Turkish power in the Balkans. Serbia's power limited by creation of Albania by Treaty of London, May 1913

Second Balkan War, 1913, ends in defeat of Bulgaria and strengthening of Serbia to a point where it could resist Austrian pressure

6 | The Outbreak of the First World War 1914

The assassination of Franz Ferdinand

On 28 June 1914, Archduke Franz Ferdinand, the heir to the Austria throne, and his wife were assassinated at Sarajevo by Gavrilo Princip, who had been recruited by the Serb terrorist group, the **Black Hand**. The assassination at last provided Austria with an excuse to eliminate the Serb threat to Bosnia and its South Slav territories. To succeed, however, Vienna needed to gain German backing in case of Russian intervention and also to move quickly while the horror of the assassination was still fresh in the minds of the European governments. The German government agreed with the Austrian analysis of the Serb threat, and the Kaiser and his Chancellor, **Bethmann Hollweg**, gave the Austrians on 5 July their unconditional support: the so-called '**blank cheque**', as it was later called.

What did they hope this would achieve? Neither was intending to unleash a major European war, but Bethmann Hollweg believed that a brief punitive war against Serbia could be kept localised. He gambled that Russia would not in the end intervene both because it was financially not ready for war and because it would see the war as justified retribution for the assassination of the heir to the Austrian throne. Bethmann Hollweg hoped that the rapid defeat of Serbia would restore the prestige of the Dual Alliance, weaken Pan Slavism and Russia, and subsequently enable Germany to exploit Austria's success to improve relations with the *Entente* powers from a position of strength.

Franz Ferdinand, and his wife Sophie one hour before their assassination in Sarajevo on 28 June 1914.

Key question
Why did Germany give Austria a 'blank cheque'?

Sarajevo incident: 28 June 1914

Key date

Key terms

Black Hand
This secret terrorist organisation was founded in May 1911 and by 1914 probably had about 2500 members. They included a considerable number of the army officers who had taken part in the Serbian revolution of 1903. Its aim was to work for the union of the Serbs living in the Austrian and Turkish Empires with Serbia.

Blank cheque
A free hand, unconditional support.

Theobold von Bethmann Hollweg (1856–1921)
A Prussian civil servant before becoming *Reich* Minister of the Interior in 1907. He was appointed *Reich* Chancellor in 1909 and forced to resign by the army in 1917.

Key figure

Key question
Why did the Austrians send an ultimatum to Serbia?

Key dates

Austria declared war on Serbia: 28 July 1914

Full Russian mobilisation ordered: 30 July 1914

Key terms

Mobilisation
Preparing the armed forces for war.

General staff
Military office which plans operations and administrates an army.

Key question
Did Russian mobilisation make the First World War inevitable?

Key question
Why did Germany declare war on Russia on 1 August 1914?

The Austrian ultimatum

Possibly, if Austria had moved quickly, the plan might have worked. On 7 July the Austro-Hungarian ministerial council met to consider what action to take. The Chancellor, Count Leopold von Berchtold (1863–1942), was ready to launch a surprise attack on Serbia but on the advice of the Hungarian Premier, Count Stephen Tisza (1861–1918), he agreed first of all to present Serbia with an ultimatum, and then only declare war if this was rejected.

The crucial part of the ultimatum insisted that Serbia should carry out under the supervision of Austrian officials a whole series of anti-terrorist measures. The Austrians calculated that Belgrade would reject this demand, as it would give Vienna effective control of Serbia's security forces, and enable it to intervene in Serbia's internal affairs. It was sent to Belgrade on 23 July.

The Serbs reject the ultimatum

The Serb reply to the ultimatum was skilfully drafted. It rejected, as Vienna expected, and indeed hoped, the crucial demand that Austrian officials should supervise the anti-terrorist measures, yet its tone was so conciliatory that it cunningly appeared to offer Austria most of what it wanted. The Austrians were not fooled by this 'masterpiece of public relations'. They broke off diplomatic relations and then on 28 July declared war on Serbia.

The reaction of the Great Powers
Russia

The Russians accepted the Austrians' right to demand an inquiry into the assassination at Sarajevo, but they were not ready to tolerate the destruction of Serbia and Austro-Hungarian domination of the Balkans. On 28 July, the day Austria declared war on Serbia, the Russian government ordered the **mobilisation** of the military districts of Odessa, Kiev, Kazan and Moscow. Two days later this was changed to full mobilisation despite the initial reservations of the Tsar and a personal appeal from the Kaiser. This move certainly heightened the tension, although it would take at least six weeks before the Russian army would be ready for war.

Germany

Russian mobilisation made German mobilisation inevitable given the Schlieffen Plan (see page 42) which depended on defeating the French *before* the Russian army was fully ready. By 28 July the German **general staff** was already urging mobilisation on their government. Germany therefore had little option but to act quickly. On 31 July it dispatched an ultimatum to Russia warning its government that unless it stopped mobilisation within 12 hours, Germany would fully mobilise its armed forces. When the ultimatum expired, Germany declared war on Russia. Politically, the fact that the Russians started general mobilisation before the Germans, enabled Bethmann Hollweg to claim that Germany was only acting defensively against the Russian threat. This was to prove an important factor in gaining the support of the German working classes for the war.

France

French reactions to the crisis were confused by the fact that both the French President and Prime Minister were at sea returning from a visit to St Petersburg and did not reach Paris until 29 July. However, the War Minister had taken the precaution of discreetly recalling soldiers from leave and moving some key units back from Morocco.

On 31 July the French cabinet ordered mobilisation to start on the following day. The German ambassador was instructed from Berlin to ask what France's attitude would be to a Russo-German war. If France chose to remain neutral, it would have to surrender the two fortresses of Toul and Verdun to Germany as a pledge of good faith. The Prime Minister merely commented that 'France will act in accordance with her interests.' In reality France had little choice. The Dual Alliance bound France to come to the help of Russia. The French could not stand back and allow the defeat of Russia, which would immeasurably increase German power.

The Germans, however, could not afford to wait for France to declare war. They had to implement the Schlieffen Plan, part of which involved a flanking attack against France through Belgium as soon as possible. On 2 August they sent an ultimatum to Belgium demanding a free passage for their troops. When this was rejected the following day, orders were given to the German army to advance into Belgium and war was declared on France.

Great Britain

As the seriousness of the crisis in the Balkans became clear, the British Foreign Minister, **Sir Edward Grey**, on 27 July suggested a conference in London to discuss the crisis. The Italians and the French backed it, but the Germans argued that only direct Austro-Russian negotiations could solve the problem. That same day the cabinet decided that the British fleet, which had just finished manoeuvres, should not be dispersed to its peacetime bases. Ominously, Grey also raised with the cabinet the possibility that Britain might declare war on Germany, should France be attacked.

With the announcement of Russian mobilisation and the German declaration of war on Russia, pressure from both France and Russia on Britain to enter the war increased, while Germany attempted to persuade Britain to remain neutral. The French argued that Britain was morally committed to back them. However, on the vital issue of peace or war the cabinet was divided. On 29 July it could only agree that 'at this stage' it was 'unable to pledge ourselves in advance either under all circumstances to stand aside or on any condition to go in'.

It was finally the German violation of Belgium on 4 August that enabled Grey and the '**war party**' to win over the majority of those in the cabinet, who still clung to the hope that Britain could keep out of the war. An ultimatum was sent to Berlin at 2 pm that afternoon and when it expired at midnight (German time) Britain was at war with Germany.

Key question
Why did France reject the German neutrality demand?

Key dates

Germany declared war on Russia:
1 August 1914

Germany declared war on France:
3 August 1914

German troops invaded Belgium:
4 August 1914

Britain declared war on Germany:
4 August 1914

Key question
Why did Britain not declare war on Germany until 4 August 1914?

Key figure

Edward Grey (1872–1933)
British Foreign Minister, 1905–16, and Liberal MP. He became a great champion of the League of Nations.

Key term

War party
A group of ministers supporting Britain's entry into the war.

Key question
Why did Italy initially
remain neutral?

Italy

Throughout the critical days in late July, Italy, despite being a
member of the Triple Alliance, refused to align itself with
Germany and Austria-Hungary. There was little public support
for Austria, who was still viewed as the 'traditional enemy' (see
page 19), and also an awareness of how vulnerable Italy's
coastline would be to British and French naval attacks. After the
war in Libya (see page 48) the army, too, needed to be
re-equipped and rested. However, the Italian Prime Minister did
not rule out eventual entry on either side if promised sufficient
territorial reward.

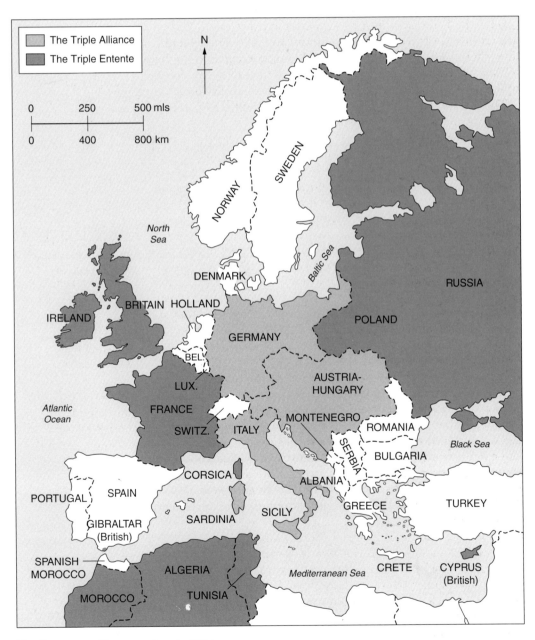

The European alliance system in 1914.

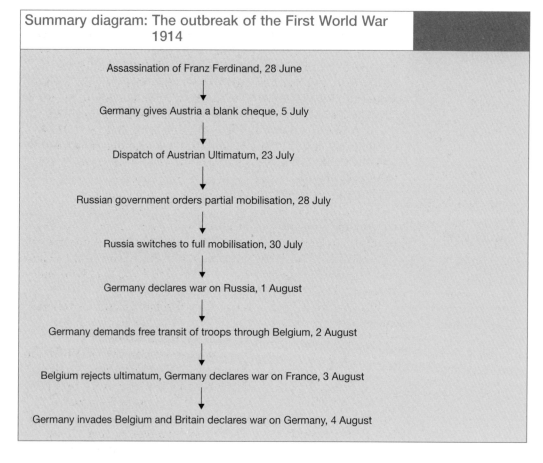

Summary diagram: The outbreak of the First World War 1914

Assassination of Franz Ferdinand, 28 June

↓

Germany gives Austria a blank cheque, 5 July

↓

Dispatch of Austrian Ultimatum, 23 July

↓

Russian government orders partial mobilisation, 28 July

↓

Russia switches to full mobilisation, 30 July

↓

Germany declares war on Russia, 1 August

↓

Germany demands free transit of troops through Belgium, 2 August

↓

Belgium rejects ultimatum, Germany declares war on France, 3 August

↓

Germany invades Belgium and Britain declares war on Germany, 4 August

7 | The Key Debate

Can it be argued that no one power alone bears the chief responsibility for the causes of the First World War?

The 'European system' 1871–1914

The causes of the First World War are one of the most controversial debates in modern history. At the Paris Peace Conference in 1919 (see pages 89 and 96) the Allied powers had little doubt that 'this responsibility rests first on Germany and Austria', but in the 1920s and 1930s this view was rejected by historians not only in Germany but in the USA, Britain and even France. They insisted that the real causes of the war were far more complex and were a result of the 'European system' that came into existence in 1871. In their opinion the key causes were:

- the Alliance system
- nationalism
- militarism
- imperialism
- the arms race
- economic rivalry.

Nationalism, militarism and imperialism certainly helped to create the atmosphere which made war acceptable and exciting.

Key terms

These ideologies radicalised large sections of public opinion in the European states, but by themselves they did not *cause* the war. In Germany, for instance, in July 1914 Bethmann Hollweg was worried that the German Socialist Party, the SPD, would not support war unless it was seen to be a defensive struggle against **autocratic** Russia. Neither did economic rivalry, despite Marx's and Lenin's teachings to the contrary, make the war inevitable. The German 'economic miracle' during the period 1890–1914 certainly challenged Britain's former economic supremacy, but both countries became each other's major trading partners, and British and German banks worked closely together.

The arms race and the alliance system both contributed towards the outbreak of war. The arms race fuelled political tension and insecurity, as did the Anglo-German navy race, for example. In Germany the generals, faced by the growing strength of the Russian and French armies, positively welcomed the chance to go war in 1914 before the strength of their potential enemies became overwhelming.

The alliance system with its **secret diplomacy** and treaties was much criticised after the war. The fact that the web of treaties which covered Europe in 1914 contained, or – equally as important – was thought to contain, secret clauses, contributed to the atmosphere of suspicion between the Triple Alliance and the Triple *Entente*. The alliance system also divided Europe up into potential friends and enemies and influenced military and strategic planning. The danger of this was that the general staffs had to take planning decisions which in a time of acute crisis could deprive their governments of both time and the freedom of action. The existence of the Schlieffen Plan, for instance, made it much more difficult for Bethmann Hollweg to avoid war in July 1914.

Autocratic
Absolute government by one person.

Secret diplomacy
Diplomatic contacts, meetings and decisions which are not made public.

Bismarckian constitution
Introduced by Bismarck in 1871; kept executive power in the hands of the Kaiser and the ministers he appointed.

Key question
What role did Germany play in the causes of the war?

Germany's role

From the 1920s to the 1960s it was generally agreed that all the Great Powers were responsible for the war, but then this consensus was challenged by a new generation of German historians led by Fritz Fischer, who argued in two key books that the German leadership by 1912 was more than ready to risk war both to make Germany into a world power and to consolidate its position at home.

Fischer certainly focused the spotlight back on Germany's role in the causes of the war. The difficulty with Germany was that it was often difficult to know 'who ruled in Berlin'. The Kaiser was no constitutional monarch and was notoriously indiscreet in what he said, while both the army and navy were not ultimately subjected to civilian politicians, as in Britain and France. Many army officers and conservatives urged a quick, victorious war both to break out of isolation and to crush the socialists and the critics of the **Bismarckian constitution**. In many ways Germany was an economic giant in the charge of a divided, chaotic government pursuing contradictory policies. Germany's position in Europe and its great power made this very dangerous.

Why did war break out in 1914?

Why did war break out in 1914 when previous crises in the
Balkans and Morocco had not led to conflict between the Dual
Alliance and the Triple *Entente*? Arguably, each crisis increased
the likelihood of war. The two Moroccan crises did much to bring
together Britain and France, while France's failure to back Russia
in the Bosnian crisis of 1908, and Russia's subsequent humiliation
at the hands of Austria and Germany, strengthened both
Poincaré's resolve to support Russia next time and Russia's
determination to stop the destruction of Serbia in July 1914.

The Great Powers did co-operate in containing the fall-out
from the two Balkan wars, but nevertheless the emergence of a
greatly strengthened Serbia in 1913 with its claims on Bosnia and
Herzegovina was a deadly threat to the Habsburg Empire, and
the following year Austria went to war to crush it.

The constant international tension had created a mood
throughout Europe that war was sooner or later inevitable, and
that the main thing was to choose the right moment for the
struggle to start. For differing reasons and at different stages that
moment seemed to have been reached in July 1914. The Sarajevo
assassinations brought together all the explosive tensions in
Europe. Germany could not allow its only reliable ally to be
humiliated by Serbia and Russia. Once Germany declared war on
Russia, France could not stand back and see Russia defeated,
while Britain, despite initial hesitations, could not afford to run
the risk of a German victory. The decisions of the statesmen were
backed for the most part by their people, who saw the war as a
struggle and a matter of honour and principle to preserve their
nations' independence, greatness and future development.

Some key books in the debate
V.R. Berghahn, *Germany and the Approach of War in 1914*
(Macmillan, 1973).
Fritz Fischer, *Germany's Aims in the First World War* (Chatto &
Windus, 1967).
R. Henig, *The Origins of The First World War*, 2nd edn (Routledge,
1993).
M. Hewitson, *Germany and the Causes of the First World War* (Berg,
2004),
J.V. Keiger, *France and the Origins of the First World War* (Macmillan,
1993).
P. Kennedy, *Rise of Anglo-German Antagonism, 1860–1914* (Allen &
Unwin, 1980).
W.L. Langer, *The Diplomacy of Imperialism, 1890–1902*, revised edn
(Knopf, 1951).
D.C. Lieven, *Russia and the Origins of the First World War*
(Macmillan, 1983).
John Lowe and Robert Pearce, *Rivalry and Accord: International
Relations, 1870–1914*, 2nd edn (Hodder, 1998).
A.J.P. Taylor, *The Struggle For Mastery in Europe* (OUP, 1954).

Study Guide: AS Question

In the style of OCR A

'Troubles in the Balkans from c1890 were the most important factor in causing the outbreak of the First World War.' How far do you agree?

Exam tips

The page references are intended to take you straight to the material that will help you to answer the question.

This question asks you to weigh up the causes of the First World War and put them in order of importance. It gives you one cause and you will be expected to examine it seriously (not dismiss it in one sentence), even if you want to argue that something else was far more important.

So you might want to start with 'troubles in the Balkans'. Do not just think of 1914. Set Balkan instability in a wider context:

- the Bosnian crisis of 1908 (pages 47–8)
- the Balkan Wars of 1912–13 (pages 48–9).

But do not just think of the Balkans. Move up a layer of explanation: the question is not about problems in the Balkans but about the role of Balkans in causing the First World War – so focus on examining Balkan troubles in a wider context:

- Austro-Russian rivalry (pages 47–8)
- the wider 'eastern question' (pages 48–9)
- the importance of Slav nationalism and increasing tensions in the early twentieth century (pages 46–7).

An answer that stopped there would not score high marks, however, because the question would not have been addressed. How Balkan troubles helped lead to a major war may have been discussed, but the relative significance of the Balkans in causing that war would have been ignored. A strong answer needs a comparative focus: weighing up the relative importance of the role of Balkan troubles compared to other causes, such as:

- the role of rivalry amongst the Great Powers (pages 34–7)
- the role of German militarism and foreign policy (pages 38–40)
- the role of the alliance system; the role of the arms races (page 44).

These must all be evaluated against each other and put in a clear hierarchy of importance.

Study Guide: A2 Question

In the style of Edexcel

'In 1914, a mismanaged Balkan crisis caused the powers to stumble into a general European war which had been avoided in 1908 and 1912.' How far do you agree with this view?

Exam tips

The page references are intended to take you straight to the material that will help you to answer the question.

This question requires you to isolate the key factors in 1914 which were different from those in the earlier crises. You should not be tempted simply to rehearse a general survey of the causes of the First World War. For example, it is legitimate to note the conditions and dispositions in 1914 – the factors of nationalism, militarism imperialism (pages 54–5) which lent themselves to conflict. But in this case you should note that they were factors present in all three crises. Similarly, the presence of the alliance system is not of itself a satisfactory explanation for war. Italy did not enter the war in 1914, in spite of its membership of the Triple Alliance, and the crisis of 1912 had also threatened to activate the alliance system. Were there key differences in 1914, or was the outbreak of war the result of miscalculations and poor diplomacy?

In the process of organising your information, you should consider which factors were primarily responsible for the avoidance of general conflict in:

- the Bosnian crisis 1908–9 (pages 47–8)
- the Balkan Wars of 1912–13 (pages 48–9).

You should then examine the crisis of 1914 (page 50) to determine whether the situation in 1914 was substantially different. Austria and Germany were not planning to unleash a European war (page 51). Why did the gamble fail?

In reaching your overall judgement you should consider:

- The impact of previous conflicts in the Balkans and Morocco in heightening tensions (page 56).
- The impact of the military and naval arms races.
- The influence and attitude of the German high command.
- The Great Powers' handling of events in 1914.

Make sure your answer ends with a clearly stated conclusion. It should focus on whether the situation was materially different in 1914 or whether the powers stumbled into war as a result of failures in diplomacy.

4 The First World War 1914–18

POINTS TO CONSIDER

Once war broke out the key decisions about the future of Europe were made on the battlefield. It was not the diplomats, but the generals and admirals who now called the tune. To understand why the war lasted so long and ended in the defeat of the Central Powers, it is necessary to examine how events on the battlefields unfolded, as well as the aims and strategies of the belligerents. This chapter therefore examines the history of the war under the following headings:

- The military and strategic background of the war 1914–15
- 1916: The deadlock still unbroken
- 1917: 'No peace without victory'
- 1918: The final year of the war
- The armistices of October and November 1918

Key dates

1914	August	Germany invaded Belgium and France
		Battle of Tannenberg
	August 23	Japan declared war on Germany
	October 28	Turkey joined Central Powers
1915	April 26	Treaty of London signed by Italy, France, Britain and Russia
	May 23	Italy declared war on Austria-Hungary
1916	Feb–Nov	Battle of Verdun
	June 1916	Battle of Jutland
	July–Nov	Battle of the Somme
1917	January	Unrestricted submarine warfare began
	February	First Russian Revolution
	April 6	USA declared war on Germany
	October	Second Russian or Bolshevik Revolution
1918	January 8	Wilson announced his Fourteen Points
	March 3	Treaty of Brest-Litovsk
	March–April	German offensive on Western Front
	November 11	German Armistice

1 | The Military and Strategic Background of the War 1914–15

Initial war plans and strategy, August–December 1914

The initial **strategy** of the German invasion of France was determined by the Schlieffen Plan (see page 42 and the map below). It was imperative for the Germans to defeat the French army, which was the most effective in the Triple *Entente*, in a lightning campaign before Russia had completed mobilisation, and then turn east to deal with Russia.

At first, the German advance under the command of **General von Moltke** (see opposite page) made good progress. The Germans swung through Belgium and Luxembourg and on into north-eastern France. The French meanwhile, in accordance with **Plan 17**, attempted to retake Alsace-Lorraine, but were repulsed with huge casualties. Soon, however, the German strategy began to go very wrong. Contrary to expectations, the Russians advanced into East Prussia. This necessitated the dispatch of two army corps from France to Prussia, although by the time they had arrived, the Russians had already been defeated at Tannenberg by Hindenburg.

The German's absence on the Western Front had fatal consequences. By the end of August the French had slowed down the German advance and prevented the encirclement of Paris. Then, together with the small British Expeditionary Force of 120,000 men, they counter-attacked across the river Marne on

Key question
Why had the war of movement turned into static trench warfare by December 1914 on the Western Front?

Key dates

Germany invaded France and Belgium: August 1914

Battle of Tannenberg: August 1914

Key terms

Strategy
The military planning and management of war.

Plan 17
The French plan to make a frontal attack on Germany if war broke out.

How the Schlieffen Plan was supposed to work in the west.

Profile: Paul von Hindenburg 1847–1934

1847	–	Born in Posen
1911	–	Retired as Corps Commander
1914	–	Recalled and won Battle of Tannenberg
	–	Promoted to Field Marshal
1914–16	–	Commander-in-Chief on the Eastern Front
1916	–	Chief of General Staff
1919	–	Retired
1925–34	–	President of the German Republic

Hindenburg became the living symbol the German army during the war. He formed a remarkable partnership with General von Ludendorff, his Chief of Staff in Russia, whose organisational skills complemented Hindenburg's great popularity. From 1917 to 1918 both men virtually controlled Germany. In 1925, largely as a result of his war record, Hindenburg was elected President of Germany. In 1933 he appointed Hitler Chancellor of Germany.

Key figure

Helmut von Moltke (1848–1914) Chief of the German general staff 1906–14. Commanded the invasion of Belgium and France, but was replaced by General von Falkenhayn after the Battle of Marne when his health broke down.

6 September and forced the Germans to retreat behind the river Aisne, where they dug in and repulsed the Allied attack.

By the autumn of 1914 the war was beginning to settle into the pattern it retained until 1918. In the west, German attempts to outflank the Allies in northern France and Belgium failed after they were halted in the first Battle of Ypres in November. The war of movement was turning into static trench warfare, and a line of makeshift trenches now ran from the sea to the Swiss border.

On the Eastern Front, East Prussia was cleared of Russian troops but the Russians were still able to invade Austria and threaten Silesia. Clearly, Russia was far from being knocked out of the war; a new Austro-German campaign would have to be mounted in 1915.

The widening war 1914–15

Japan declares war on Germany

Key question
Why did Japan declare war on Germany?

Japan quickly seized the chance to declare war on Germany on 23 August 1914 to capture German territory in the Chinese province of Shantung as well as the German Pacific islands. Japan refused to send any troops to the Western Front but its navy helped Britain to ensure the security of the Pacific Ocean. Japan's primary interest was to strengthen its hold on China.

Turkey joins the Central Powers

Key question
Why did Turkey join the Central Powers?

Key dates

Japan declared war on Germany: 23 August 1914

Turkey joined Central Powers: 28 October 1914

Both the Germans and the Allies also attempted to secure Turkish support, at least by rival offers of concessions. In the end, the Germans were able to outbid their enemies by promising their support for the Turkish annexation of Russian border territory and possibly the restoration of the Aegean islands, which had been ceded to Greece. Britain also seriously damaged its bargaining position by refusing to hand over two Turkish warships which had just been constructed in British dockyards. Turkey declared war on the *Entente* Powers on 28 October 1914.

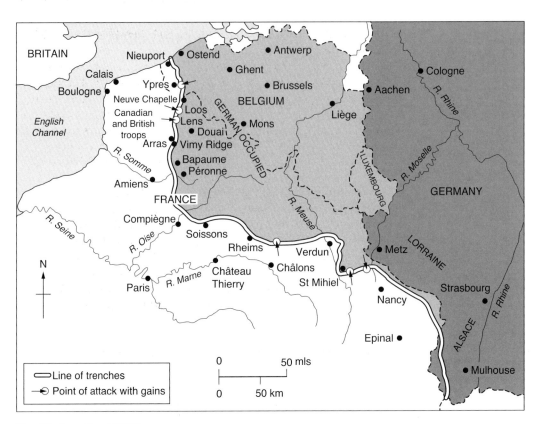

The Western Front 1915.

Turkey's entry into the war was a direct threat to Britain's position in Egypt and led to the dispatch of the **Anzac** Corps to defend the Suez Canal. In November an Anglo-Indian force captured Basra to secure Britain's oil supplies from the Persian Gulf. From there, British forces over the next three years advanced ever deeper in **Mesopotamia**. Despite a defeat at Kut in April 1916, Baghdad was finally occupied nearly a year later.

Italy abandons neutrality

Throughout the winter of 1914–15 the Italian government negotiated with both the Central Powers and the Allies to gain the maximum concessions for abandoning neutrality. In the end, Italy entered the war on the Allied side in May 1915, and by the Treaty of London was promised not only the Austrian territories of South Tyrol, Istria and nearly half the Dalmatian coastline, but also territory in Africa and the Middle East.

Key dates

Treaty of London signed by Italy, France, Britain and Russia: 26 April 1915

Italy declared war on Austria-Hungary: 23 May 1915

Key question
Why did Italy enter the war on the Allied side?

Anzac
Australian and New Zealand Army Corps.

Key term

Key question
What were the main features of trench warfare?

Key term

Mesopotamia
An ancient Greek term literally meaning the land between two rivers: the Tigris and Euphrates. Today this area consists of Iraq, as well as some parts of north-eastern Syria, south-eastern Turkey and south-western Iran.

Key question
How did the belligerents seek to use technology and science to overcome the restraints of trench warfare?

Key term

Creeping barrage
Friendly artillery fire aimed to eliminate opposition in front of advancing troops.

Military stalemate in the west: the development of trench warfare

By 1915 the key element of the defensive war on the Western Front was the trench. Only through the construction of trenches could troops gain protection from enemy firepower. The trenches were protected with massive barbed-wire entanglements and machine guns. Over the course of the next three years the trench system on both sides of the Western Front became far more elaborate. They were shored up with timber and sand bags and deep concrete dug-outs were built.

In 1915 both Allied and German attacks followed a depressingly similar pattern. Air reconnaissance first located the enemy machine-gun nests and trench system which were then pounded with heavy artillery shells. The infantry then went 'over the top' in waves about 100 yards apart with men only six to eight yards distant from each other. The attackers often took the first line of trenches but were then repulsed by a counter-attack. In 1915 no British or French attack managed to gain more than three miles of land.

Attempts to use science and technology to break the deadlock

To break the trench warfare deadlock both sides attempted to develop new techniques and new weapons.

Artillery

From the early days of the war it had been clear that only artillery could effectively destroy trench defences and give a frontal attack some chance of success. Throughout 1915 both sides sought to improve their deficiencies in heavy guns and devise new techniques for their use, such as the **creeping barrage**. By 1916

British troops in sandbagged trenches in France in 1917.

A British soldier stands among a massive pile of artillery shells – the remains of what was fired into German lines.

the Germans had developed enormous **howitzers** –'Big Berthas' as they were called – which could fire a shell weighing nearly a ton.

Gas

As early as October 1914 the German Second Army was considering employing gas as a means to achieve a breakthrough, but it was not until April 1915 that it was first used at Ypres. It failed, largely because the Germans did not exploit the initial surprise and panic. Later, with the development of gas masks, the impact of gas was minimised, but it marked another stage in the development of modern scientific warfare.

Tanks

Essentially, at this stage of the war, military technology favoured defence rather than attack. However, in March 1915 an eventual technical solution to the problem of barbed wire, trenches and machine guns was foreshadowed by the invention of the tank. It linked two ideas: the use of armour plating to protect soldiers while advancing and caterpillar tracks to help them cross trenches and surmount barbed wire. Trials were first held in February 1916, but it was not until the battle of Cambrai in November 1917 that tanks first effectively displayed their potential (see page 72).

Howitzer
A gun for firing shells at relatively high trajectories, with a steep angle of descent.

Key term

Key question
What did Britain hope
to achieve at
Gallipoli?

Key terms

China Squadron
Units of the
German navy used
for protecting their
possessions in the
Far East.

Official historian
A historian
appointed by the
government to write
the history of the
war.

The use of sea power 1914–15: the Gallipoli landing

By January 1915 the Royal Navy unquestionably controlled the seas. The flow of British and Empire troops to France and the Middle East was unimpeded. The German **China Squadron** under Graf von Spee, after some brilliant successes against the British, had been destroyed and Germany itself was blockaded.

Given the stalemate on the Western Front, British politicians increasingly wondered whether sea power could somehow break the military deadlock and lead to a speedy end to the war. Inspired by Winston Churchill, the decision was taken to force the Dardanelles. The plan, according to the British **official historian**, was 'one of the few great strategical conceptions of world war'. It would have knocked Turkey out of the war, opened up Russia to military supplies from western Europe and the USA and in turn enabled it to export wheat supplies to Britain. It could well have altered the course of the war and perhaps even have prevented the Russian Revolution. British and Anzac troops landed on 25 April on Gallipoli but an earlier naval bombardment had deprived them of the element of surprise. The campaign rapidly degenerated into another trench war and the troops were withdrawn in December.

The failure of the campaign showed that there was no 'easy fix' and that only on the Western Front could a decision be obtained.

Profile: Winston Churchill 1874–1965

1874	– Born in Blenheim Palace, Oxfordshire
1898	– Fought in the Battle of Omdurman
1900	– Entered parliament as a Conservative
1904	– Joined the Liberal Party
1910	– Home Secretary
1911–15	– First Lord of the Admiralty
1917	– Minister of Munitions
1918–21	– Secretary for War and Air
1924	– Rejoined Conservative Party
1924–9	– Chancellor of the Exchequer
1940–45	– Prime Minister
1951–55	– Prime Minister
1965	– Died

Churchill was one of the most original and gifted politicians of the twentieth century. He had great energy and powers of leadership, but at the same time these gifts could lead him into making disastrous errors of judgement. During the 1930s he was excluded from government because he opposed concessions to Indian nationalists and irritated the government with his repeated warnings about the dangers of German rearmament. In May 1940 he was appointed Prime Minister and proved to be a charismatic wartime leader, leading Britain to victory in 1945.

The Germans attempt to achieve a decision in the east

In France the Germans remained on the defensive throughout 1915. Eight German divisions were removed from the Western to the Eastern Front and formed the basis of a new German army there. The intention was that they, together with Austrian troops, would deliver a knockout blow against Russia. A brilliantly successful attack was launched against the Russians in southern Poland in early May. The Central Powers broke through the Russian lines between Gorlice and Tarnow and advanced 95 miles within two weeks. In August, Warsaw was taken and by September the Central Powers' troops had advanced 125 miles to the east of Warsaw. Again, as in the autumn of 1914, spectacular results were achieved. The Russians suffered nearly two million casualties.

One consequence of this success was that Bulgaria joined the Central Powers in September. However, great as this success was, Russia had not been defeated. By the autumn the Russians had consolidated their positions. The Central Powers were still locked in a two-front war with no decisive victory in sight.

Key question
What advantages would the defeat of Russia bring to the Central Powers?

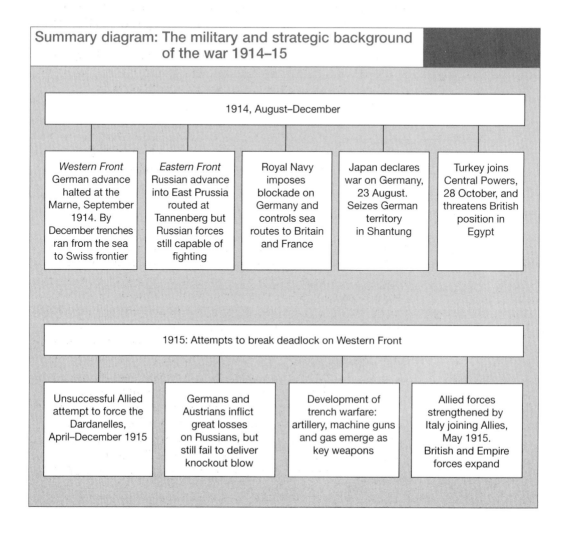

Summary diagram: The military and strategic background of the war 1914–15

1914, August–December

| *Western Front* German advance halted at the Marne, September 1914. By December trenches ran from the sea to Swiss frontier | *Eastern Front* Russian advance into East Prussia routed at Tannenberg but Russian forces still capable of fighting | Royal Navy imposes blockade on Germany and controls sea routes to Britain and France | Japan declares war on Germany, 23 August. Seizes German territory in Shantung | Turkey joins Central Powers, 28 October, and threatens British position in Egypt |

1915: Attempts to break deadlock on Western Front

| Unsuccessful Allied attempt to force the Dardanelles, April–December 1915 | Germans and Austrians inflict great losses on Russians, but still fail to deliver knockout blow | Development of trench warfare: artillery, machine guns and gas emerge as key weapons | Allied forces strengthened by Italy joining Allies, May 1915. British and Empire forces expand |

2 | 1916: The Deadlock Still Unbroken

Allied plans

Key question
What plans did the Allies have for an offensive in 1916?

What options had the Allied and Central Powers in January 1916? Both had failed to achieve a decisive breakthrough in 1915. The Allies needed to bring to bear on Germany their huge reserves of strength. France had been weakened but its army was still the most effective on the Allied side. The British Empire was mobilising its resources effectively and the British now had over a million men in France. Italy too was an ally, while Russia had unlimited reserves of manpower if only they could be exploited.

The answer, of course, was to plan a co-ordinated attack on the Central Powers by all four Allied nations, which was agreed on in principle at the Inter-Allied Military Conference at Chantilly in December 1915.

German plans

Key question
What were the German plans for 1916?

Key figure

Erich von Falkenhayn (1861–1922)
German Chief of the General Staff until August 1916. He then commanded armies on the Eastern Front and in Mesopotamia.

For the Germans and Austrians the situation was more difficult. They had limited manpower resources and needed to force one of their enemies out of the war. Should they renew the offensive against Russia, concentrate on weakening France to the point where it could no longer take the strain of fighting or eliminate Britain or France?

General von Falkenhayn, the German Chief of Staff, argued that if France could be defeated, 'England's best sword' would be knocked out of its hand. To achieve this he came to the conclusion that:

> Within our reach behind the French sector of the Western Front there are objectives for the retention of which the French general staff would be compelled to throw in every man they have. If they do so, the forces of France will bleed to death …

Verdun

Key question
What did the Germans achieve at Verdun?

Key date

Battle of Verdun: February–November 1916

The place Falkenhayn chose for his decisive attack was the historic fortress of Verdun. He calculated correctly that, while it had only limited military value, its defence would become a priority because its fall would be perceived by the French to be a major defeat and so weaken the fighting morale of the nation. Falkenhayn's plan was simple: the Germans would mount a series of limited attacks. These, preceded by short intense artillery bombardments, would allow the Germans to make short advances and then consolidate their positions before the French counter-attacked. Falkenhayn calculated that the French would be destroyed by the 'mincing machine' of the German artillery.

The attack began on 21 February. The French did indeed suffer terribly, but as the siege wore on until it ended in a German withdrawal in November, it became clear that the Germans too had been sucked into a 'mincing machine'. The Germans sustained some 336,831casualties and the French some 362,000.

France's allies attack

To relieve the pressure on Verdun, the Italians, the Russians and the British all launched offensives in the summer of 1916. The Italians attacked on the Trentino front in May. The Russian attack under General Brussilov (1856–1926) was launched in June and on 1 July the British army advanced on the German positions north of the Somme.

The Italians were quickly halted by 10 June. The Russians initially achieved a brilliant success against the Austrians on the Carpathian front, taking some quarter of a million prisoners, which persuaded Romania to join the war on the side of the Allies and forced Falkenhayn to transfer reserves from the Western Front. However, Brussilov's success was not exploited by any of the other Russian army corps and ground to a halt in the autumn.

The British attack on the Somme in July was successful in taking some of the pressure off the French. It was, too, the first battle in which a small number of tanks were used, but when the advance halted in November it had cost about 415,000 British casualties for the gain of a strip of land of some 30 miles with a maximum depth of seven miles.

The Battle of Jutland

There was also a possibility that the Germans could achieve a major naval success by severely damaging the British fleet, even if in the process the German navy was itself defeated. This would, as the Germans put it in 1898, 'so substantially weaken the enemy that, in spite of a victory he might have obtained, his own position in the world would no longer be secured by an adequate fleet'. In other words, Britain would find it much more difficult to

Key question
How did France's allies try to relieve the pressure on the French?

Key dates

Battle of the Somme: July–November 1916

Battle of Jutland: June 1916

Key question
How indecisive was the battle of Jutland?

The German fleet is deflected from bombarding the British coast by Admiral Beatty's battle cruiser squadron, which forms a protective screen during the Battle of Jutland in June 1916.

Key term

Unrestricted submarine warfare
Sinking by German submarines (called U-boats) of all merchant ships, Allied or neutral, engaged in carrying goods to or from Allied states.

Key dates

Unrestricted submarine warfare began: January 1917

USA declared war on Germany: 6 April 1917

find sufficient ships to escort troops and supplies to France and the Middle East. Admiral Jellicoe, the Commander-in-Chief of the Grand Fleet, was aware of this risk and appreciated that if he led the fleet into defeat he could 'lose the war in a single afternoon'!

On 31 May, Rear-Admiral von Scheer succeeded in tempting the British fleet out of its bases. Although in the subsequent Battle of Jutland, he inflicted more damage on the British than his own fleet sustained, he rapidly withdrew back to the German North Sea bases. He may have given the Royal Navy a bloody nose but strategically the situation was not changed. The German fleet was not destroyed but it was confined to its bases in northern Germany. The British fleet retained its overwhelming numerical superiority, and the blockade was still in place. As one US newspaper observed: 'The German fleet has assaulted its jailor, but it is still in jail'!

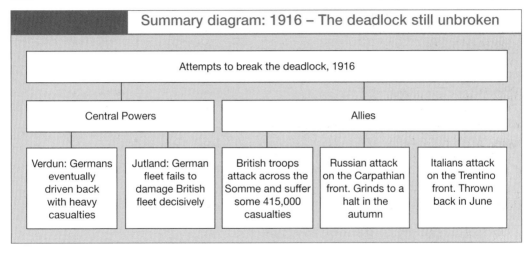

Summary diagram: 1916 – The deadlock still unbroken

Attempts to break the deadlock, 1916

Central Powers — Allies

Verdun: Germans eventually driven back with heavy casualties

Jutland: German fleet fails to damage British fleet decisively

British troops attack across the Somme and suffer some 415,000 casualties

Russian attack on the Carpathian front. Grinds to a halt in the autumn

Italians attack on the Trentino front. Thrown back in June

3 | 1917: 'No Peace without Victory'

The declaration of unrestricted submarine warfare, January 1917

Key questions
Why did the Germans declare unrestricted submarine warfare against the Allies? Why did the USA enter the war in April 1917?

Key term

Associated power
The USA was not bound by any treaties with Britain and France, 1917–19, and was free, if necessary, to pursue its own policies.

Bethmann Hollweg was reluctant to risk a rupture with the USA. Yet in January 1917, against his better judgement, he was pushed by the German high command into sanctioning **unrestricted submarine warfare** against all shipping trading with the Allies, on the optimistic assumption that this would rapidly defeat Britain. Inevitably this ran the risk of drawing the USA into the war on the Allied side, because since 1914 the US economy had become increasingly dependent on exporting to the Allies munitions, food and a wide range of industrial products.

Predictably, US shipping and commerce suffered severely from the U-boat attacks. On 6 April President Wilson declared war on the Central Powers as an '**associated power**' rather than ally of Britain and France. Potentially this was a development of immense importance because the manpower reserves and

Profile: Woodrow Wilson 1856–1924

1856	– Born in Virginia
1890–1902	– History Professor at Princeton University
1902–10	– President of Princeton University
1911–12	– Democratic Governor of New Jersey
1913–21	– President of the USA
1924	– Died

Wilson was an academic who had been President of Princeton University. He entered politics in 1911 and was elected President of the USA in 1912. He pursued a policy of strict neutrality in the war and in 1916 was re-elected on the slogan 'Keep us out of the war'. The USA was, however, forced into the war by the resumption of the unrestricted submarine warfare by Germany. On 8 January he issued his Fourteen Points as the basis for a negotiated peace. In 1919 he was welcomed as a hero in Europe, but at the Peace Conference he was forced to compromise his ideals by Clemenceau and Lloyd George. His hopes that the League of Nations would eventually correct the injustices of the treaty were dashed by the **Senate's** refusal to ratify the treaty. He was struck down by a stroke while campaigning to win public support for the League, and was an invalid until his death in 1924.

> **Key term**
> **Senate**
> The upper house of the US Congress.

economic strength of the USA would now be available to the Allies. On the other hand, it would take the USA at least a year to train and equip an army that could fight in France.

The development of the convoy system

Initially Germany's gamble that unrestricted submarine warfare would drive Britain out of the war appeared to be paying off. By April a million tons of Allied shipping had been lost, and Admiral Jellicoe told his US counterpart that 'it was impossible for us to go on with the war if losses like this continue'.

However, in May the **convoy system** was introduced, and by the autumn with the help of the US navy, Allied shipping was escorted in both directions across the Atlantic and the Mediterranean. This, combined with the introduction of rationing in Britain, prevented starvation and thwarted German hopes that they could knock Britain out of the war.

> **Key question**
> Why did the German submarine campaign fail?

> **Key term**
> **Convoy system**
> Group of ships travelling together under escort.

The Hindenburg line

At the end of 1916 General Ludendorff (see page 61) told Bethmann Hollweg that if the war were prolonged without the collapse of one of the Allies, Germany would inevitably be defeated. He feared above all that a renewed offensive on the scale of the Somme would break clean through the German lines. As a result of this advice, in north-eastern France the Germans constructed a strongly fortified line, the Hindenburg line, to

> **Key question**
> Why did the Germans retire to the Hindenburg line?

which they retreated in March 1917. The line would also save the Germans manpower because they would require 13 fewer divisions to defend it.

Key question
What were the consequences of the failure of the Nivelle offensive?

The Nivelle offensive and the exhaustion of the French army

The strength of the Hindenburg line forced the Allies to abandon plans for a fresh attack across the Somme. Instead they were persuaded by the new Commander-in-Chief of the French armies, General Nivelle, that a massive attack, just south of the Hindenburg line, composed of over 50 French divisions would drive right through the German lines and roll them up in a mere 48 hours.

The attack opened on 16 April. Once again, to quote the military historian John Terraine, 'the machine guns … survived the bombardment – machine guns in undreamt-of-numbers, spaced in depth to trap and decimate the French infantry'. Such was the slaughter that by the middle of May the French army was paralysed by a series of mutinies. By the beginning of June there were only two reliable divisions on the French central front covering Paris.

A French collapse was prevented by Nivelle's replacement, **General Pétain**, who managed by a well-judged combination of firmness and improvement in the living conditions of the French soldier to restore morale and discipline. Miraculously the extent of the mutinies was concealed from both the Germans and France's allies.

Key figure

Philippe Pétain (1856–1951)
Commander-in-Chief of the French army 1917–18, appointed Prime Minister in June 1940 and concluded an armistice with Hitler. He was Head of State of Vichy France and in 1945 was tried as a traitor.

Past a twisted iron bed frame, a relic of the civilian world that once existed here, and the body of a French soldier fallen on the edge of a shell hole, German troops advance through smoke and fire. This head-on combat photograph, including the action of a man about to hurl a potato-masher grenade, was taken as Hindenburg's army overran Allied lines near the Somme in March 1918.

On the Western Front the main burden of the war now fell on the British, who launched a major offensive at Ypres in July, but by early November, when it ended, only a few miles had been gained. The Germans had suffered heavy losses of over 200,000 men, and Ludendorff was concerned about 'the demoralising effect of the battle' on his troops, but the British losses of 245,000 were even higher.

The Battle of Cambrai

Key question
Why was the Battle of Cambrai a pointer to the future?

Briefly, in November 1917, the future was glimpsed in the battle of Cambrai: 381 British tanks attacked the Hindenburg line at Cambrai. The tank force was divided up into groups of 12 machines each supported by infantry. The tanks carried great bundles of brushwood. These were dropped in the enemy trenches and served as bridges for the tanks to pass over. The German were caught completely by surprise and their front lines, which had been considered impregnable, were overrun. The barbed wire was crushed flat and the tanks rolled forward to a depth of four to six miles on a six-mile front. However, owing to a lack of tank and infantry reserves, the attack ran out of steam and over the next week the Germans won back nearly all the land they had lost.

The Russian Revolutions, February–October 1917

Key question
How did the Russian Revolutions weaken the Allies?

In Russia the February Revolution had swept away the Tsarist regime. The new **Provisional Government** initially promised to fight a '**people's war**' against the Germans. It hoped that carrying on the war under a new democratic regime would ignite a great burst of popular enthusiasm, but the Russian army was in no state to fight. Its morale was low and discipline was undermined by the Bolsheviks. In July a badly planned attack against the Austrians in Galicia ended in a rout. In October the Bolsheviks seized power and were determined to pull Russia out of the war.

First Russian Revolution: February 1917

Second Russian or Bolshevik Revolution: October 1917

Key dates

Why was it impossible to end the war in 1917 through a negotiated peace?

In 1917 there seemed a brief window of opportunity for peace negotiations. Karl, the new Austrian Emperor, desperate to save his empire from disintegration, had already put out peace feelers to the Allies in the autumn of 1916. The Pope also appealed to the warring powers in August 1917, as did the International Socialist Conference, which met in Stockholm in June. In Germany the *Reichstag* in July 1917 actually passed a resolution 'for a peace of understanding'.

Both sides were suffering from the war of attrition. Why then did the war not end in 1917? In the past such a situation of mutual exhaustion would have led to a compromise peace, but the First World War was not a war waged by professional armies and diplomats. On the contrary, it was a people's war where whole nations were mobilised against each other. To persuade them to work, fight and ultimately to die for their country, the popular nationalism, militarism and imperialism of the pre-war period (see pages 2–3) had to be appealed to and exploited. The

Provisional Government
A government in power until the holding of elections.

People's war
Popular war fought by the mass of the people.

Key terms

enemy had to be demonised, and the population inspired with the prospect of an absolute victory that would make worthwhile their present suffering. If that failed, then the population might indeed turn against the war and the regime which had led them into war.

In Russia, war weariness did produce revolution, but in 1917 the key belligerents, Britain, France and Germany, were not yet ready to make peace. The entry of the USA into the war gave Britain and France the hope of ultimate victory. In December 1916 Lloyd George (see page 85) came to power to head a political coalition with a mandate to fight on for victory. In France, too, 11 months later Georges Clemenceau (see page 84) was appointed Prime Minister, and was committed to waging total war against the Central Powers.

In Germany the collapse of Russia also held out the prospect of eventual victory, which would make the struggle worthwhile after all. Generals Hindenburg and Ludendorff, backed by a mass nationalist party, the **Fatherland's Party**, reacted to the *Reichstag*'s peace resolution by insisting on the dismissal of Bethmann Hollweg in July 1917 and his replacement by a chancellor who was essentially a puppet of the high command.

Key term

Fatherland's Party
The party was founded close to the end of 1917 and represented political circles supporting the war. By the summer of 1918 it had around 1,250,000 members.

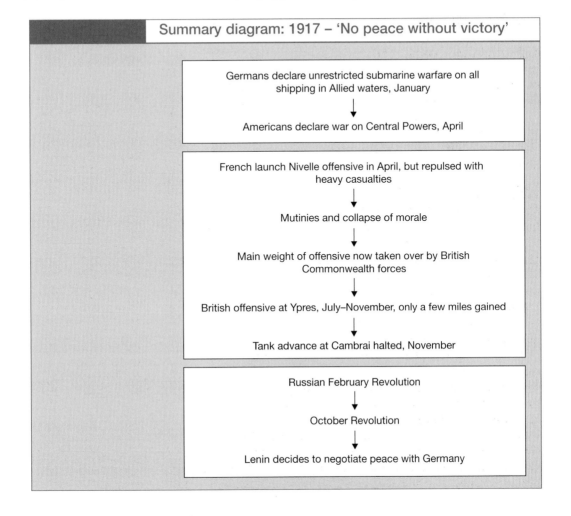

Summary diagram: 1917 – 'No peace without victory'

Germans declare unrestricted submarine warfare on all shipping in Allied waters, January

↓

Americans declare war on Central Powers, April

French launch Nivelle offensive in April, but repulsed with heavy casualties

↓

Mutinies and collapse of morale

↓

Main weight of offensive now taken over by British Commonwealth forces

↓

British offensive at Ypres, July–November, only a few miles gained

↓

Tank advance at Cambrai halted, November

Russian February Revolution

↓

October Revolution

↓

Lenin decides to negotiate peace with Germany

4 | 1918: The Final Year of the War

The impact of the Bolshevik Revolution

In Russia the Bolsheviks overthrew the Provisional Government in October 1917. This not only led to a two-year civil war, but also gave the Germans their best chance of victory since August 1914. **Lenin**, the Bolshevik leader, although hoping that the revolution in Russia would trigger similar revolts throughout Europe, realised that if his regime were to survive he needed to make immediate peace with Germany.

On 22 December Lenin began negotiations with the Germans at Brest-Litovsk after announcing to the world that he supported a peace without annexations or reparations. As the Allies ignored his calls for a general peace, Lenin had no option but to sign the Treaty of Brest-Litovsk. Russia was forced to give independence to Poland, the Baltic provinces, the Ukraine, Finland and the Caucasus.

Key question
How did the Germans benefit from the Bolshevik Revolution?

Treaty of Brest-Litovsk: 3 March 1918

German offensive on Western Front: March–April 1918

Key dates

The final German offensive, March–July 1918

In January 1918 on the Western Front, the initiative now lay with Germany. The majority of German troops on the Russian front had been had been moved to France, and by early March there were 193 German divisions as against 173 Allied. Despite warnings of an imminent offensive, the Allies were slow to withdraw troops from other fronts to make up this deficiency.

Ludendorff's intention was to split the Allied armies and push the British back to the coast. The Germans attacked at the juncture between the British and French fronts where they had a local superiority of 69 divisions to 33. Specially trained groups of stormtroopers armed with light machine guns, light trench mortars and flame throwers infiltrated the enemy trenches and

Key question
Why did the German offensive of March–July fail?

V.I. Lenin (1870–1924)
Leader of the Bolshevik Party from 1903. In 1917 the Bolsheviks seized power but were then faced with a bitter civil war, which they won under Lenin's leadership. In 1922–3 he suffered a series of strokes and power passed to Stalin, Zinoviev and Kamenev.

Key figure

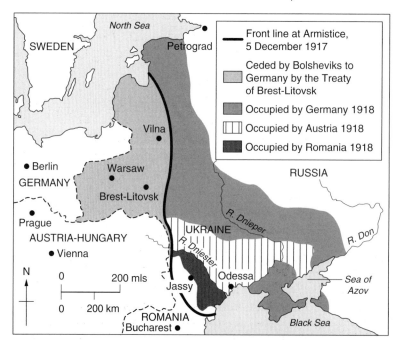

The gains of the Central Powers and Romania 1917–18.

The Allied generals photographed in Alsace-Lorraine in 1918. From left to right: Joffre (France), Foch (France), Haig (UK), Pershing (USA), Gillain (Belgium), Albricci (Italy) and Haller (Poland).

Key figure

Ferdinand Foch (1851–1929) Commanded a French army group on the Somme, 1916, then in 1917 Chief of Staff to Pétain, and in April 1918 appointed Commander-in-Chief of the Allied armies on the Western Front. He played a prominent part in the Paris Peace Conference and retired in 1920.

managed to penetrate to the artillery. By the end of March the Germans had advanced nearly 40 miles.

The Allies responded by setting up a joint command under **General Foch**, which was able to co-ordinate military operations against the Germans. Troops were recalled from the other theatres and for the first time US divisions were committed to battle. By mid-July the Allies were in a position to counter-attack. On 8 August a Franco-British force attacked east of Amiens using over 400 tanks and overwhelmed the forward German divisions. Ludendorff was later to describe this as 'the blackest day of the German army in the history of the war … it put the decline of our fighting power beyond all doubt'.

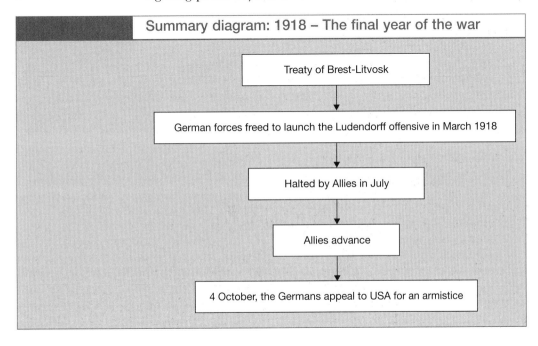

Summary diagram: 1918 – The final year of the war

Treaty of Brest-Litvosk

↓

German forces freed to launch the Ludendorff offensive in March 1918

↓

Halted by Allies in July

↓

Allies advance

↓

4 October, the Germans appeal to USA for an armistice

5 | The Armistices of October and November 1918

On 28 September, after further military defeats in the west, Ludendorff and Hindenburg conceded defeat and advised the Kaiser to form a new **parliamentary government**, which would impress President Wilson with its democratic credentials and facilitate the negotiation of an armistice on the basis of the Fourteen Points. Summing these points up in February 1918, Wilson had proclaimed that the USA wanted a peace of 'no annexations, no contributions, no punitive damages'.

Key term

Parliamentary government
A government responsible to and elected by parliament.

Wilson's Fourteen Points consisted of the following proposals:

1. Open covenants [agreements], openly arrived at … diplomacy shall always proceed frankly and in the public view.
2. Absolute freedom of navigation upon the seas, outside territorial waters …
3. The removal, so far as possible, of all economic barriers …
4. Adequate guarantees given and taken that national armaments will be reduced to the lowest point consistent with domestic safety.
5. A free, open-minded, and absolutely impartial adjustment of all colonial claims … the interests of the populations concerned must have equal weight with the equitable claims of the government whose title is to be determined.
6. The evacuation of all Russian territory …
7. Belgium, the whole world will agree, must be evacuated and restored, without any attempt to limit the sovereignty, which she enjoys in common with all other free nations.
8. All French territory should be freed and the invaded portions restored, and the wrong done to France by Prussia in 1871 in the matter of Alsace-Lorraine … should be righted …
9. A readjustment of the frontiers of Italy should be effected along clearly recognisable lines of nationality.
10. The peoples of Austria-Hungary, whose place among the nations we wish to see safeguarded and assured, should be accorded the freest opportunity of autonomous development.
11. Romania, Serbia and Montenegro should be evacuated … Serbia afforded free and secure access to the sea; and the relations of the several Balkan states to one another determined by friendly council along historically established lines of allegiance and nationality …
12. The Turkish portions of the present Ottoman Empire should be assured a secure sovereignty, but the other nationalities … should be assured an absolutely unmolested opportunity of autonomous development, and the Dardanelles should be permanently open as a free passage to the ships and commerce of all nations …
13. An independent Poland should be erected which should include the territories inhabited by indisputably Polish populations, which should be assured a free and secure access to the sea …
14. A general association of nations must be formed under specific covenants for the purpose of political independence and territorial integrity to great and small states alike …

Key dates

Wilson announced his
Fourteen Points:
8 January 1918

German Armistice:
11 November 1918

Key question
Why were the terms
of the armistice
agreement with
Germany so severe?

Key terms

Neutral zone
A belt of territory
which would be
occupied by neither
German nor Allied
troops.

Soviets
Elected councils.

Key question
Why had the German
government little
option but to accept
the Allied armistice
terms on
11 November?

Key question
Why was the Austrian
Empire dissolved on
1 November 1918?

On 4 October the new German government asked Wilson for 'an immediate armistice' on the basis of the Fourteen Points. Similar requests then came from Bulgaria, Austria-Hungary and the Ottoman Empire, all of which faced imminent defeat by Allied forces.

The armistice agreement with Germany

Germany's hopes of dividing its enemies were dashed when Wilson asked the Allies to draft the details of the armistice agreements. They produced tough terms, which anticipated their key aims at the coming Peace Conference:

- In the west the Germans were to evacuate all occupied territory, including Alsace-Lorraine, and to withdraw beyond a 10-kilometre wide **neutral zone** to the east of the Rhine.
- Allied troops would move in and occupy the west bank of the Rhine.
- In eastern Europe all German troops were similarly to be withdrawn from the occupied territories.
- The German navy was also to be interned in either a neutral or a British port.

Events in Germany, October–November 1918

Once news of the armistice negotiations became public, the demand for peace by the German people after the years of deprivation caused by the Allied blockade and false hopes of victory became unstoppable.

Rashly, on 28 October, the German Admiralty ordered the fleet out on a suicide mission against the British. In protest, the sailors at the Wilhelmshaven base mutinied. When the ringleaders were arrested, their colleagues organised mass protest meetings and formed **soviets**, which by the evening controlled all the naval bases and prevented the fleet from setting sail. Over the next few days unrest spread, and soviets also sprang up in the cities. On 9 September the Kaiser was forced to abdicate and the German government had little option but to accept the armistice on 11 November.

The armistice agreement with Austria-Hungary

In the summer of 1918, under US pressure, the Allies decided to abandon their former policy of dealing with Austria-Hungary as a sovereign state. Instead they recognised the right of its subject peoples, especially the Czechs and the Yugoslavs, to independence. In Paris, the exiled leaders of the Austrian Yugoslavs had already agreed to form a South Slav state (later to be called Yugoslavia), together with the Serbs, Croats and Slovenes. In October, Wilson brushed aside attempts by Vienna to negotiate on behalf of its empire, and the Czechs and Yugoslavs seized the chance to declare their independence. On 1 November the Austro-Hungarian Empire was dissolved, and two days later the former Imperial High Command negotiated an armistice with the Italians.

The Turkish armistice

In the meantime the Turkish armistice was signed at Mudros on 30 October. The Turks surrendered their remaining garrisons outside **Anatolia**, and gave the Allies the right to occupy forts controlling the Straits of both the Dardanelles and the Bosphorus. The Ottoman army was demobilised, and ports, railways and other strategic points were made available for use by the Allies. In the Caucasus, Turkey had to withdraw its troops back to its pre-war borders.

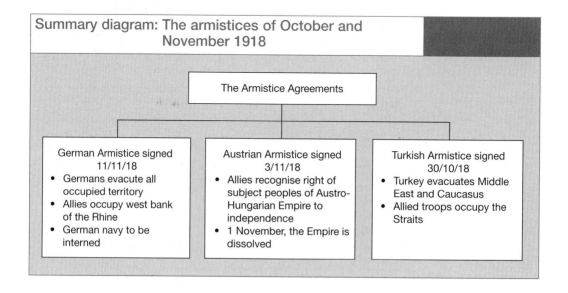

Summary diagram: The armistices of October and November 1918

The Armistice Agreements

German Armistice signed 11/11/18
- Germans evacute all occupied territory
- Allies occupy west bank of the Rhine
- German navy to be interned

Austrian Armistice signed 3/11/18
- Allies recognise right of subject peoples of Austro-Hungarian Empire to independence
- 1 November, the Empire is dissolved

Turkish Armistice signed 30/10/18
- Turkey evacuates Middle East and Caucasus
- Allied troops occupy the Straits

Key question
What were the terms of the armistice negotiated with Turkey?

6 | The Key Debate

Why did the First World War last so long before Germany was defeated?

The First World War occurred at a time when military technology favoured defence rather than attack. A well dug-in and defended army was virtually impossible to defeat. After the failure of the Schlieffen Plan in September 1914, the war in France settled down to static siege warfare from the Belgian coast to the Swiss frontier. Only at the end of the war was the domination of the defensive being challenged by the tank, aircraft and motorised transport.

For the Allies, the logic of the war was that Germany could only be defeated by battles of **attrition** on the Western Front. Potentially, time favoured the Allies with their preponderance of manpower and access to the world's raw materials. Britain did not realise its full military potential until 1917, while the USA's would not have been reached until 1919.

Time did not, however, favour Germany with its two weak allies, Turkey and Austria. Out of desperation in January 1917,

Anatolia
The core territory of the Turkish Empire, covering most of the modern Turkish republic.

War of attrition
A war in which both sides seek to exhaust and wear each other down.

Key terms

Germany tried to knock Britain out of the war by declaring unrestricted submarine warfare on all merchant ships in Allied waters. This backfired and enormously strengthened the Allies by bringing in the USA. Only in October, with the Bolshevik Revolution, was Germany at last able to concentrate forces on the Western Front. The subsequent Ludendorff offensive was a race against time before the Americans could mobilise their strength fully, but by July 1918 Germany had lost this race. Ultimately Germany was defeated because it was locked into conflict with a coalition that it could not destroy.

The war could not have lasted so long without the enormous industrial strength of Germany and the ingenuity of German scientists who were able to help lessen the impact of the British blockade. Munitions production was one of the great triumphs of the German war industry, and right up to October 1918, despite the Allied blockade, its army never wanted for munitions.

Popular support for the war on both sides was also an important factor that prolonged the struggle. The war united whole populations behind their governments and generals. It inflamed nationalism and militarism and led to the belief that victory at all costs had to be achieved. In 1917 in their different ways Generals Hindenburg and Ludendorff, Clemenceau and Lloyd George inspired their compatriots to make even greater sacrifices.

Some key books in the debate

R. Chickering, *Imperial Germany and the Great War, 1914–1918* (CUP, 1998).

David Stevenson, *The First World War and International Politics* (OUP, 1998).

John Terraine, *The First World War, 1914–18* (Papermac, 1985).

Study Guide: AS Question

In the style of OCR A

To what extent were generals to blame for the long stalemate on the Western Front?

Exam tips

The page references are intended to take you straight to the material that will help you to answer the question.

Success in answering this question depends on deciding:

- what the reasons for long stalemate were; and
- how far it was the generals who were responsible.

When a question gives you one factor, always take it seriously, even if you intend to reject it in favour of another that you judge to be more important. You may want to argue that generals on both sides helped to contribute to the stalemate by the strategies and tactics they adopted (pages 63–4). If so, back up what you say with evidence. If you do not refer to particular failed offensives and show how lack of progress can be attributed to commanders, your answer will be a series of assertions, not a well-argued case.

But do not forget that the question is 'To what extent ... ?'
A strong answer will examine other factors that contributed to the long stalemate:

- the scale of warfare and the limitations placed on strategy by mass armies (page 63)
- the nature of weapons and the constraints placed on strategy by technology (pages 63–4)
- the constraints placed on strategy by defensive systems (page 63)
- the lack of alternative strategies and tactics (pages 67–8).

With these too, use examples from particular campaigns to support your points. Wherever possible, point out linkages between one factor and another. Above all, remember that to score well your job is to judge the relative importance of the causes of stalemate and give a clear answer about the role of the generals.

5 The Peace Settlements 1919–23

POINTS TO CONSIDER

This chapter looks at the peace settlements of 1919–23 and the aims and motives of the participants. It also assesses how fair and effective these complex settlements were and what their immediate impact on Europe and the Middle East was. It analyses these problems by examining the following topics:

- Problems faced by the peacemakers
- The aims and principles of the victorious Great Powers
- The organisation of the Paris Peace Conference
- The settlement with Germany
- The settlements with Austria, Hungary and Bulgaria
- The settlement with Turkey 1919–23
- Enforcing the Treaty of Versailles 1920–3

Key dates

1919	January 18	Peace Conference opened at Paris
	June 28	Treaty of Versailles signed with Germany
	September 10	Treaty of St Germain signed with Austria
	November 27	Treaty of Neuilly signed with Bulgaria
1920	January 10	Treaty of Versailles and League of Nations came into force
	June 4	Treaty of Trianon signed with Hungary
	August 10	Treaty of Sèvres signed with Turkey
1921	March	Plebiscite in Upper Silesia
	April	German reparations fixed at 132 billion gold marks
1922	April	Geneva Conference and Rapallo Treaty between Germany and USSR
	Sept–Oct	Chanak incident
1923	January 11	French and Belgian troops occupied the Ruhr
	July 23	Treaty of Lausanne

1 | Problems Faced by the Peacemakers

In January 1919 the statesmen of the victorious powers were confronted with a Europe in turmoil. The sudden and complete defeat of the Central Powers had made Europe vulnerable to the spread of communism from Russia. Germany for much of the winter of 1918–19 seemed poised on the brink of revolution. With the disintegration of the Austrian, Turkish and Russian empires there was no stable government anywhere east of the Rhine. In March, when the communists temporarily seized power in Hungary, it seemed to the Allied leaders that the door to the heart of Europe was now open to communism.

The fear of revolution was intensified by the influenza **pandemic** which by the spring of 1919 had caused the deaths of millions of people, and by the near famine conditions in central and eastern Europe. The problems facing the statesmen in Paris were thus not only the negotiation of peace and the drawing up of new frontiers, but also the pressing need to avert economic chaos and famine. As one Allied official observed, 'There was a veritable race between peace and anarchy.'

The task of rebuilding a peaceful and prosperous Europe was made more difficult by the continued strength of nationalist feeling among the populations of the victorious powers. Public opinion in Britain, the USA, France and Italy viewed the peace conference as the final phase of the war in which their leaders must ruthlessly consolidate the gains made on the battlefields and smash the enemy forever.

The greatest blow to the prospects for real peace in Europe were delivered when the **Congressional elections** in the USA in November 1918 gave the Republicans, who opposed the Democratic President Woodrow Wilson, a majority. The Republicans were determined to campaign for a hard peace with Germany and simultaneously insist that the USA should become involved neither in guaranteeing it nor in financing any expensive schemes for European reconstruction.

Key question
Why did the economic, political and social conditions of the time make it so much more difficult to negotiate a just and balanced peace settlement?

Key terms

Pandemic
An epidemic on a global scale.

Congressional elections
The elections to the US Senate and House of Representatives took place on 5 November 1918. The Republicans secured an overall majority of two seats in the Senate and 50 in the House.

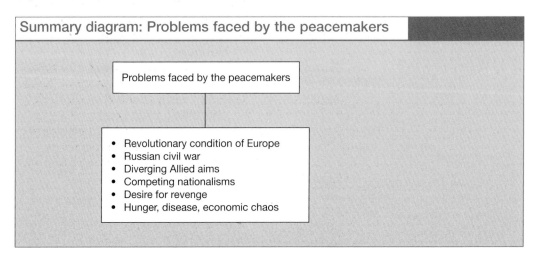

Summary diagram: Problems faced by the peacemakers

Problems faced by the peacemakers

- Revolutionary condition of Europe
- Russian civil war
- Diverging Allied aims
- Competing nationalisms
- Desire for revenge
- Hunger, disease, economic chaos

2 | Aims and Principles of the Victorious Great Powers

Key question
What did the individual Allied and Associated powers hope to achieve from the peace treaties?

The peace negotiations in Paris are often interpreted as a struggle between the proponents of reconciliation, led by Wilson and Lloyd George, and the ruthless advocates of a peace of revenge, represented by Clemenceau, the French Prime Minister. The reality, however, was much more complicated.

The USA: Wilson's efforts to implement the Fourteen Points

Key question
Why did the Allies disagree about the Fourteen Points?

Although President Wilson strongly believed that Germany needed to be punished for its part in starting the war and that it should be put on 'probation' before joining the League, he was determined to ensure that the Fourteen Points (see page 76) served as a basis for the coming peace negotiations and to anchor the **Covenant** of the League of Nations in the text of the peace treaties. He was convinced that this was the key to creating a just and lasting peace.

This was, however, an optimistic assessment. There was general agreement among the victors to set up independent **nation-states** in eastern Europe and the Balkans and confine Turkey to its ethnic frontiers, all of which was anticipated by points 10–13. Points 7 and 8, covering the liberation of Belgium and the return of Alsace-Lorraine to France, had already been fulfilled at the start of the Armistice.

On other issues, Wilson was ready to compromise. Britain, for instance, was assured that point 2, which demanded the 'freedom of the seas', did not mean the immediate lifting of the blockade against Germany. The French and Belgians were promised US support for German reparations, despite the absence of any such clause in the Fourteen Points, and Italy was promised the award of former Austrian territory up to the Brenner frontier, even though this would include over 200,000 Germans. Wilson was also ready to compromise with Britain over the former German colonies and the Middle Eastern possessions of Turkey. These territories would be the ultimate responsibility of the new League of Nations but would be handed over as '**mandates**' to the appropriate powers to administer.

These concessions did not go far enough to turn the Fourteen Points into a practicable **inter-Allied consensus** for the coming peace negotiations. They failed to overcome imperialist rivalries between Britain and France in the Middle East or between the USA, Japan and Britain in the Far East. Nor did they provide a solution to the rival claims in 1919–20 of Italy and the new 'kingdom of the Serbs, Croats and Slovenes' (which later became Yugoslavia) to Dalmatia (see page 98).

Key terms

Covenant
Rules and constitution of the League of Nations.

Nation-state
A state consisting of an ethnically and culturally united population.

Mandates
Ex-German or Turkish territories entrusted by the League of Nations to one of the Allied powers to govern in accordance with the interests of the local population.

Inter-Allied consensus
Agreement between the Allies.

France's priorities

More importantly, the Fourteen Points failed to impress the French Premier, Clemenceau, who was convinced that only an effective balance of power in Europe could contain Germany. He was painfully aware that France, with its reduced birth rate and a total number of casualties of 1.3 million dead and another 2.8 million wounded, faced a Germany which, as a consequence of the collapse of Austria-Hungary and Tsarist Russia, was potentially stronger than in 1914.

Clemenceau was anxious to enforce maximum disarmament and reparation payments on the Germans, to set up strong independent Polish, Czechoslovak and Yugoslav states, and in addition an independent Rhineland state. He also wanted an alliance with Britain and the USA and to continue inter-Allied financial and economic co-operation into the post-war years. He was ready to make considerable concessions to achieve his aims. For instance, in the Middle East, he offered to cede Palestine and the Mosul oilfields to the British in the hope of gaining their support in Europe.

Great Britain: a satisfied power?

In contrast to France, Britain, even before the Great Powers met in Paris, had already achieved many of its aims: the German fleet had surrendered, German trade rivalry was no longer a threat and Germany's colonial empire was liquidated, while the German

Key question
What were France's aims at the Peace Conference?

Vittorio Orlando (1860–1952)
Professor of law and Italian Prime Minister 1917–19. Withdrew from politics when Mussolini came to power in 1922.

Key figure

Key question
To what extent had Britain achieved its war aims by December 1919?

Profile: Georges Clemenceau 1841–1929

1841	– Born in the Vendée, France
1876–1903	– A member of the Radical Party in the French parliament
1906–9	– Prime Minister of France
1917–20	– Became Prime Minister again and rallied France
1919	– Presided over the Paris Peace Conference
1920	– Retired
1929	– Died

Clemenceau came from a Republican and atheistic background. He was mayor of Montmartre in Paris during the Prussian siege of 1870–1, and in 1876–1893 a radical Liberal deputy whose outspokenness won him the title of 'the tiger'. He championed captain Dreyfus who was falsely accused of spying for the Germans, and in October 1906 became Prime Minister. During the first three years of the war he was a fierce critic of the government, and in November 1917 became a charismatic war leader, who inspired France to rise to the challenges of 1918. He presided over the Paris Peace Conference of 1919, but lost power in 1920. He foresaw the re-emergence of Germany as a great power and even predicted war in 1940.

Key terms

Reparations
Compensation paid by a defeated power to make good the damage it caused in a war.

War guilt
Carrying the blame for starting the war.

Dominions
The British Dominions of Australia, Canada, New Zealand and South Africa were self-governing, but part of the British Empire and Commonwealth, of which to this day they are still members.

Key question
What did both Italy and Japan hope to gain from the peace treaty?

armies in western Europe had been driven back into the *Reich*. Britain's territorial ambitions lay in the Middle East, not Europe.

Lloyd George realised that a peaceful, united Germany would act as a barrier against the spread of Bolshevism from Russia. Above all, he wanted to avoid long-term British commitments on the continent of Europe and prevent the annexation of German minorities by the Poles or the French creating fresh areas of bitterness, which would sow the seeds of a new war. Inevitably, then, these objectives were fundamentally opposed to the French policy of securing definite guarantees against a German military revival either by negotiating a long-term Anglo-American military alliance or by a partial dismemberment of Germany.

The logic of British policy pointed in the direction of a peace of reconciliation rather than revenge, but in two key areas, **reparations** and the question of German **war guilt**, Britain adopted a much harder line. Lloyd George and Clemenceau agreed in December 1918 that the Kaiser should be tried by an international tribunal for war crimes. Under pressure from the **Dominions**, who also wanted a share of reparations, the British delegation at Paris was authorised 'to secure from Germany the greatest possible indemnity she can pay consistently with the well-being of the British Empire and the peace of the world without involving an army of occupation in Germany for its collection'.

Italy and Japan
Italy
The Italian Prime Minister, **Orlando** (see opposite page), was anxious to convince the voters that Italy had done well out of the war, and concentrated initially on attempting to hold the *Entente* to their promises made in the Treaty of London (see page 62), as well as demanding the port of Fiume in the Adriatic.

Profile: David Lloyd George 1863–1945
1890	– Elected to parliament as a Liberal
1908–15	– Chancellor of the Exchequer
1916–22	– Prime Minister and brilliant war leader
1923–45	– Never again held any office of state
1945	– Died

Lloyd George was brought up in north Wales, and in 1890 was elected MP for Carnarvon for the Liberals. He was bitterly critical of the Boer War. In 1905 he joined the cabinet of the Liberal government and successfully recommended a series of major social reforms. During the First World War he made his reputation as a brilliant Minister of Munitions. In December 1916 he combined with the Conservatives to overthrow Asquith, the Liberal leader and Prime Minister. He was an inspirational war leader and remained in power until 1922. After his fall he never returned to power and died in 1945.

Japan

Japan wanted recognition of the territorial gains made in the war (see page 61). The Japanese also pushed hard, but ultimately unsuccessfully, to have a racial equality clause included in the covenant of the League of Nations. Japan hoped that this would protect Japanese immigrants in the USA.

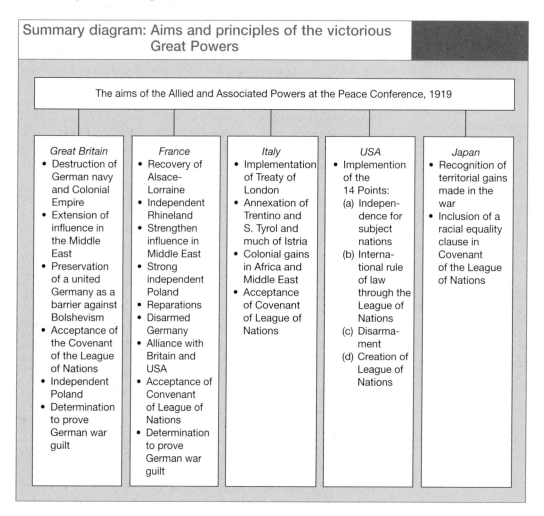

Summary diagram: Aims and principles of the victorious Great Powers

The aims of the Allied and Associated Powers at the Peace Conference, 1919

Great Britain	France	Italy	USA	Japan
• Destruction of German navy and Colonial Empire • Extension of influence in the Middle East • Preservation of a united Germany as a barrier against Bolshevism • Acceptance of the Covenant of the League of Nations • Independent Poland • Determination to prove German war guilt	• Recovery of Alsace-Lorraine • Independent Rhineland • Strengthen influence in Middle East • Strong independent Poland • Reparations • Disarmed Germany • Alliance with Britain and USA • Acceptance of Convenant of League of Nations • Determination to prove German war guilt	• Implementation of Treaty of London • Annexation of Trentino and S. Tyrol and much of Istria • Colonial gains in Africa and Middle East • Acceptance of Covenant of League of Nations	• Implemention of the 14 Points: (a) Independence for subject nations (b) International rule of law through the League of Nations (c) Disarmament (d) Creation of League of Nations	• Recognition of territorial gains made in the war • Inclusion of a racial equality clause in Covenant of the League of Nations

3 | The Organisation of the Paris Peace Conference

Key question
How effective was the organisation of the Peace Conference?

Compared to the Vienna Congress of 1814–15, the Paris Conference was a showpiece of sophisticated organisation. The British delegation, for instance, which was composed of 207 officials, as compared to a mere 17 in 1814, had its own printing press, telephone lines to London and the capitals of the British Empire, and a direct daily air link to Croydon airfield.

Yet despite this impressive evidence of outward efficiency, the conference got off to a slow start and for the first two months little progress was made towards a German settlement. The reasons for this were partly organisational and partly that the Allied statesmen formed what Lloyd George called a 'Cabinet of Nations', which could not ignore the pressing problems of immediate post-war Europe. They had to consider the emergency consignments of food to central and eastern Europe, set up the **Supreme Economic Council** to deal with the financial and economic problems affecting both occupied and unoccupied Germany, and negotiate the easing of the food blockade of Germany in exchange for the surrender of the German merchant fleet. Above all, they ceaselessly monitored the progress of the civil war in Russia and weighed up the pros and cons of Allied military intervention.

The Council of Ten

When the Peace Conference opened on 18 January 1919 the delegates of 27 states attended, but in reality power lay with the 'big five': Britain, France, Italy, Japan and the USA. Each, with the exception of Japan, which to a great extent relied on its professional diplomats, was at first represented by its wartime leaders in the Council of Ten (two representatives per country). Neither Russia nor the defeated enemy powers attended. Russia was torn by a civil war between the Bolsheviks and the **White Russians**. At first, the Allies attempted to secure Russian representation at Paris, but their efforts to negotiate a truce between the factions in the civil war failed.

Right up to April the Allies were not sure whether to follow the pattern of previous peace conferences and plan for a preliminary peace with Germany and the other Central Powers, which would only contain the disarmament terms and the outlines of the territorial settlement. Then, at a later date, when passions had cooled, an international congress would be called to which the ex-enemy states would be invited.

Thus, unsure in their own minds whether they were working on a preliminary or final treaty, the members of the Council of Ten grappled with the intricate problems of peace-making. Fifty-eight committees were set up to draft the clauses of not only the German treaty but also the treaties with Austria, Bulgaria, Hungary and Turkey. Their work was handicapped by the absence of any central co-ordinating body, and consequently the different committees worked in isolation from each other, sometimes coming up with contradictory solutions.

The emergence of the Council of Four

It was not until 24 March that the organisation of the conference was streamlined as a result of Lloyd George's controversial Fontainbleau memorandum. Inspired by the fear that the Allies might drive Germany into the arms of the Bolsheviks, this urged major concessions to Berlin, and so raised important issues which could only be resolved by secret discussions among Clemenceau, Lloyd George, Orlando and Wilson. This 'Council of Four' proved so effective that it became the key decision-making committee of the conference. It briefly became the Council of Three when

Key question
What problems faced the Council of Ten?

Key date
Peace Conference opened in Paris: 18 January 1919

Key terms

Supreme Economic Council
Allied body with the power to deal with economic issues.

White Russians
The name given to members and supporters of the counter-revolutionary 'White' armies, which fought against the Bolshevik Red Army in the Russian Civil War (1918–21).

Key question
Why did the organisation of the Paris Peace Conference have to be streamlined?

Orlando left it in protest against its refusal to agree to Italian claims in Fiume and Dalmatia (see page 98).

As most of the territorial committees had finished their reports by March, it was also decided to drop the idea of a preliminary peace and to proceed quickly to a final settlement with Germany. Inevitably, this decision had serious repercussions on the drafting of the treaty and possibly for the future peace of Europe. Harold Nicolson, a member of the British delegation in Paris, argued in 1933 that:

> Many paragraphs of the treaty, and especially in the economic section, were in fact inserted as 'maximum statements' such as would provide some area of concession to Germany at the eventual congress. This congress never materialised: the last weeks flew past us in a hysterical nightmare; and these 'maximum statements' remained unmodified and were eventually imposed by ultimatum.

On the other hand, it is arguable that such were the problems the Allied statesmen faced in 1919 that, as the historian Max Beloff has observed, it is surprising 'not that the treaties were imperfect but that they were concluded at all'.

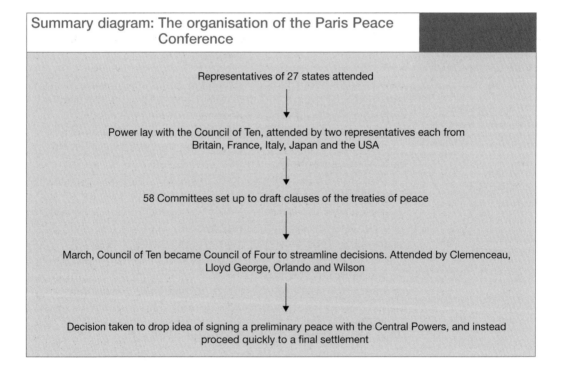

Summary diagram: The organisation of the Paris Peace Conference

Representatives of 27 states attended

↓

Power lay with the Council of Ten, attended by two representatives each from Britain, France, Italy, Japan and the USA

↓

58 Committees set up to draft clauses of the treaties of peace

↓

March, Council of Ten became Council of Four to streamline decisions. Attended by Clemenceau, Lloyd George, Orlando and Wilson

↓

Decision taken to drop idea of signing a preliminary peace with the Central Powers, and instead proceed quickly to a final settlement

4 | The Settlement with Germany

All the peace settlements were to a greater or lesser extent the result of compromises between the Allied powers. Versailles was no exception. Its key clauses were the result of fiercely negotiated agreements, which were often only reached when the conference appeared to be on the brink of collapse. The first 26 articles

Key question
To what extent was the Treaty of Versailles a harsh treaty?

(which appeared in all the other treaties as well) contained the covenant of the League of Nations (see pages 119–20) and were agreed unanimously.

German war guilt

Despite some US and Italian reservations, which were eventually overcome by Lloyd George and Clemenceau, about the legality of demanding the surrender of the Kaiser and other German leaders for trial for committing acts against 'international morality', there was universal agreement amongst the victorious powers that Germany was guilty of having started the war. It was this principle of war guilt which was to provide the moral justification for the reparations clauses of the treaty, as was stressed in Article 231:

> The Allied and associated governments affirm and Germany accepts the responsibility of Germany and her allies for causing all the loss and damage to which the Allied and associated governments and their nationals have been subjected as a consequence of the war imposed up them by the aggression of Germany and her allies.

Reparations

Although there was general agreement that Germany should pay compensation to the victors, there was considerable debate about the amount to be paid, the nature of the damage deserving compensation and how Germany could raise such large sums of money without rebuilding an export trade which might then harm the Allied industries. Essentially, the major issue behind the Allied demands was the compelling need to cover the costs of financing the war. Britain had covered one-third of its war expenditure through taxation; France just one-sixth. At a time of severe social unrest, no Allied country could easily face the prospect of financing debt repayments by huge tax increases and savage cuts in expenditure. Initially it was hoped that the USA could be persuaded to continue wartime inter-Allied economic co-operation and, above all, cancel the repayment of Allied war debts, but by the end of 1918 it was obvious that this was not going to happen, as Wilson dissolved all the agencies for inter-Allied co-operation in Washington. Without US participation the British Treasury was reluctant to continue its wartime co-operation with the French Finance Ministry and in March 1919 all further financial assistance from Britain to France was stopped. France had no option therefore but to seek financial reparation from Germany.

French demands for reparations

The French Finance Minister, **Louis Klotz**, backed by the press and the Chamber of Deputies, urged a policy of maximum claims, and coined the slogan that 'Germany will pay' (for everything). Behind the scenes, however, **Loucheur**, the Minister for Reconstruction, pursued a more subtle policy and informed

---

Key question
Why were Anglo-French demands for reparations so high?

Key figures

Louis-Lucien Klotz (1868–1930)
A French journalist and politician and Minister of Finance 1917–20.

Louis Loucheur (1872–1931)
French Minister of Munitions 1917–18 and Minister of Industrial Re-construction until 20 January 1920. In 1921 he negotiated the Wiesbaden Agreement on reparations with Walther Rathenau.

the Germans that such was the need of the French economy for an immediate injection of cash, that his government would settle for a more moderate sum which the Germans would be able to raise quickly through the sale of bonds on the world's financial markets. The German government, however, suspected that these overtures were merely a means of dividing Germany from the USA, which was seen in Berlin as the country potentially most sympathetic to the German cause. The USA's reparation policy was certainly more moderate than either Britain's or France's as it recommended that a modest fixed sum should be written into the treaty.

British reparation demands

The British delegation consistently maximised their country's reparation claims on Germany. Some historians explain this in terms of the pressure exerted on the government by the electorate. On the other hand, Lloyd George himself claimed that 'the imposition of a high indemnity … would prevent the Germans spending money on an army'. It was arguable that a high indemnity would also ensure that there would be money left over for Britain and the Dominions after France and Belgium had claimed their share. To safeguard Britain's percentage of reparations, the **Imperial War Cabinet** urged that the cost of war pensions should be included in the reparation bill. By threatening to walk out of the conference, Lloyd George then forced the Council of Four to support his arguments.

Key question
Why did the British demand the maximum reparations from Germany?

Setting up the Reparation Commission

The British pension claims made it even more difficult for the Allied financial experts to agree on an overall figure for reparations. Consequently, at the end of April, it was agreed that the Reparation Commission should be set up to assess in detail by 1 May 1921 what the German economy could afford. In the meantime, the Germans would make an interim payment of 20 **milliard** (or billion) gold marks and raise a further 60 milliard through the sale of bonds. It was not until December 1919 that Britain and France agreed on the ratio 25:55 as the percentage of the total reparations which each power should eventually receive. Belgium was the only power to be awarded full compensation for its losses and priority in payment of the first sums due from Germany, largely because it too had threatened to withdraw from the conference in May at a time when Italy had already walked out and the Japanese were also threatening to do so (see page 93).

Key question
What was the task of the Reparation Commission?

Imperial War Cabinet
A cabinet made up of Prime Ministers of the self-governing Commonwealth countries.

Milliard
One thousand million; now largely superseded by the term billion.

Key terms

German disarmament

As with reparations, the Allied and associated nations agreed on the necessity for German disarmament, but there were differences in emphasis. The British and Americans wished to destroy in Germany the tradition of conscription, which they regarded as 'the taproot of militarism'. Instead they wanted a small professional army created along the lines of the British or US

Key question
Why did Foch disagree with the British and Americans over the abolition of conscription?

Key terms

Inter-Allied commissions
Allied committees set up to deal with particular tasks.

Plebiscite
A referendum, or vote by the electorate on a single issue.

Key question
What was the territorial settlement with Germany?

Key question
Why did Wilson and Clemenceau disagree over the Saarland?

Key question
What were French aims in the Rhineland?

peacetime armies. General Foch, more wisely as it turned out, feared that a professional German army would merely become a tightly organised nucleus of trained men which would be capable of quick expansion when the opportunity arose.

Foch was overruled and the Council of Ten accepted in March proposals for the creation of **inter-Allied commissions** to monitor the pace of German disarmament, the abolition of the general staff, the creation of a regular army with a maximum strength of 100,000 men, the dissolution of the air force and the reduction of the navy to a handful of ships.

The territorial settlement

It was accepted, even by many Germans, that the predominantly Danish northern Schleswig, annexed by Bismarck in 1866, should be returned to Denmark. There was therefore general agreement that a **plebiscite** should be held to determine the size of the area to be handed back. The former German territories of Eupen and Malmedy, together with Moresnet, which before 1914 had been administered jointly by Germany and Belgium, were ceded to Belgium, and the neutrality of the Grand Duchy of Luxembourg was confirmed.

The Saarland

The French proposals for the future of the Saarland proved more controversial. Clemenceau insisted on the restoration to France of that part of the Saar which was given to Prussia in 1814. He also aimed to detach the mineral and industrial basin to the north, which had never been French, and place it under an independent non-German administration. Finally he demanded full French ownership of the Saar coalmines to compensate for the destruction of the pits in northern France by the Germans.

Wilson immediately perceived that here was a clash between the national interests of France and the principle of self-determination as enshrined in the Fourteen Points. While he was ready to agree to French access to the coalmines until the production of their own mines had been restored, he vetoed outright other demands. To save the conference from breaking down, Lloyd George persuaded Wilson and Clemenceau to accept a compromise whereby the mines would become French for 15 years, while the actual government of the Saar would be entrusted to the League. After 15 years the people would have the right to decide in a plebiscite whether they wished to return to German rule. (In 1935 the plebiscite was duly held and the territory reverted to German control.)

The Rhineland

Over the future of the Rhineland there was an equally bitter clash between Britain and France. The British had no ambitions on the Rhine, but to the French, the occupation of the Rhine was a unique opportunity to weaken Germany permanently by making the whole region independent of Berlin. This would deprive Germany of the natural defensive line of the Rhine. The British feared that this would not only create a new area of tension between France and Germany but also tilt the balance of power in Europe decisively towards France.

Only after heated and often bitter arguments was a compromise at last reached. Clemenceau agreed to limit the Allied occupation of the Rhineland to a 15-year period in return for an Anglo-American treaty guaranteeing France against a new German attack. The Rhineland would be divided into three zones, which would be evacuated after five, 10 and 15 years. Thereafter the Rhineland would be permanently **demilitarised**. Lloyd George was unwilling to accept even this length of occupation, and right up to the signature of the treaty he sought to evade the commitment.

Demilitarised Having all military defences removed.

Key term

Germany's eastern frontiers

Anglo-French disagreements again dominated negotiations on Germany's eastern frontiers. The Commission on Polish Affairs recommended on 12 March that Danzig, Marienwerder and

Key question What was Lloyd George's solution to the Danzig problem?

| Land lost by Germany | Lost by Russia | To Greece 1920 Recovered by Turkey 1923 |
| Lost by Austria and Hungary | Lost by Bulgaria | |

Central Europe after the peace settlements 1919–23.

Upper Silesia should all be included in the new Polish state, so as to give it access to the sea and make it economically viable. Only the future of Allenstein would be decided by plebiscite. Lloyd George vigorously opposed the inclusion of Danzig and Marienwerder as he feared the long-term resentment of the local, and predominantly German-speaking, population and dreaded that an embittered Berlin might turn to Bolshevik Russia for help. By threatening to withdraw from the Anglo-American guarantee pact, he forced Clemenceau to agree to the holding of a plebiscite in Marienwerder and the establishment of a free and autonomous city of Danzig. The city was to be presided over by a High Commissioner appointed by the League of Nations and to form a **customs union** with Poland. It was also to be linked with Poland through a narrow corridor of territory – the Danzig, or Polish, corridor.

Key term

Customs union
An economic bloc, the members of which trade freely with each other.

Germany's colonies

Key question
How were Germany's colonies divided up between the victorious powers?

President Wilson insisted that the League should also have ultimate control over the former German colonies. This was accepted only reluctantly by the British Dominions of New Zealand, Australia and South Africa, each arguing that the outright annexation by themselves of the South Pacific islands, Samoa and South West Africa, respectively, was vital for their security. In May, agreement was reached on the division of the German colonies. Britain, France and South Africa were allocated most of the former German colonial empire in Africa, while Australia, New Zealand and Japan secured the mandates for the scattered German possessions in the Pacific. Italy was awarded control of the Juba valley in East Africa, and a few minor territorial adjustments were made to its Libyan frontier with Algeria. Essentially Britain, the Dominions and France had secured what they wanted, despite paying lip service to the League by agreeing to mandated status for the former German colonies.

Japan and former German territory in Shantung

Key question
Why did Japan and the USA disagree over the future of former German territory in China?

Key term

Kiaochow
In 1897 the Germans seized Kiachow in revenge for the murder of two missionaries. They also secured mining rights in the neighbouring province of Shantung.

A more serious clash arose between Japan and the USA. The Japanese were determined to hold on to the ex-German leasehold territory of **Kiaochow** (see page 61) in Shantung in China. The Chinese government, however, on the strength of its declaration of war against Germany in 1917, argued that all former German rights should automatically revert to the Chinese state, despite the fact that in 1915 it had agreed to recognise Japanese rights in Shantung. Wilson was anxious to block the growth of Japanese influence in the Pacific and supported China, but Lloyd George and Clemenceau, wanting to protect their own rights in China, backed Japan. Wilson, already locked in conflict with the Italians over their claims to Fiume (see page 98) and facing Japanese threats to boycott the conference and sign a separate peace with Germany, had no option but to concede. It is arguable that this humiliating defeat did much to turn the US Senate against the Treaty of Versailles.

The German reaction

While the Allies were working on the treaty, the German government could only prepare for the time when it would be summoned to Paris to receive the draft terms. Optimistically in what one German intellectual, Ernst Troeltsch, called 'the dreamland of the armistice period', Berlin hoped that it would be able to protect Germany from excessive reparation claims and so keep the way open for a rapid economic recovery. Germany had become a republic in November 1918 and in elections held in January voted for a democratic coalition government in which the moderate socialist **SPD** was the largest party.

On 7 May the draft peace terms were at last presented to the Germans, who were given a mere 15 days to draw up their reply. The German government bitterly criticised the treaty on the basis that it did not conform to the Fourteen Points and demanded significant concessions:

- immediate membership of the League of Nations
- a guarantee that Austria and the ethnic Germans in the Sudetenland, which was a part of the new Czechoslovak state, should have the chance to decide whether they wished to join Germany (see the map on page 92)
- and the setting up of a neutral commission to examine the war guilt question.

Key question
How justified was German criticism of the Treaty of Versailles?

SPD
Social Democratic Party of Germany. Its leaders were hostile to Bolshevism and believed in parliamentary government.

Key term

Allied and US concessions to the Germans

These demands, which if met, would have strengthened Germany's position in central Europe, were rejected outright by the Allied and associated powers, but nevertheless some ground was conceded. Lloyd George, fearful that the Germans might reject the treaty, persuaded the French to agree to a plebiscite in Upper Silesia. He failed to limit the Rhineland occupation to five years, but did manage to secure the vague assurance, which later became Article 431 of the treaty, 'that once Germany had given concrete evidence of her willingness to fulfil her obligations', the Allied and associated powers would consider 'an earlier termination of the period of occupation'.

Key question
What concessions were made to Germany?

The signature of the Treaty of Versailles

On 16 June the Germans were handed the final version of the treaty incorporating these concessions. Not surprisingly, given the depth of opposition to it among the German people, it triggered a political crisis splitting the cabinet and leading to the resignation of the Chancellor. Yet in view of its own military weakness and the continuing Allied blockade, the Berlin government had little option but to accept the treaty, although it made very clear that it was acting under duress:

> Surrendering to superior force but without retracting its opinion regarding the unheard of injustice of the peace conditions, the government of the German Republic therefore declares its readiness to accept and sign the peace conditions imposed by the Allied and associated governments.

Key question
Why did the Germans sign the Treaty?

Treaty of Versailles signed with Germany: 28 June 1919

Treaty of Versailles and League of Nations came into force: 10 January 1920

Key dates

In the Hall of Mirrors in Versailles, French Prime Minister Georges Clemenceau adds his signature to the Treaty of Versailles on 28 June 1919.

On 28 June 1919 the treaty was signed in the Hall of Mirrors at Versailles, where in 1871 the German Empire had been proclaimed (see page 13).

The American refusal to ratify the treaty

By January 1920 the treaty had been **ratified** by all the signatory powers with the important exception of the USA. In Washington, crucial amendments had been put forward by a coalition of **isolationists**, led by **Senator Lodge**, rejecting the Shantung settlement and seriously modifying the covenant of the League. In essence the isolationists feared that if the USA joined the League, it could be committed to defend the independence of other League members from aggression, even if this meant going to war. They therefore proposed that Congress should be empowered to veto US participation in any League initiative that clashed with the USA's traditional policy of isolationism and independence. Wilson felt that these amendments would paralyse the League and so refused to accept them. He failed twice to secure the necessary two-thirds majority in the Senate.

This was a major defeat for Wilson, and the consequences for Europe were serious. Without US ratification, the Anglo-American military guarantee of France lapsed and the burden of carrying out the Treaty of Versailles fell on Britain and France (see pages 102–5).

Key question
Why did the Americans not ratify the treaty?

Key terms

Ratified
Having received formal approval from parliament.

Isolationists
US politicians who were opposed to any US commitments or entanglements in Europe or elsewhere.

Key figure

Henry Cabot Lodge (1850–1924)
A US statesman, a Republican politician and a historian. He was chairman of the Senate Foreign Relations Committee.

Summary diagram: The settlement with Germany

The settlement with Germany

Territorial changes	Reparations	Disarmament	League of Nations
Independent Poland	Reparation Commission fixes amount of 132 billion gold marks in May 1921	Abolition of conscription	Collective security
Plebiscites in Upper Silesia, Schleswig and West Prussia		Regular German army of 100,000	New principle of mandates
Alsace-Lorraine to France	Prolonged struggle to force Germany to pay, 1921–3	Very small fleet	Weakened by absence of USA
Saar administered by League of Nations	France occupies Ruhr in Jan. 1923	Allied control commissions in Germany until 1927	Germany and defeated powers initially excluded
Germany loses colonies and foreign investments	Dawes Commission Jan. 1924	Rhineland occupied for 15 years	

5 | The Settlements with Austria, Hungary and Bulgaria

After the ceremony at Versailles the Allied leaders returned home, leaving their officials to draft the treaties with Germany's former allies. The outlines of a settlement in eastern Europe and the Balkans were already clear: Austria-Hungary and the Tsarist Russian empire had collapsed, the Poles and Czechs had declared their independence and the South Slavs had decided to federate with Serbia to form what was later to be called Yugoslavia. The bewildering diversity of races in the Balkans, who were in no way concentrated in easily definable areas, would ensure that however the Great Powers drew the frontiers, the final settlement would be full of contradictions. The three defeated powers, Austria and Hungary (both treated as the heirs to the former Austro-Hungarion Empire) and Bulgaria, all had to pay reparations, disarm and submit to the humiliation of a war guilt clause. The basis of the settlement in south-central Europe and the Balkans was the creation of the new Czecho-Slovak state and Serbo-Croat-Slovene state, or Yugoslavia.

The Treaty of St Germain, 10 September 1919

The Treaty of St Germain split up the diverse territories which before the war had been part of the Austrian Empire. Rump Austria was now reduced to a small German-speaking state of some six million people:

- Italy was awarded South Tyrol, despite the existence there of some 230,000 ethnic Germans.
- Bohemia and Moravia were ceded to Czechoslovakia. Any second thoughts the British or Americans had about handing over to the Czechs the three million Germans who made up nearly one-third of the population of these provinces were

Key question
What were the main terms of the Treaty of St Germain?

Key date

Treaty of St Germain signed with Austria: 10 September 1919

quickly stifled by French opposition. The French wanted a potential ally against Germany to be strengthened by a defensible frontier and the possession of the Skoda munitions works in Pilsen, both of which entailed the forcible integration of large German minorities into Czechoslovakia.

- Slovenia, Bosnia-Herzegovina and Dalmatia were handed over to Yugoslavia.
- Galicia and Bukovina were ceded to Poland and Romania, respectively.
- Only in Carinthia, where the population consisted of German-speaking Slovenes who did not want to join Yugoslavia, did the Great Powers consent to a plebiscite. This resulted in 1920 in the area remaining Austrian.
- To avoid the dangers of an *Anschluss* with Germany, Article 88 (which was identical to Article 80 in the Treaty of Versailles) stated that only the Council of the League of Nations was empowered to sanction a change in Austria's status as an independent state. Effectively this meant that France, as a permanent member of the Council, could veto any proposed change (see the map on page 92).

Key terms

Anschluss
The union of Austria with Germany.

Magyar
Ethnic Hungarians.

Key question
What were the main terms of the Treaty of Trianon?

Key dates

Treaty of Trianon signed with Hungary: 4 June 1920

Treaty of Neuilly signed with Bulgaria: 27 November 1919

The Treaty of Trianon, 4 June 1920

Of all the defeated powers in 1919 it is arguable that Hungary suffered the most severely. By the Treaty of Trianon Hungary lost over two-thirds of its territory and 41.6 per cent of its population. It was particularly vulnerable to partition, as essentially only the heartlands of Hungary, the great Central Plain, were **Magyar**. Its fate was sealed, when, in November 1918, Serb, Czech and Romanian troops all occupied the regions they claimed. The completion of the treaty was delayed by the communist coup in March 1919 (see page 82), but was resumed after its defeat. The Treaty of Trianon was signed in June 1920:

- Most of the German-speaking area in the west of the former Hungarian state was ceded to Austria.
- The Slovakian and Ruthenian regions in the north went to Czechoslovakia.
- The east went to Romania.
- The south went to Yugoslavia (see the map on page 92).

The Treaty of Trianon was justified by the Allies according to the principle of national self-determination, but in the context of Hungary this was a principle almost impossible to realise. C.A. Macartney, an expert on Hungary and the successor states, observed in 1937:

> … the ethical line was practically nowhere clear cut … long centuries of interpenetration, assimilation, migration and internal colonisation had left in many places a belt of mixed and often indeterminate population where each national group merged into the next, while there were innumerable islands of one nationality set in seas of another, ranging in size from the half-million of Magyar-speaking Szekely in Transylvania through many inter-determinate groups of fifty or a hundred thousand down to communities of a

single village or less … No frontier could be drawn which did not leave national minorities on at least one side of it.

Wherever there was a clash of interests between Hungary and the **successor states** or Romania, the Allies ensured that the decision went against Hungary.

Successor states States that were created after the collapse of Austria-Hungary.

Key term

The Treaty of Neuilly, 27 November 1919

The same principle operated in the negotiations leading up to the Treaty of Neuilly with Bulgaria, which was signed on November 1919. Essentially Britain and France regarded Bulgaria as the **'Balkan Prussia'** which needed to be restrained. They were determined, despite reservations from Italy and America, to reward their allies, Romania, Greece and Serbia (now part of Yugoslavia) at its expense. Thus southern Dobruja, with a mere 7000 Romanians out of a total population of 250,000, was ceded to Romania and western Thrace was given to Greece (see the map on page 92).

Key question What were the main terms of the Treaty of Neuilly?

Fiume, Istria and Dalmatia

These post-war settlements were accompanied by bitter quarrels between the Allied and associated powers. The most serious clash of opinions took place between Italy and the USA over Italian claims to Fiume, Istria and Dalmatia (see the map on page 92). Orlando was desperate to prove to the Italian electorate that Italy was not a **'proletarian nation'** which could be dictated to by the Great Powers, and insisted on its right to annex both Albania and the port of Fiume in which, it could be argued, there was a bare majority of ethnic Italians, if the Croat suburb of Susak was conveniently left out of the picture. The Italian annexation of Fiume would have the added bonus of denying Yugoslavia its only effective port in the Adriatic, thereby strengthening Italy's economic grip on the region. Agreement could have been achieved, especially as Orlando was ready in April 1919 to accept Fiume as a compromise for giving up Italian claims on Dalmatia; but Wilson made the major political mistake of vetoing this option publicly in a statement in the French press. After compromising over the Saar and Shantung, Wilson was stubbornly determined to make a stand on the Fourteen Points in the Adriatic. Orlando and Sonnino, his Foreign Secretary, walked out of the Peace Conference in protest and did not return until 9 May 1919.

Orlando's resignation and his replacement by Nitti in June opened the way up for secret negotiations in Paris, but the lynching of nine French troops in Fiume by an Italian mob in July and then the seizure of the city in September by the Italian nationalist poet **d'Annunzio** merely prolonged the crisis. It was not until November 1920 that Yugoslavia and Italy agreed on a compromise and signed the Treaty of Rapallo. Istria was partitioned between the two powers, Fiume was to become a self-governing free city, while the rest of Dalmatia went to Yugoslavia. In December Italian troops cleared d'Annunzio out of Fiume, although in late 1923 Mussolini ordered its reoccupation.

Key question Why could Orlando and Wilson not agree on the future of Fiume, Istria and Dalmatia?

'Balkan Prussia' Bulgaria was compared to Prussia, which in the eyes of the Allies had an aggressive and militarist reputation.

Proletarian nation A nation that lacked an empire and raw materials. Like the proletariat (workers) it was poor.

Key terms

Gabriele D'Annunzio (1863–1938) Italian nationalist poet, writer and leader of the coup in Fiume.

Key figure

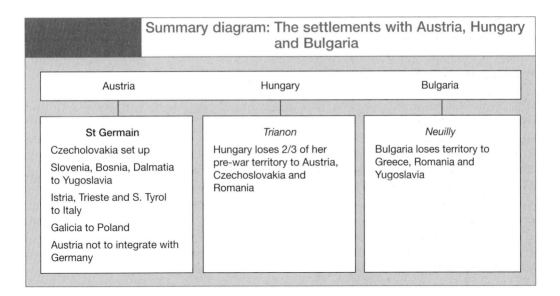

Summary diagram: The settlements with Austria, Hungary and Bulgaria

Austria	Hungary	Bulgaria
St Germain	*Trianon*	*Neuilly*
Czecholovakia set up	Hungary loses 2/3 of her pre-war territory to Austria, Czechoslovakia and Romania	Bulgaria loses territory to Greece, Romania and Yugoslavia
Slovenia, Bosnia, Dalmatia to Yugoslavia		
Istria, Trieste and S. Tyrol to Italy		
Galicia to Poland		
Austria not to integrate with Germany		

6 | The Settlement with Turkey 1919–23

Key question
To what extent was the Treaty of Sèvres so harsh that it was bound to provoke a backlash?

Key date
Treaty of Sèvres signed with Turkey: 10 August 1920

The Treaty of Sèvres was another Anglo-French compromise. Lloyd George hoped drastically to weaken Turkey, not only by depriving it of Constantinople and of the control of the Straits, but also by forcing it to surrender all territories where there was no ethnic Turkish majority. He now envisaged Greece, which entered the war on the Allied side in 1917, rather than Italy, as filling the vacuum left by the collapse of Turkish power and, in effect, becoming the agent of the British Empire in the eastern Mediterranean. The French, on the other hand, concerned to protect their pre-war investments in Turkey, wished to preserve a viable Turkish state. Above all, they wanted the Turkish government to remain in Constantinople where it would be more vulnerable to French pressure.

The end product of this Anglo-French compromise was a harsh and humiliating treaty. Constantinople remained Turkish, but Thrace and most of the European coastline of the Sea of Marmara and the Dardanelles were to go to Greece. In the Smyrna region the Greeks were also given responsibility for internal administration and defence, while an Armenian state was to be set up with access across Turkish territory to the Black Sea. The Straits were to be controlled by an international commission, and an Allied financial committee was to have the right to inspect Turkey's finances. By a separate agreement zones were also awarded to France and Italy in southern Turkey (see the map on page 100).

The division of Turkey's Arabian territories

Key question
Why was Britain able to revise the Sykes–Picot Agreement to suit its own interests?

The Sykes–Picot Agreement
In May 1916 Britain and France signed the Sykes–Picot Agreement. By this they committed themselves to dividing up Mesopotamia, Syria and the Lebanon into Anglo-French spheres

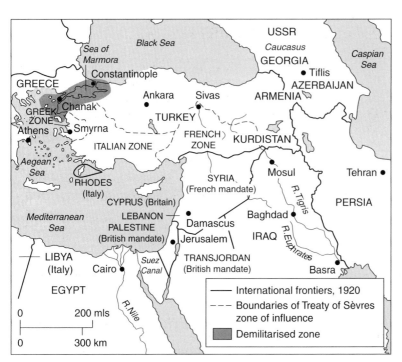

The Near and Middle East after the Treaty of Sèvres.

of interest once the war against Turkey had been won. Britain, however, was the only power with a large army in the Middle East, and consequently was able to revise the Sykes–Picot Agreement unilaterally. In 1917 Britain insisted on claiming the whole of Palestine, which was quite contrary to the agreement. By announcing support for the **Zionists**' ambition to establish a national home for the Jews in Palestine through the **Balfour Declaration**, Britain cleverly managed to secure the USA's backing for its aims.

The Middle East mandates

In February 1919, in deference to Wilson and the Fourteen Points, Britain and France agreed that they could only exercise power over these territories in the name of the League of Nations. It took several more months of bitter argument before the British agreed to a French mandate in Syria and also French access to the oil wells in Mosul in Iraq. The frontiers between the British mandates of Palestine and Iraq and the French mandate of Syria were then finalised in December (see the map above).

Mustapha Kemal and the revision of the treaty

Of all the treaties negotiated in 1919–20, Sèvres, signed on 10 August 1920, was the most obvious failure as it was never put into effect by the Turkish government. When the Allies imposed it, they took little account of the profound changes in Turkey brought about by the rise of Mustapha Kemal, the leader of the new nationalist movement. Kemal had set up a rebel government which controlled virtually the whole of the Turkish interior, and

Key terms

Zionists
Supporters of Zionism, a movement for re-establishing the Jewish state.

Balfour Declaration
A communication to the Zionists by A.J. Balfour, the British Foreign Secretary, declaring British support for establishing a national home for the Jews in Palestine.

Key question
Why was Kemal able to force the revision of the Treaty of Sèvres?

Profile: Mustapha Kemal 1880–1938

1880	– Born in Salonika
1908	– As an army officer he originally supported attempts to modernise Turkey by the Young Turks
1915	– Commander of Turkish troops at Gallipoli
1919	– Became leader of a nationalist revolution
1922	– Ejected Greeks from Smyrna and forced Britain and France to renegotiate the Treaty of Sèvres
1922–38	– Ruled Turkey as a dictator

Mustapha Kemal created the Turkish Republic in 1923. He was a great moderniser who emancipated women, introduced a Latin alphabet and encouraged Western-style dress. He also began to industrialise Turkey and to free it from traditional Islamic loyalties.

Key dates

Chanak incident: September–October 1922

Treaty of Lausanne: 23 July 1923

Key term

Straits zone
The shores along the Straits of Dardanelles and Bosphorus were occupied by Allied troops.

was determined not to accept the treaty. The long delay until August 1920 ensured that growing Turkish resentment, particularly at the Greek occupation of Smyrna (see page 99), which the Allies had encouraged in May 1919, made its enforcement an impossibility.

By settling the dispute over the Russo-Turkish frontier in the Caucasus, Kemal was able to concentrate his forces against the Greeks without fear of Russian intervention from the north. By August 1922 he was poised to enter Constantinople and the **Straits zone**, which were still occupied by Allied troops. Both the Italians and French rapidly withdrew leaving the British isolated. Kemal, however, avoided direct confrontation with the British forces and negotiated an armistice, which gave him virtually all he wanted: the Greeks withdrew from eastern Thrace and Adrianople, and the British recognised Turkish control over Constantinople and the Straits (see the map on page 100).

In 1923 an international conference met at Lausanne to revise the Treaty of Sèvres. Kemal, anxious not to be dependent on Russia, agreed to the creation of small demilitarised zones on both sides of the Straits and the freedom of navigation through them for Britain, France, Italy and Japan. He also insisted on the abolition of foreign control over Turkish finances. This was a serious blow to the French hopes of re-establishing their pre-war influence over Turkish finances, and arguably they, apart from the Greeks, lost more than any other power as a consequence of the new Treaty of Lausanne. The Chanak crisis did not affect the fate of Turkey's former Arab provinces, which remained under the control of Britain and France.

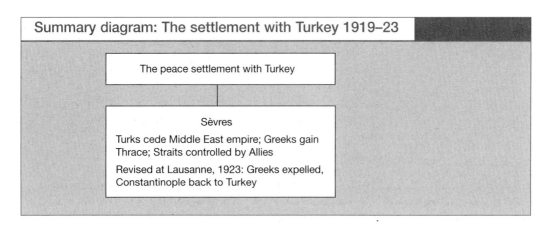

Summary diagram: The settlement with Turkey 1919–23

The peace settlement with Turkey

Sèvres

Turks cede Middle East empire; Greeks gain Thrace; Straits controlled by Allies

Revised at Lausanne, 1923: Greeks expelled, Constantinople back to Turkey

7 | Enforcing the Treaty of Versailles 1920–3

The organisation for carrying out the treaties

Once the Treaty of Versailles had been ratified the victorious powers set up a series of inter-Allied commissions to organise the plebiscites, monitor German disarmament and examine Germany's financial position with a view to payment of its reparations. These reported to the **Conference of Ambassadors** in Paris, which represented the Allied powers, but the real decisions were taken by the Allied prime ministers, who between January 1920 and January 1924 met 24 times to review progress made in carrying out the Treaty of Versailles.

Anglo-French differences

Both Britain and France had conflicting ideas of how best to ensure that Germany carried out the Treaty of Versailles. Essentially Britain, as the centre of a worldwide empire, wanted to see a balance of power in Europe that would prevent either French or German domination and leave it free to deal with the growing challenges to its power from nationalist movements in India, Egypt and Ireland. Britain was also convinced that only a prosperous and peaceful Germany could pay reparations and play its part in Europe as one of the main engines of the European economy.

For France, the German problem was an overriding priority. French policy swung uneasily between occasionally exploring the possibilities of economic co-operation with Germany, and more usually of applying forceful measures designed permanently to weaken Germany and to force it to fulfil the treaty.

Drawing up Poland's borders

The eastern frontier with Russia

The Poles exploited the chaos caused by the Russian civil war to extend their eastern frontier deep in the Ukraine and Belorussia. In December 1919 they rejected the proposed eastern frontier based on recommendations put forward by Lord Curzon, the British Foreign Minister, and in early 1920 embarked on a full-scale invasion of the Ukraine.

Key question
What was the machinery for carrying out the Treaty of Versailles?

Key question
Why did Britain's and France's views on how to implement the Treaty of Versailles conflict?

Conference of Ambassadors Standing committee set up to supervise the carrying out of the Treaty of Versailles.

Key term

Key question
Why did it take so long to regulate Poland's eastern frontier with Russia?

By August, Bolshevik forces had pushed the Poles back to Warsaw. However, with the help of French equipment and military advisers, the Poles rallied and managed to inflict a decisive defeat on the Red Army just outside Warsaw. Soviet troops were pushed back, and in March 1921 Poland's eastern frontiers were at last fixed by the Treaty of Riga. Poland annexed a considerable area of Belorussia and the western Ukraine (see the map on page 92), all of which lay well to the east of the proposed Curzon line.

Upper Silesia

By the end of 1920 the Marienwerder and Allenstein plebiscites had been held, in both of which the population voted to stay in Germany, and Danzig had became a free city under the administration of the League of Nations in November 1920.

Fixing the Upper Silesian frontiers, however, proved to be a much greater problem. Upper Silesia had a population of some 2,280,000 Germans and Poles, who were bitterly divided along ethnic lines, and a concentration of coal mines and industries that were second only in size to the Ruhr.

The plebiscite on 17 March 1921 produced an ambiguous result which did not solve the Anglo-French disagreements over Poland. The British argued that its result justified keeping the key industrial regions of the province German, while the French insisted that they should be awarded to Poland. Fearing that once again British wishes would prevail, the Poles seized control of the industrial area, and an uprising broke out in May 1921. Order was eventually restored by British and French troops in July 1921 and the whole question was handed over to the League of Nations in August. In 1922 the League, bowing to French pressure, decided to hand over most of the industrial areas to Poland.

Reparations

By far the most difficult problem facing the British and French governments was the reparation problem. Both the British and French hoped to solve the problem by fixing a global total as soon as possible on the assumption that once Germany knew the full sum of its debts it would be able to raise money in the USA from the sale of government bonds and begin payments.

At the end of April 1921 the Reparation Commission at last fixed a global total for reparations of 132 billion gold marks to be paid over a period of 42 years. When this was rejected by Germany, on the grounds that the sum was too high, an ultimatum was dispatched to Berlin giving the Germans only a week to accept the new payment schedule, after which the Ruhr would be occupied.

To carry out the London ultimatum a new government was formed by Joseph Wirth (1879–1956) on 10 May. Assisted by **Walther Rathenau**, his Minister for Reconstruction, he was determined to pursue a policy of negotiation rather than confrontation. The first instalment was paid, and Rathenau made some progress in persuading the French to accept the payment of a proportion of reparations in the form of the delivery of industrial

---

Key question
Why did the British and French disagree about the Upper Silesian frontier?

Key dates

Plebiscite in Upper Silesia: March 1921

German reparations fixed at 132 billion gold marks: April 1921

Key question
Why did all efforts to solve the reparation questions fail by the end of 1922?

Key figure

Walther Rathenau (1867–1922)
The son of the founder of the German electrical company AEG. In 1914–15 he saved Germany from the impact of the British blockade by setting up the German Raw Materials Department. He was murdered by German nationalists in 1922.

goods and coal. However, by the end of the year the German government dropped a bombshell by announcing that, as a consequence of escalating inflation, it could not raise sufficient hard currency to meet the next instalment of reparation payments.

The Geneva Conference, April 1922

This gave Lloyd George the opportunity to launch a major initiative. He was convinced that Germany needed a temporary **moratorium**, to put its economy in order, while in the longer term the key to the payment of reparations and a European economic revival lay in creating a European group of industrial nations, including Germany, to rebuild Russia. He hoped that this would generate an international trade boom, which would also benefit Germany, and enable it to pay reparations without damaging the commerce of the other European nations.

Raymond Poincaré (see page 45), who had just became French Prime Minister again, grudgingly consented to holding an international conference at Geneva, to which both the USSR and Germany would be invited to discuss these plans, but he vetoed any concession on reparations. The Soviets agreed to attend, but were highly suspicious of Lloyd George's plans for opening up their economy to foreign capital.

During the conference they pulled off a major diplomatic triumph by secretly negotiating the Rapallo Agreement with Germany, whereby both countries agreed to write off any financial claims on each other dating from the war. Germany also pledged to consult with Moscow before participating in any international plans for exploiting the Soviet economy.

Rapallo effectively killed Lloyd George's plan. It is hard not to see Rapallo as a miscalculation by the Germans. While it helped Germany to escape from isolation, it did so at the cost of intensifying French suspicions of its motives. In many ways these were justified, as a **secret annex** signed in July allowed Germany to train its soldiers in Soviet territory, thereby violating the terms of the Treaty of Versailles.

The Ruhr occupation

In July 1922 a major confrontation between France and Germany seemed inevitable when the German government requested a three-year moratorium. At the same time Britain announced that, as the USA was demanding the repayment of British wartime debts, it must in turn insist on the repayment of money loaned to former allies, particularly France. To the French, Britain's demand for these repayments contrasted painfully with the concessions Lloyd George was ready to offer the Germans.

On 27 November the Poincaré cabinet decided finally that the occupation of the Ruhr was the only means of forcing Germany to pay reparations, and on 11 January French and Belgian troops moved into the Ruhr. Significantly, Britain did not join in but adopted a policy of '**benevolent neutrality**' towards France.

For nine months the French occupation of the Ruhr was met by **passive resistance** and strikes which were financed by the

Key question
Why did the Geneva Conference fail?

Key date

Geneva Conference and Rapallo Treaty between Germany and USSR: April 1922

Key terms

Moratorium
Temporary suspension of payments.

Secret annex
Secret addition to a treaty.

Benevolent neutrality
Favouring one side while not officially supporting them.

Passive resistance
Refusal to co-operate, stopping short of actual violence.

Key question
Why did the Ruhr crisis mark a turning point in post-war European history?

Key date

French and Belgian troops occupied the Ruhr: 11 January 1923

Key terms

Hyperinflation
Massive daily increases in the prices of goods and in the amount of money being printed.

Rhineland separatism
A movement favouring separation of the Rhineland from Germany.

German government. This increased the cost of the occupation, but it also triggered **hyperinflation** in Germany. In September, Germany was on the brink of collapse and the new Chancellor, Gustav Stresemann, called off passive resistance.

France, too, had exhausted itself and seriously weakened the franc in the prolonged Ruhr crisis. France's attempts to back **Rhineland separatism** and to create an independent Rhineland currency were unsuccessful. Separatist leaders were assassinated by German nationalist agents from unoccupied Germany or lynched by angry crowds. Poincaré had thus little option but to co-operate with an Anglo-American initiative for setting up a commission chaired by the US financier Charles G. Dawes. Its two committee experts, one to study Germany's capacity for payment, and the other to advise on how it could best balance the budget and restore its currency, began work in early 1924.

As one French official accurately observed, the time was now past for dealing with Germany as 'victor to vanquished'. The Ruhr crisis marked the end of the attempts to carry out the Treaty of Versailles by force and the beginning of the gradual revision of the treaty itself.

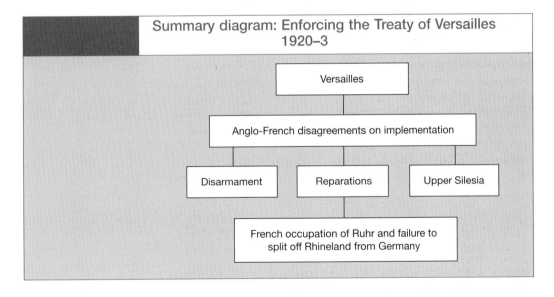

Summary diagram: Enforcing the Treaty of Versailles 1920–3

8 | The Key Debate

> To what extent did the peace settlements of 1919–20 contain the seeds of their own destruction?

The peace treaties of 1919–20 were seen by some contemporaries as a triumph of democracy, the rule of law, self-determination and collective security against militarism, and yet by others as a hypocritical act of vengeance and economic ignorance. The treaties contained a unique combination of idealism and morality with old-fashioned **power politics**.

Increasingly, as a result of the devastating criticisms in *The Economic Consequences of the Peace*, which was a brilliant analysis of

Key term

Power politics
International relations that are based on force rather than moral principles.

the Versailles Treaty written in 1919 by **Keynes**, an economist who had been a member of the British delegation in Paris, public opinion in Britain and the USA began to turn against the peace. Keynes summarised his arguments as follows:

1) ... the treaty ignores the economic solidarity of Europe and by aiming at the destruction of the economic life of Germany it threatens the health and prosperity of the Allies themselves.

2) ... the German economic system as it existed before depended on ... i) Overseas commerce as represented by her Mercantile marine [most of which had to be handed over to the Allies], her colonies, her foreign investments, her exports ... ii) The exploitation of her coal and iron and the industries built upon them ... The Treaty aims at the systematic destruction of [this system].

To the Germans, Keynes' arguments seemed to provide the final proof that the Allies were out to destroy their country. Yet viewed from the perspective of 1945 the Treaty of Versailles does not appear as harsh as it did in 1919. Germany was still potentially a Great Power.

Unlike the Vienna settlement of 1815, the peace treaties failed to create a new balance of power in Europe. The Austrian Empire was replaced by several smaller unstable states. Italy felt cheated by the peace and was to remain a revisionist power in the Mediterranean and the Adriatic. Even Britain and France, who gained most from Versailles, in fact secured only short-term advantages as they were too divided by mutual suspicions effectively to implement the treaties in the crucial post-war years.

A major weakness of the settlements of 1919–20 was that the USA, which had played such a part in negotiating them, was prevented by the vote in the Senate from helping to implement them. One US historian, Paul Birdsall, argued that:

the defection of the United States destroyed the Anglo-American preponderance which above all could have stabilised Europe. It impaired the authority and prestige of the League at its birth and it precipitated an Anglo-French duel which reduced Europe to the chaos from which Hitler emerged to produce new chaos ...

While it is debatable whether the US Senate can be held responsible for the rise of Hitler and the Second World War, there is no doubt that the USA's active presence in the Supreme Council of the Allies between 1920 and 1923 and its participation in a military guarantee of France's frontiers would have had a decisive influence on European stabilisation in the immediate post-war years.

John Maynard Keynes (1883–1946)
A British economist and civil servant who represented the Treasury at the Paris Conference. He was a bitter critic of the Versailles Treaty and in the 1930s became famous for his views on dealing with unemployment. During the Second World War he was financial advisor to the British government.

Key figure

Some key books in the debate:
R. Henig, *Versailles and After, 1919–33*, 2nd edn (Routledge, 1995).
M. Macmillan, *Peacemakers* (John Murray, 2001).
A.J. Mayer, *Politics and Diplomacy in Peacemaking: Containment and Counter-revolution at Versailles* (Weidenfeld and Nicolson, 1968).
Alan Sharp, editor, *Makers of the Modern World: The Paris Peace Conferences 1919–23* (Haus Publishing, 2009).

Study Guide: AS Question

In the style of OCR A

'A compromise that satisfied nobody.' How far do you agree with this verdict on the Treaty of Versailles?

Exam tips

The page references are intended to take you straight to the material that will help you to answer the question.

You are given a claim and your job is to judge it. You may agree or disagree with it. As long as you argue using examples to back up what you say you will score well. Note that the question is broad. To answer properly, you must assess the degrees of satisfaction with the treaty felt by the individual Allied powers and Germany. You can answer this in two ways. One approach would be to judge the level of satisfaction state by state against the aims and expectations of that protagonist in the war. Alternatively, you could look individually at the particular terms of the treaty and judge how well each one satisfied each power. Whichever approach you take, be clear that the levels of satisfaction varied from nation to nation:

- Germany was unlikely to be satisfied because it was the defeated power (pages 94–5).
- France's attitude must be considered, and that will allow you to balance mixed attitudes: satisfaction that Germany was punished severely, but dissatisfaction that it was not crippled and France still felt vulnerable (pages 84 and 89–90).
- Discussion of Britain will also force you to handle complex feelings: the dissatisfaction of some people convinced that Germany's punishment was too harsh, set against the dissatisfaction of others that its punishment was not harsh enough (pages 84–5 and 90).
- Do not forget the USA. Did failure to ratify the treaty show dissatisfaction there as well (pages 83 and 95)?

However you choose to argue, your essay will score well if you evaluate the satisfaction levels of the various states involved. In each case, you can only do that if you show why their level of satisfaction was as it was – and that means using examples for each. As you do this, beware of wandering off the point into a description of the treaty's terms.

Study Guide: A2 Question

In the style of Edexcel

'It was shaped by the French determination to exact revenge and to ensure Germany's permanent weakness.' How far do you agree with this view of the post-war settlement with Germany in 1919?

Exam tips

The page references are intended to take you straight to the material that will help you to answer the question.

In order to answer this question you will need to examine the military, financial and territorial terms of the settlement (pages 88–93) for evidence of the extent to which they reflect a French desire for revenge and/or an attempt to constrain the future power of Germany. You will also need to consider how far they were shaped by French aims and how far by other considerations. For example:

- the principle of self-determination enshrined in President Wilson's Fourteen Points (page 83)
- British interests (pages 84–5).

In the process of reaching an overall judgement, remember to take account of the settlement related to German colonial possessions (page 93) as well as the European situation. Also pay particular attention to instances where the aims of France and the others drawing up the settlement were in conflict. For example:

- the issue of Danzig (pages 92–3)
- the Rhineland, Saarland and Upper Silesia (pages 92–3).

You should reach a conclusion offering a clear judgement that is in line with the argument you have advanced in the body of your answer.

6 Reconciliation and Disarmament 1924–30: The Locarno Era

POINTS TO CONSIDER

This chapter covers the period after the failure of the Ruhr occupation. Confrontation was now slowly replaced with co-operation between Britain, France and Germany. It looks at:

- The impact of the Dawes Plan
- The Locarno Treaties
- The 'Locarno spirit' and Germany's re-emergence as a Great Power
- Russia and eastern Europe during the Locarno era
- The development of the League of Nations
- Progress made towards disarmament

As you read this chapter ask yourself both why the League was at last able to function more effectively and to what extent Europe by 1928–9 had recovered from the consequences of the First World War. Also consider whether the USA had in practice given up isolation.

Key dates

1921	March	Franco-Polish Alliance
1921–2		Washington Conference and Five Power Naval Convention
1925	October	Locarno Conference
1926	January	Allies evacuated Cologne zone
	April	German–Soviet Treaty of Friendship
	September	Germany joined the League of Nations
1928	August 27	Kellogg–Briand Pact signed by 15 states
1929	August	Hague Conference
	October 29	Wall Street Crash

1 | The Impact of the Dawes Plan

Key question
What were the terms of the Dawes Plan, and why did it help to stabilise Europe after the Ruhr crisis?

The Dawes Plan played a crucial part in ending the bitter conflict over reparations which had nearly escalated into open war during the Ruhr occupation.

The recommendations of the Dawes Plan

- Although the plan did not alter the overall reparation total, which had been fixed in 1921, it did recommend a loan of 800 million gold marks, which was to be raised mainly in the USA, to assist the restoration of the German economy. This was a crucially important component of the plan because it opened the way for US investment in Germany.
- Annual reparation payments were to start gradually and rise at the end of five years to their maximum level. These payments were to be guaranteed by the revenues of the German railways and of several key industries.
- A committee of foreign experts sitting in Berlin under the chairmanship of a US official was to ensure that the actual payments were transferred to Britain, France and Belgium in such a way that the German economy was not damaged. The plan was provisional and was to be renegotiated over the next 10 years.

Key question
What were the recommendations of the Dawes Plan?

The reaction to the Dawes Plan

The British

It was welcomed enthusiastically in April 1924 by the British Treasury as 'the only constructive suggestion for escape from the present position, which if left must inevitably lead to war, open or concealed, between Germany and France'. It also had the advantage of involving the USA in the whole process of extracting reparations from Germany.

Key question
What was the reaction of the British, French and Germans to the Dawes Plan?

The French

There was much that the French disliked about the plan. For instance, it was not clear to them how the Germans could be compelled to pay if they again defaulted and refused to pay, as they had in 1922. However, with the defeat of Poincaré in the elections of June 1924 their willingness to co-operate markedly increased. Essentially, if the French were ever to receive any reparation payments and to avoid isolation, they had little option but to go along with the Dawes Plan.

The Germans

The Germans also disliked the Plan as it placed their railways and some of their industry under international control and did nothing about scaling down their reparation debts. Stresemann, who, after the fall of his cabinet in November 1923, was now Foreign Minister, realised, however, that Germany had no alternative but to accept the plan if the French were to be persuaded to evacuate the Ruhr sooner rather than later.

The London Conference

Agreement to implement the Dawes Plan and to withdraw French and Belgian forces from the Ruhr within 12 months was achieved at the London Conference in August 1924. The new balance of power in Europe was clearly revealed when Britain and the USA devised a formula for effectively blocking France's ability to act

Key question
What steps were taken to ensure that France would not again be able to act alone if Germany defaulted on reparation payments?

Profile: Gustav Stresemann 1878–1929

1878	–	Born in Berlin
1906	–	Elected to the *Reichstag* as a National Liberal
1917	–	Succeeded to party leadership
1923	–	Chancellor
1924–9	–	Foreign Secretary
1929	–	Died

During the war Stresemann was an ardent nationalist and close supporter of Hindenburg and Ludendorff. After 1922 he moderated his position and aimed to win the confidence of the Western Powers by carrying out the Treaty of Versailles. In August 1923 he called off passive resistance in the Ruhr. Between 1924 and 1929, as Foreign Minister, he had considerable success in restoring Germany's position in Europe through the Locarno Treaties and by securing Germany a seat on the council of the League of Nations. He was hated by the nationalists in Germany, but he believed that Germany would eventually dominate Europe through peaceful means.

Key term

Permanent Court of International Justice
An institution set up at The Hague, the Netherlands, by Article 14 of the Covenant of the League of Nations in 1920.

alone against Germany in the event of another default in reparation payments. If Germany again refused to pay, it was agreed that Britain as a member of the Reparation Commission would have the right to appeal to the **Permanent Court of International Justice** at The Hague, and that a US representative would immediately join the Reparation Commission. Joint Anglo-American pressure would then be more than enough to restrain France from reoccupying the Ruhr. Deprived of much of their influence on the Reparation Commission, the French had undoubtedly suffered a major diplomatic defeat at the London Conference.

Summary diagram: The impact of the Dawes Plan

Recommendations	• 800 million mark loan to Germany • A committee under American chairmanship set up in Berlin to arrange transfer of reparation payments • Payments to start gradually to reach maximum level after 5 years
Reaction of the Great Powers: Britain France Germany	 Welcomed it to break the reparation deadlock After failure of the Ruhr occupation, France had no option but to accept it The Germans too had to accept if the French were to quit the Ruhr
	Dawes Plan implemented at the London Conference, 1924

2 | The Locarno Treaties

France's need for security

The Dawes Plan, by bringing the Ruhr crisis to an end, had, together with the **German measures to stabilise the mark**, made Germany an attractive prospect for US investment. To a certain extent, one of the preconditions for a European economic recovery was now in place, but investment was to come from individuals and banks and was not guaranteed by the US government. Nor was it accompanied by offers of military security to the French. Thus, should a new economic crisis blow up, US money could melt away and France could be left facing a strong and aggressive Germany.

Initially, the French had little option but to continue to insist, in as far as they still could, on the literal implementation of the Treaty of Versailles. They refused, for instance, to agree to the evacuation of the Cologne zone, which was due in January 1925 (see page 92), on the grounds that Germany had not yet carried out the military clauses of the treaty 'either in the spirit or in the letter'.

Negotiating the Locarno Treaties 1925

The urgent need to reassure the French of Germany's peaceful intentions, and so secure the evacuation of Cologne, prompted Gustav Stresemann, on the unofficial advice of the British ambassador in Berlin, to put forward a complex scheme for an international guarantee by the European great powers of the Rhineland and of the status quo in western Europe.

Austen Chamberlain, the British Foreign Secretary, at first suspected the proposals of being an attempt to divide France and Britain. Then he rapidly grasped that it was potentially a marvellous opportunity to square the circle by achieving both French security and the evacuation of Cologne without committing Britain to a military pact with France, which the cabinet would never tolerate. Aristide Briand, now back in power, was aware that only within the framework of an international agreement on the lines put forward by Stresemann could he in any way commit Britain to coming to the assistance of France if it were again attacked by Germany.

In the ensuing negotiations Briand successfully persuaded Chamberlain and Stresemann to widen the international guarantee to cover the Belgian–German frontier. He also attempted to extend it to Germany's eastern frontiers, but this was rejected by both Stresemann and Chamberlain. However, Stresemann did undertake to refer disputes with Poland and Czechoslovakia to arbitration, although he refused to recognise their frontiers with Germany as permanent. Chamberlain was quite specific that it was in Britain's interests only to guarantee the status quo in western Europe. He told the House of Commons in November 1925, in words that were to return to haunt the British government (see page 169), that extending the guarantee to the Polish corridor would not be worth 'the bones of a British grenadier'.

Key question
How did France seek to gain security from future German aggression?

Key figure

Austen Chamberlain (1863–1937)
Member of Lloyd George's government 1919–21 and then British Foreign Secretary 1924–9. He was the half-brother of Neville Chamberlain.

Key question
What were the terms of Locarno Treaties?

Key term

German measures to stabilise the mark
In November 1924 the devalued German currency was replaced temporarily by the *Rentenmark* and then in August 1924 by the new *Reichsmark*, which was put on the gold standard. Theoretically this meant that paper bank notes could be converted into agreed, fixed quantities of gold.

Key date

Locarno Conference: October 1925

Profile: Aristide Briand 1862–1932

1862	–	Born in Nantes
1906	–	Resigned from Socialist Party
1906–9	–	Cabinet minister
1909–29	–	Headed 11 governments and was a strong supporter of the League of Nations and reconciliation with Germany
1932	–	Died

Briand started off his political career as a socialist, but when he joined a left-wing liberal coalition government in 1906, he was expelled from the party. Between 1906 and 1929 Briand headed 11 governments and was also Foreign Minister from 1925 to 1932. As a wartime Prime Minister he lacked energy and charisma, but he came into his own after the war when between 1924 and 1929 as Prime Minister and Foreign Minister he supported the League of Nations and Franco-German reconciliation. He was awarded the Nobel Peace Prize jointly with Gustav Stresemann.

The negotiations were completed at the Locarno Conference, 5–16 October 1925, and resulted in a number of treaties that were signed on 1 December. The most important of these were agreements confirming the **inviolability** of the Franco-German and Belgian–German frontiers and the demilitarisation of the Rhineland.

The treaties were underwritten by an Anglo-Italian guarantee to assist the victims of aggression. If a relatively minor incident on one of the frontiers covered by Locarno occurred, the injured party (for example, France) would first appeal to the Council of the League of Nations (see page 120), and if the complaint was

Key term

Inviolability
Not to be changed or violated.

The signatories of the Treaties of Locarno in the garden of 10 Downing Street, London. Prime Minister Stanley Baldwin is on the far right, French Foreign Minister Aristide Briand in the front row, centre, and Winston Churchill back row, right.

upheld, the guarantors would assist the injured state to secure compensation from the aggressor (for example, Germany). In the event of a serious violation of the treaty the guarantors could act immediately, although they would still eventually refer the issue to the council.

Assessing the agreements

Key question
What did Britain, France and Germany gain from the Locarno Agreements?

Throughout western Europe and the USA the Locarno Treaties were greeted with enormous enthusiasm. It appeared as if real peace had at last come. Had France now achieved the security it had for so long been seeking? Of all the great powers the French gained least from Locarno. It is true that France's eastern frontier was now secure, but under Locarno it could no longer threaten to occupy the Ruhr in order to bring pressure to bear on Berlin in the event of Germany breaking the Treaty of Versailles. The British had managed to give France the illusion of security, but the provision for referring all but major violations of the Locarno Agreements to the League before taking action ensured that the British government would in practice be able to determine, through its own representative on the Council, what action, if any, it should take. For Britain there were two main advantages to Locarno: it tied France down and prevented it from repeating the Ruhr occupation. Also, by improving relations between Germany and the Western Powers and by holding out the prospect of German membership of the League, it discouraged any close co-operation between Moscow and Berlin.

Locarno was deeply unpopular with the German nationalists, but for Stresemann it was the key to the gradual process of revising the treaty. He wrote to the former heir to the German throne on 7 September 1925:

> There are three great tasks that confront German foreign policy in the more immediate future. In the first place the solution of the reparation question in a sense tolerable for Germany, and the assurance of peace, which is essential for the recovery of our strength. Secondly the protection of the Germans abroad, those 10–12 millions of our kindred who now live under a foreign yoke in foreign lands. The third great task is the readjustment of our Eastern frontiers: the recovery of Danzig, the Polish frontier, and a correction of the frontier of Upper Silesia.

By assuring Germany of peace in the west, and by not placing its eastern frontiers with Poland under international guarantee, Locarno left open the eventual possibility of revision of the German–Polish frontier. Stresemann's aims were therefore diametrically opposed to Briand's, but both desired peace and therein lay the real importance of Locarno. It was a symbol of a new age of reconciliation and co-operation. Locarno, as Ramsay MacDonald (1866–1937), the leader of the British Labour Party, observed, brought about a 'miraculous change' of psychology on the continent.

Summary diagram: The Locarno Treaties

Locarno Conference, October 1925
attended by Chamberlain, Stresemann and Briand

Locarno Treaties signed, December 1925

Arbitration treaties signed between Germany and France, Belgium, Czechoslovakia and Poland

Agreement guaranteeing Franco-German and Belgo-German frontiers and demilitarisation of the Rhineland signed by France, Germany and Belgium. Guaranteed by Italy and Britain

Key question
To what extent did the Locarno Treaties lead to a revision of the Treaty of Versailles?

Key term

Locarno spirit
The optimistic mood of reconciliation and compromise that swept through Europe after the signing of the Locarno Treaties.

3 | The 'Locarno Spirit' and Germany's Re-emergence as a Great Power

The '**Locarno spirit**' was an elusive concept which was interpreted differently in London, Paris and Berlin. All three powers agreed that it involved goodwill and concessions, yet the scope and timing of these concessions were a matter of constant and often bitter debate. Both Stresemann and Briand had to convince their countrymen that the Locarno policy was working. Briand had to show that he was not giving too much away, while Stresemann had to satisfy German public opinion that his policy of '**fulfilment**' was resulting in real concessions from the ex-Allies. It can be argued that the survival not only of Stresemann's policy but of the German Republic itself depended on ever more ambitious diplomatic successes. What would happen once these were unobtainable?

Key question
How much had Stresemann achieved by the end of 1927?

Key terms

Fulfilment
A policy aimed by Germany at extracting concessions from Britain and France by attempting to fulfil the Treaty of Versailles.

Détente
A process of lessened tension or growing relaxation between two states.

Stresemann's initial successes and failures 1925–7

The atmosphere of *détente* created by Locarno quickly led to the evacuation of the Cologne zone in January 1926, and in September 1926 Germany at last joined the League of Nations and received a permanent seat on the Council.

Stresemann exploited every opportunity both inside and outside the League to accelerate the revision of Versailles. In 1926 he attempted to exploit France's financial weakness by proposing that Germany pay the French nearly one-and-a-half billion gold marks, most of which Germany would raise in the USA by the sale of bonds. In return France would evacuate the Rhineland and give back the Saar and its coalmines to Germany. Despite initial interest, the plan was rejected in December. The French government's finances had, contrary to expectation, improved, and it also emerged that the US government was not ready to approve the sale of more German bonds to US investors.

Stresemann did, however, manage to extract further concessions from both Britain and France. In January 1927 the Allied Disarmament Commission was withdrawn from Germany, and in the following August Britain, France and Belgium withdrew a further 10,000 troops from their garrisons in the Rhineland.

The Young Plan and the evacuation of the Rhineland

Two years later Stresemann achieved his greatest success when he managed to negotiate a permanent reduction in reparations with an Anglo-French evacuation of the Rhineland five years before the Treaty of Versailles required it. At the Hague Conference in 1929 the overall reparation sum was reduced from 132 billion gold marks to 112 billion, to be paid over the course of 59 years, and Britain and France agreed to evacuate the Rhineland in 1930.

The agreement to end the Rhineland occupation helped to make the Young Plan acceptable in Germany, but even so in December the government faced a referendum forced on them by the Nazi and Nationalist parties declaring that its signature would be an act of high treason on the grounds that Germany was still committed to paying reparations. This was easily defeated and the Young Plan was officially implemented on 20 January 1930.

Proposals for a European customs union and a common currency

With the evacuation of the Rhineland, Germany's restoration to the status of a great European power was virtually complete. Briand, like his successors in the 1950s, appears to have come to the conclusion that Germany could only be peacefully contained through some form of European federation. At the tenth assembly of the League of Nations in 1929, he outlined an ambitious, but vague scheme for creating 'some kind of federal link … between the peoples of Europe'.

Stresemann reacted favourably and urged both a European customs union and a common currency. Briand was then entrusted by the 27 European members of the League with the task of formulating his plan more precisely; but when it was circulated to the chancelleries of Europe in May 1930, the whole economic and political climate had dramatically changed. Stresemann had died and the political crisis in Germany caused by the onset of the Depression brought to power a government under **Heinrich Brüning** that was more interested in a customs union with Austria than in a European **federation**. The German cabinet finally rejected the memorandum on 8 July 1930. A week later it was also rejected by Britain.

It is tempting to argue that Briand's plans for a European federation, which were killed off by the economic crisis that was eventually to bring Hitler to power, was one of the lost opportunities of history. On the other hand, it would be a mistake to view them through the eyes of early twenty-first century European federalists. Essentially, Stresemann hoped that it would open the door to an accelerated revision of the Treaty of Versailles, while Briand calculated that it would have the opposite effect. Perhaps under favourable circumstances it could at least have provided a framework within which Franco-German differences could have been solved.

Key question
What did Stresemann achieve at the Hague Conference?

Key dates

Allies evacuated Cologne zone: January 1926

Germany joined League of Nations: September 1926

Hague Conference: August 1929

Wall Street Crash: 29 October 1929

Key question
Why did Briand's proposals for a European federation fail?

Key figure

Heinrich Brüning (1885–1970)
Leader of the German Centre Party and Chancellor of Germany 1930–2.

Key term

Federation
A system of government in which several countries or regions form a unity but still manage to remain self-governing in internal affairs.

Summary diagram: The 'Locarno spirit' and Germany's re-emergence as a Great Power

The Locarno era				
The London Conference, 1924, inaugurates Dawes Plan	Locarno Agreements, September 1925	Kellogg–Briand Pact, August 1928	Young Plan and evacuation of the Rhineland, 1929–30	Briand's proposal for European Union, 1929

4 | Russia and Eastern Europe During the Locarno Era

Russia and Germany

Key question
What were the aims of Russian foreign policy towards Germany, 1924–9?

Key date
German–Soviet Treaty of Friendship: April 1926

The Soviet government, which after the death of Lenin in January 1924 increasingly fell under the control of Stalin (see page 144), viewed the progress made in stabilising western Europe through the Dawes Plan and the Locarno Agreements with both dismay and hostility, as it feared that this would strengthen the anti-Bolshevik forces in Europe and delay revolution in Germany. The Russians initially attempted to deflect Stresemann from his Locarno policy, first with the offer of a military alliance against Poland, and then, when that did not work, with the contradictory threat of joining with France to guarantee Poland's western frontiers.

Stresemann, aware of Russia's attempts to stir up revolution in Germany in 1923, was not ready to abandon the Locarno policy, but he was anxious to keep open his links with Moscow and consolidate the Rapallo Agreement of 1922 (see page 104), if only as a possible insurance against Anglo-French pressure in the west. Thus, the Russians were able first to negotiate a commercial treaty with Germany in October 1925. Then in April 1926, at a time when the Poles and the French were trying to delay Germany's membership of the League council, they persuaded Stresemann to sign the German–Soviet Treaty of Friendship (the Berlin Treaty). Essentially, this was a neutrality pact in which both powers agreed to remain neutral if either party was attacked by a third power.

Anglo-Russian relations

Key question
Why were relations so bad between Britain and Russia 1924–9?

Relations between Russia and Britain sharply deteriorated when the incoming Conservative government refused in October 1924 to ratify the Anglo-Soviet General Treaty which had been negotiated by the outgoing Labour administration. In 1927, after ordering a raid on the offices of the official Soviet trading company, Arcos, in an attempt to discover evidence of espionage, the British government severed all official relations with Russia.

Only in 1929, with the return of Labour, were ambassadors again exchanged. This outbreak of the first 'Anglo-Soviet cold war', as the American historian Jacobson has called it, strengthened Stalin's determination to cut Russia off from the West. Increasingly, the main thrust of Soviet foreign policy in the late 1920s was to exploit anti-Western feeling in the Middle East, China and India.

France and eastern Europe

With the victory of the Bolsheviks in the Russian Civil War, the French began to build up a series of alliances in eastern Europe to take the place of their original pre-war alliance with Tsarist Russia (see page 33). In March 1921 they concluded an alliance with Poland which, because it was hated by Russia and Germany and was on bad terms with Czechoslovakia and Lithuania, was the most vulnerable of the east European states. Further French attempts to strengthen it met with little success. Paris failed to persuade Stresemann to agree to a guarantee of Poland's frontiers or to ensure that Poland gained a permanent seat on the League council. In 1925–6 it even looked as if the Polish state would suffer financial collapse, but by 1927 its financial position stabilised and for the time being the USSR and Germany had to tolerate its existence.

The French were less successful in organising the other new states created by Versailles into a defensive alliance against Germany. In August 1920 Czechoslovakia and Yugoslavia signed a pact which became known as the Little *Entente*, and were joined by Romania in 1921. However, it was primarily directed against Hungary and was designed to prevent the return of the Habsburgs and the revision of the Trianon Treaty. Only in 1924 did Paris succeed in concluding a treaty with Czechoslovakia but, again, it was not strictly an anti-German alignment. It would only come into operation in the event of a restoration of the royal families of Austria or Germany or of an Austrian *Anschluss* with Germany. Despite attempts by Italy to challenge French influence in the Balkans, the French government was able to exploit the suspicions caused by the growth of Italian influence in Albania to sign first a treaty with Romania guaranteeing its frontiers (1926) and then a treaty of friendship with Yugoslavia (1927). By the end of the decade French influence was preponderant in the Balkans.

Key question
To what extent did France consolidate its influence in eastern Europe?

Key date
Franco-Polish Alliance: March 1921

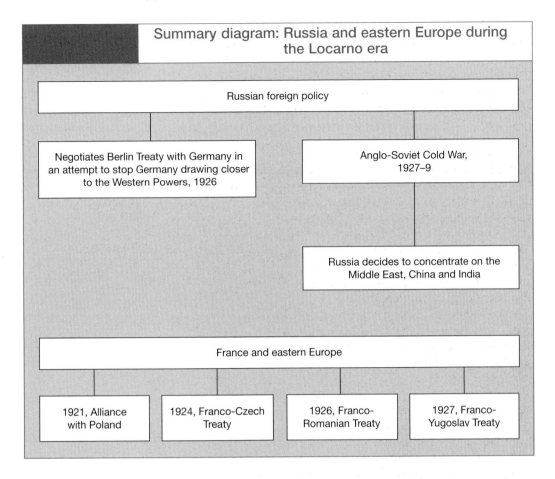

Summary diagram: Russia and eastern Europe during the Locarno era

Russian foreign policy

Negotiates Berlin Treaty with Germany in an attempt to stop Germany drawing closer to the Western Powers, 1926

Anglo-Soviet Cold War, 1927–9

Russia decides to concentrate on the Middle East, China and India

France and eastern Europe

1921, Alliance with Poland

1924, Franco-Czech Treaty

1926, Franco-Romanian Treaty

1927, Franco-Yugoslav Treaty

5 | The Development of the League of Nations

Key question
How successful was the League of Nations?

The League was a part of the international settlements negotiated in 1919–20. Inevitably, the tensions and divisions inherent in these were also present in the League. The absence in 1920 of three Great Powers from the League reflected the reality of the international situation where both Germany and the USSR licked their wounds in defensive isolation, while the US government, after having played such a key role in negotiating the new peace settlement, had been forced by Congress to disengage from most of its international responsibilities. The League's ultimate success or failure was dependent on the progress made by the great powers in stabilising Europe after the First World War. Not surprisingly, the League's golden age coincided with the new stability created by the Locarno era.

The Covenant of the League of Nations

Key question
How did the League of Nations work?

In retrospect, it is possible to argue that the League's Covenant or constitution provided too many loopholes for war, supported the status quo which favoured the Great Powers and, in the final analysis, lacked the machinery for collective action against an aggressor. Yet even if it had had a theoretically perfect constitution, would its history have been any different? Perhaps the official British commentary on the Covenant was realistic when it pointed out:

> If the nations of the future are in the main selfish, grasping and warlike, no instrument or machinery will restrain them. It is only possible to establish an organisation which may make peaceful co-operation easy and hence customary, and to trust in the influence of custom to mould opinion.

The organs of the League of Nations

The initial members of the League were the 32 Allied states which had signed the peace treaties and 12 neutral states. By 1926 all the ex-enemy states including Germany had joined, but Soviet Russia did not do so until 1934, and the USA never did. The League at first consisted of three main organs: the Assembly, the Council and the Permanent Secretariat.

The Assembly

The Assembly was essentially a **deliberative chamber** where each state, regardless of its size, was allotted three representatives. It was a jealously guarded principle that even the smallest state had the right to be heard on international issues.

The Council

The Council in 1920 had four permanent members: Britain, France, Italy and Japan. In 1926 this was increased by one when Germany joined. The smaller states were represented by a changing rota of four temporary members, later increased to seven, who were all selected by the Assembly. As the Council met more frequently than the Assembly and was dominated by the Great Powers, it gradually developed as an **executive committee** or 'cabinet' of the Assembly, and worked out the details and

Key question
What roles did the organs of the League play?

Key terms

Deliberative chamber
An assembly appointed to debate or discuss issues.

Executive committee
A committee which can take key decisions.

Ambassadors from around the world assemble in the Reformation Hall at Geneva's Palais de Nations for the first session of the League of Nations in November 1920.

implementation of policies which the Assembly had endorsed in principle. Decisions in both bodies were normally taken by unanimous vote. The votes of states involved in a dispute under discussion by the League were discounted when the Assembly and Council voted on recommendations for its settlement. In this way they could be prevented from vetoing an otherwise unanimous decision.

Permanent Secretariat

The routine administrative work of the League was carried out by the Permanent Secretariat which was staffed by a relatively small **international civil service**.

Permanent Court of International Justice

In 1921 a fourth organ was added to the League when the Permanent Court of International Justice was set up at The Hague in the Netherlands with the task of both advising the council on legal matters and judging cases submitted to it by individual states.

Key term

International civil service

A permanent administration made up of officials from all the member states.

Key question
How effective were the League's powers for solving international disputes?

What powers did the League of Nations possess to solve international disputes?

The heart of the covenant, Articles 8–17, was primarily concerned with the overriding question of the prevention of war. The League's long-term strategy for creating a peaceful world was summed up in the first section of Article 8:

> The members of the League recognise that the maintenance of peace requires the reduction of national armaments to the lowest point consistent with national safety, and the enforcement by common action of international obligations.

The process for solving disputes between sovereign powers was defined in Articles 12–17. Initially (Article 12) disputes were to be submitted to some form of arbitration or inquiry by the League. While this was happening, there was to be a cooling off period of three months. By Article 13 members were committed to carrying out the judgements of the Permanent Court of International Justice or the recommendations of the Council. Even if a dispute was not submitted to arbitration, the Council was empowered by Article 15 to set up an inquiry into its origins. The assumption in these articles was that states would be only too willing to eliminate war by making use of the League's arbitration machinery. If, however, a state ignored the League's recommendations, Article 16 made it clear that:

> I. … it shall … be deemed to have committed an act of war against all other members of the League, which hereby undertake immediately to subject it to the severance of all trade or financial relations …
> II. It shall be the duty of the council in such case to recommend to the several governments concerned what effective military, naval

or air force the members of the League shall severally contribute
to the armed forces to be used to protect the covenants of the
League.

In Article 17 the League's powers were significantly extended by
its right to intervene in disputes between non-members of the
League, while in Article 11 member states were encouraged to
refer to the assembly or council any international problem which
might threaten the peace.

In theory, the League seemed to have formidable powers, but it
was not a world government in the making, with powers to coerce
independent nations. Its existence was based, as Article 10 made
clear, on the recognition of the political and territorial
independence of all member states. Article 15, for instance,
recognised that if a dispute arose from an internal issue, the
League had no right to intervene. There were, too, several gaps
in the League Covenant which allowed a potential aggressor to
wage war without sanction. War had to be officially declared
before the League could act effectively. It had, for instance, no
formula for dealing with acts of guerrilla warfare, which the
instigating state could disown. Even in the event of a formal
declaration of war, if the International Court or the Council could
not agree on a verdict, then League members were free to
continue with their war.

The League of Nations struggles to find a role

In January 1920 the governments of the Great Powers viewed the
League with either cynicism or open hostility. The French
doubted its ability to outlaw war, while the Germans saw it as a
means for enforcing the hated Versailles Treaty. For a short time
after the Republican victory in November 1920 the US
government was openly hostile to the League and its officials
were instructed to avoid any co-operation with the organisation.

Under the Treaty of Versailles the League was responsible for
the administration of the Saar and Danzig (see pages 91–3). This
inevitably involved the danger of it becoming too closely
associated with the policy of the Allies. Indeed, in the Saar, it
made the mistake of appointing a French chairman to the
governing commission which then administered the territory in
the interests of France. The League was also the guarantor of the
agreements, signed by the Allies and the successor states created
in 1919, which were aimed at ensuring that the various racial
minorities left isolated behind the new frontiers enjoyed full civil
rights.

> **Key question**
> What problems faced
> the League in 1920?

The mandates

Article 22 of the Covenant marked a potentially revolutionary
new concept in international affairs:

> To those colonies and territories, which as a consequence of the
> late war have ceased to be under the sovereignty of the states
> which have formerly governed them, and which are inhabited by

> **Key question**
> Was the mandate
> system merely a
> façade for colonialism
> in a new form?

peoples not yet able to stand by themselves under the strenuous conditions of the modern world, there should be applied the principle that the well-being and development of such peoples should form a sacred trust of civilisation, and that securities for the performance of this trust should be embodied in this Covenant.

When the Allies distributed the former German and Turkish territories among themselves, they were divided into three groups according to how developed they were. The most advanced were in the Middle East, while the most backward were the ex-German islands in the Pacific. The League's greatest task was to avoid becoming a façade for colonialism in a new form. Thus, mandate powers were required to send in annual reports on their territories to the League's Permanent Mandates Commission, which rapidly gained a formidable reputation for its expertise and authority.

The League's attitude towards the mandates was by modern standards paternalistic and condescending, but nevertheless, as the historian F.S. Northedge has argued, 'it helped transform the entire climate of colonialism', since the imperialist powers were forced by moral pressure to consider the interests of the native populations and to begin to contemplate the possibility of their eventual independence.

Key question
How effective was the League's welfare, medical and economic work?

Key terms

Protection
Stopping foreign goods by levying tariffs or taxes on imports.

Free trade zone
An area where countries can trade freely without restrictions.

The League's welfare, medical and economic work
Economic and financial work
The League was excluded from dealing with the key financial issues of reparations and war debts, but nevertheless in 1922 its Financial Committee was entrusted by the Allied leaders with the task of rebuilding first Austria's and then Hungary's economy. Its Economic Committee had the far greater task of attempting to persuade the powers to abolish **protection** and create a worldwide **free trade zone**. It organised two world economic conferences, held in 1927 and 1933, which both Soviet Russia and the USA attended. But not surprisingly, given the strongly protectionist economic climate of the times, it failed to make any progress towards free trade.

The International Labour Organisation
One of the greatest successes of the League was the International Labour Organisation (ILO). This had originally been created as an independent organisation by the Treaty of Versailles, but it was financed by the League. In some ways it was a league in miniature. It had its own permanent labour office at Geneva, staffed by 1000 officials. Its work was discussed annually by a conference of labour delegates. Right up to 1939 the ILO turned out an impressive stream of reports, recommendations and statistics which provided important information for a wide range of industries all over the world.

Health Organisation
The League's Health Organisation provided an invaluable forum for drawing up common policies on such matters as the treatment

of diseases, the design of hospitals and health education. The League also set up committees to advise on limiting the production of opium and other addictive drugs, on the outlawing of the sale of women and children for prostitution and on the effective abolition of slavery.

The League as peacemaker and arbitrator 1920–5

Until 1926, when the Foreign Ministers of Britain, France and Germany began to attend the meetings of the Council and turn it into a body which regularly discussed the main problems of the day, the League of Nation's role in the many post-war crises was subordinated to the Allied leaders and the Conference of Ambassadors, which had been set up to supervise the carrying out of the Treaty of Versailles (see page 102). For the most part it therefore dealt with minor crises only.

In 1920 the inability of the League to act effectively without the backing of the great powers was clearly demonstrated when it failed to protect Armenia from a joint Russo-Turkish attack, as neither Britain, France nor Italy was ready to protect it with force. One of the French delegates caustically observed in the Assembly that he and his colleagues were 'in the ridiculous position of an Assembly which considers what steps should be taken, though it is perfectly aware that it is impossible for them to be carried out'.

Key question
How effective was the League in solving international disputes 1920–5?

Polish–Lithuanian quarrel over Vilna

In October 1920, in response to appeals from the Polish Foreign Minister, the League negotiated an armistice between Poland and Lithuania, whose quarrel over border territories was rapidly escalating into war. The ceasefire did not, however, hold, as shortly afterwards **General Zeligowski** with a Polish force, which the Warsaw government diplomatically pretended was acting on its own initiative, occupied the city of Vilna and set up the new puppet government of Central Lithuania under his protection. The League first called for a plebiscite and then, when this was rejected, attempted in vain to negotiate a compromise settlement. In March 1922 Poland finally annexed Vilna province. A year later, after it was obvious that the League could not impose a solution without the support of the Great Powers, the Conference of Ambassadors took the matter into its own hands and recognised Polish sovereignty over Vilna. Britain, France and Italy, by failing to use the machinery of the League to stop Polish aggression, had again effectively marginalised it.

Key question
Why did the League fail to solve the Vilna dispute?

Lucjan Zeligowski (1865–1947)
A Polish General of Lithuanian origin. He fought in both the First World War and the Polish–Soviet War.

Key figure

The Aaland Islands dispute

In less stubborn disputes, however, where the states involved were willing to accept a verdict, the League did have an important role to play as mediator. The League enjoyed a rare success in the dispute between Finland and Sweden over the Aaland Islands. These had belonged to the Grand Duchy of Finland when it had been part of the Russian Empire. Once Finland had broken away from Russia in 1917, the islanders, who were ethnically Swedish, appealed to Stockholm to take over the islands. When Sweden

Key question
How was the League able to solve this problem successfully?

began to threaten to use force, the British referred the matter to the League. In 1921 the League supported the status quo by leaving the islands under Finnish sovereignty, but insisted on itself ensuring the civil rights of the Swedish population there. Neither government liked the verdict, but both accepted it and, what is more important, made it work.

Albania, Upper Silesia, Memel and the Ruhr

Key question
To what extent did the role of the League in these crises indicate that it was essentially subordinated to the Conference of Ambassadors?

In the second half of 1921 the League did serve as a useful means of focusing the attention of the Great Powers on the plight of Albania when it urgently appealed for help against Greek and Yugoslav aggression. As the Conference of Ambassadors had not yet finally fixed its frontiers, the Greeks and Yugoslavs were exploiting the ambiguous situation to occupy as much Albanian territory as they could. The Council responded by dispatching a commission of inquiry, but it took a telegram from Lloyd George, the British Prime Minister, both to galvanise the Conference of Ambassadors into finalising the frontiers and to push the League Council into threatening economic sanctions against Yugoslavia if it did not recognise them. When this was successful, the League was then entrusted with supervising the Yugoslav withdrawal. Thus, in this crisis the League had played a useful but again secondary role to the Allied powers. The fact that the Conference of Ambassadors then made Italy the protector of Albania's independence indicates where the real power lay.

In August 1921 the League played a key role in solving the bitter Anglo-French dispute over the Upper Silesian plebiscite, which was referred to the League Council (page 103). It again proved useful in the protracted dispute over Memel. When the Lithuanians objected to the decision by the Conference of Ambassadors to internationalise the port of Memel, and seized the port themselves in 1923, the League was the obvious body to sort out the problem. Its decision for Lithuania was accepted by Britain and France.

Attempts by Britain and Sweden to refer the question of the Ruhr occupation of 1923 (see pages 104–5) to the League were blocked by the French, who had no intention of allowing the League to mediate between themselves and the Germans.

The Corfu incident

Key question
To what extent did the Corfu incident show the continuing ability of the Great Powers to ignore the League and to take unilateral action when it pleased them?

In the Corfu incident of August–September 1923 the League's efforts to intervene were yet again blocked by a major power. The crisis was triggered by the assassination in Greek territory near the Albanian frontier of three Italians, who were part of an Allied team tracing the Albanian frontiers for the Conference of Ambassadors. Mussolini, the Italian Fascist Prime Minister, who had come to power the preceding October, immediately seized the chance to issue a deliberately unacceptable ultimatum to Athens. When the Greeks rejected three of its demands, Italian troops occupied Corfu. The Greeks wanted to refer the incident to the League, while the Italians insisted that the Conference of Ambassadors should deal with it. The Conference, while initially

Profile: Benito Mussolini 1883–1945

1883	– Born in Romagna
1904–14	– Socialist agitator and journalist
1915–18	– Supported the war against Germany
1919	– Founded the Italian Fascist Party
1922–43	– Gained power in Italy and gradually established a Fascist dictatorship
1943–5	– After the Allied invasion of Italy he was kept in power in northern Italy by the Germans
1945	– Captured and shot by Italian partisans

Mussolini was the son of a blacksmith and originally a socialist, but was expelled from the party when he supported Italy's entry into the war. He created the Fascist Party in 1919 and successfully exploited the post-war economic crisis, fear of Bolshevism and disappointment with the peace treaties to gain power in 1922. By 1929 he had consolidated his position and established a one-party government. Mussolini was determined to re-establish the Roman Empire and turn the Mediterranean into an 'Italian lake'. His fatal mistake was to enter the war as an ally of Hitler's in June 1940 on the assumption that Germany would win. After a series of defeats in Greece and North Africa the Germans had to send troops to stop Italy from being knocked out of the war. From that point on Italy became a German satellite. In the 1930s Hitler had been a great admirer of Mussolini and in many ways regarded him as a role model.

accepting some assistance from the League, nevertheless ultimately settled the case itself and insisted that Greece should pay 50 million lire in compensation to Italy. Once this was agreed, Italian forces were withdrawn from Corfu. The Corfu incident, like the Ruhr crisis, underlined the continuing ability of the major powers to ignore the League and to take unilateral action when it pleased them.

The League's successes: Mosul and the Greco-Bulgarian dispute

In 1924 the League was confronted with another crisis involving a greater power and a lesser power. On this occasion it was able to mediate successfully. It provided a face-saving means of retreat for Turkey in its dispute with Britain over the future of Mosul, which according to the Treaty of Lausanne (see page 101) was to be decided by direct Anglo-Turkish negotiations. When these talks broke down and the British issued in October 1924 an ultimatum to Turkey to withdraw its forces within 48 hours, the League intervened and recommended a temporary demarcation line, behind which the Turkish forces withdrew. It then sent a commission of inquiry to consult the local Kurdish population, which, as total independence was not an option, preferred British to Turkish rule. The League's recommendation that Mosul should

Key question
Why was the League able to deal with these disputes successfully?

become a mandate of Iraq for 25 years was then accepted. As Iraq was a British mandate, this effectively put it under British control.

In October 1925, the League's handling of the Greco-Bulgarian conflict, like its solution to the Aaland Islands dispute, was to be a rare example of a complete success. When the Bulgarians appealed to the Council, its request for a ceasefire was heeded immediately by both sides. So too was the verdict of its commission of inquiry, which found in favour of Bulgaria.

It was an impressive example of what the League could do, and in the autumn of 1925 this success, together with the new 'Locarno spirit', seemed to auger well for the future. Briand was able to claim at the meeting of the Council in October 1925 that 'a nation which appealed to the League when it felt that its existence was threatened, could be sure that the Council would be at its post ready to undertake its work of conciliation'.

The League was not put to the test again until the Manchurian crisis of 1931. Unfortunately Briand's optimism was then shown to be premature (see pages 186–90). The League could function well only if the Great Powers were in agreement.

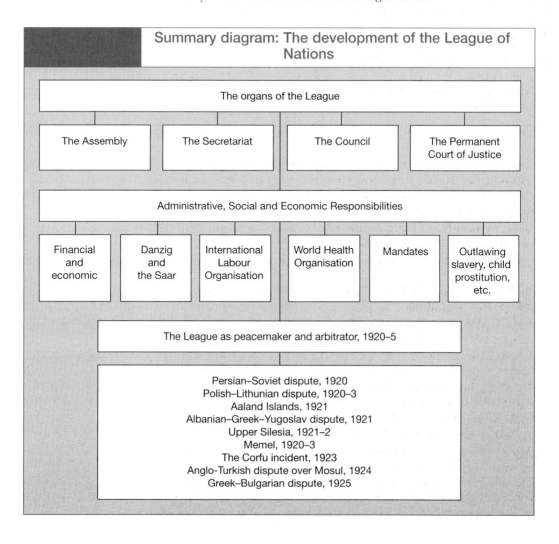

Summary diagram: The development of the League of Nations

The organs of the League

| The Assembly | The Secretariat | The Council | The Permanent Court of Justice |

Administrative, Social and Economic Responsibilities

| Financial and economic | Danzig and the Saar | International Labour Organisation | World Health Organisation | Mandates | Outlawing slavery, child prostitution, etc. |

The League as peacemaker and arbitrator, 1920–5

Persian–Soviet dispute, 1920
Polish–Lithunian dispute, 1920–3
Aaland Islands, 1921
Albanian–Greek–Yugoslav dispute, 1921
Upper Silesia, 1921–2
Memel, 1920–3
The Corfu incident, 1923
Anglo-Turkish dispute over Mosul, 1924
Greek–Bulgarian dispute, 1925

6 | Progress Made Towards Disarmament

The Geneva Protocol

One of the major tasks of the League was to work out an acceptable world disarmament programme. Disarmament, however, could not be divorced from the question of security, for if a state did not feel secure, it would hardly disarm. To solve this problem the League in 1924 drafted an ambitious **collective security** agreement, the Geneva Protocol, but this was rejected by Britain, who feared that it would commit it to policing the world.

The Washington Four Power Treaty and Naval Convention 1922

With the USA outside the League the twin problems of growing Anglo-American naval rivalry and deteriorating American–Japanese relations in the Pacific could only be tackled by negotiations between the powers concerned. By 1919 the USA had become alarmed by the rise of Japanese power in the Pacific. Japan, already possessing the third largest navy in the world, had begun a major naval construction programme. The Americans responded by forming a Pacific fleet and embarking on their own formidable building programme, which, when completed, would make the US navy the largest in the world.

In turn this pushed Britain in early 1921 into announcing its own naval programme, but privately it told Washington that it desired a negotiated settlement as it could not afford a naval race. **President Harding** was anxious both to reduce armaments and to economise, but he would only negotiate with Britain if it agreed to terminate the 20-year-old Anglo-Japanese Alliance, which, theoretically at least, could have involved Britain as Japan's ally in a war against the USA (see page 37). As the treaty was due for renewal in July 1921, the British and Japanese agreed under pressure from Washington to replace it by a new four-power treaty, which committed Britain, France, Japan and the USA to respect each other's possessions in the Pacific and to refer any dispute arising out of this agreement to a conference of the four signatory powers.

With the Anglo-Japanese Treaty out of the way, the first Washington Naval Convention was signed in February 1922 for a duration of 14 years. It halted the building of capital ships for 10 years, provided for the scrapping of certain battleships and battle cruisers, and, for those capital ships which were spared the breaker's yard, established a ratio of three for Japan and 1.67 each for Italy and France to every five for Britain and the USA. In 1929 Britain, Japan and the USA in the London Naval Treaty agreed to extend the main principle of this agreement to smaller fighting ships.

Key questions
What role did the USA play in the disarmament question 1921–33?

Why did Britain reject the Geneva Protocol?

Key question
Why did the USA want Britain to terminate the Anglo-Japanese Treaty?

Key date
Washington Conference and Five Power Naval Convention: 1921–2

Key term
Collective security
Security gained through joining an alliance or signing an agreement where the security of each state is guaranteed by the others.

Key figure
Warren Harding (1865–1923)
US President 1921–3. He was a Republican and had been an opponent of President Wilson's internationalism.

Key question
How important was the Kellogg–Briand Pact?

Key date

Kellogg–Briand pact signed by 15 states: 27 August 1928

Key term

Carnegie Endowment for International Peace An organisation founded by the industrialist Andrew Carnegie. It describes itself as being dedicated to advancing co-operation between nations.

The Kellogg–Briand Pact

From 1922 onwards the USA's attitude towards the League began to alter. The Americans saw the value of participating in some of the League's committees on social, economic and health matters, and President Harding even considered US membership of the Permanent Court of International Justice in 1923, but the Senate again vetoed it. When the League set up a Preparatory Commission in 1926 to prepare for a world disarmament conference, both the USA and Soviet Russia participated.

Peace movements, such as the **Carnegie Endowment for International Peace**, put considerable moral pressure on the US government to play a greater role in the disarmament question. In March 1927, Professor Shotwell, a director of the Carnegie Endowment, on a visit to Paris persuaded Briand to propose a Franco-American pact that would outlaw war. **Frank B. Kellogg**, the US Secretary of State, replied cautiously in December and suggested a general pact between as many states as possible, rejecting war 'as an instrument of national policy'. On 27 August 1928 the Kellogg–Briand Peace Pact was signed by 15 states, and by 1933 a further 50 had joined it.

Optimists saw the pact as supplementing the Covenant. It outlawed war, while the League had the necessary machinery for setting up commissions of inquiry and implementing cooling off periods in the event of a dispute. Pessimists, however, pointed to the fact that it was just a general declaration of intention, which did not commit its members. Perhaps, in reality, all that could be said for it was that it would give the US government a moral basis on which it could intervene in world affairs, should it desire to do so.

Key question
Why did the World Disarmament Conference fail?

Key figure

Frank B. Kellogg (1856–1937) US lawyer, statesman, senator and Secretary of State. For his part in negotiating the Kellogg–Briand Pact he was awarded the Nobel Peace Prize in 1929.

The World Disarmament Conference 1932–4

In 1930 the Preparatory Commission, after protracted discussions on different models of disarmament, produced its final draft for an international convention. The League council called the long-awaited World Disarmament Conference in February 1932 at Geneva. It could not have been convened at a more unfortunate time: the Manchurian crisis (pages 186–90) had weakened the League, the rise of nationalism in Germany was making France and Poland less likely to compromise over German demands for equality in armaments, while the impact of the Depression on the USA was reviving the isolationist tendencies of the early 1920s. Long before the Germans withdrew in November 1933 (page 138) it was clear that the conference would fail.

Summary diagram: Progress made towards disarmament	

Washington Four Power Treaty and Naval Convention, 1922	Halted building of capital ships for ten years. Established ratio of capital ships comprising three for Japan and 1.67 for Italy and France to every five for Britain and the USA
Geneva Protocol, 1924	Attempted to provide worldwide security by obliging members of the League to come to the assistance of any state which was the victim of aggression and was situated in the same continent as themselves – rejected by Britain
Kellogg–Briand Pact, 1928	Rejected war as a 'national instrument' – by 1933 65 states had signed it
World Disarmament Conference, 1932–4	Failed to achieve any agreement. November 1933 Germany withdrew

7 | The Key Debate

> To what extent did the Locarno Agreements mark the beginning of a new era of conciliation?

The acceptance of the Dawes Plan and the signature of the Locarno Agreements together marked a fresh start after the bitterness of the immediate post-war years. For the next four years the pace of international co-operation quickened and the League of Nations, despite a hesitant start, grew in authority and influence. After Germany joined the League in 1926 a new framework for Great Power co-operation evolved. The Foreign Ministers of Britain, France and Germany (Austen Chamberlain, Aristide Briand and Gustav Stresemann) regularly attended the meetings of the League Council and Assembly and played a key part in drawing up their agenda and influencing their decisions. The partnership of these three statesmen came to symbolise the new era of peace and apparent stabilisation. All three were awarded the Nobel Peace Prize. As long as the three European Great Powers co-operated, the League, too, had a chance of working.

Were these men really the great peacemakers they seemed or were they pursuing the same aims as their predecessors, although somewhat more subtly? Stresemann, particularly, is a controversial figure. Initially in the 1950s a debate raged over whether he was a great European statesman or in fact a German nationalist who just went along with Locarno as it suited Germany's interests at that point. Certainly up to 1920 Stresemann had been an uncompromising German nationalist, but in 1923 the gravity of the Ruhr crisis did convince him that only through compromise could Germany achieve the revision of Versailles and the re-establishment of its power in Europe. In a sense, as his most recent biographer, Jonathan Wright, has shown, the logic of Germany's position began to push Stresemann down the road of

European integration. Neither had Briand, who had threatened Germany with the occupation of the Ruhr in April 1921 (see page 103), really changed his fundamental aims. He still sought security against German aggression, but after the failure of Poincaré's Ruhr policy, he was determined to achieve it by co-operation with Britain and Germany itself. In many ways Briand was the right man for the moment. He had a genius for compromise or, as the French historian J. Neré has observed, 'for creating the half-light conducive to harmony'. Chamberlain, too, pursued the same policies as his predecessors, but he had a much stronger hand to play.

As a consequence of France's failure in the Ruhr, the USA's refusal to play a political role in Europe and Soviet Russia's isolation, the Dawes Plan and the Locarno Treaties made Britain the virtual arbiter between France and Germany. In that enviable but temporary position Britain could simultaneously advise the Germans to be patient and the French to compromise, while retaining the maximum freedom to attend to the pressing problems of its empire.

Some key books in the debate:

C.S. Maier, *Recasting Bourgeois Europe* (Princeton University Press, 1988).

F.S. Northedge, *The League of Nations: Its Life and Times* (Leicester University Press, 1986).

Zara Steiner, *The Lights That Failed* (OUP, 2005).

J. Wright, *Gustav Stresemann: Weimar's Greatest Statesman* (OUP, 2002).

Study Guide: AS Question

In the style of OCR A

How far were the Locarno Treaties the most important reason why there were no major conflicts in the 1920s?

Exam tips

The page references are intended to take you straight to the material that will help you to answer the question.

The focus of this question is on the international impact of Locarno (pages 112–14). You will need, therefore, to judge the significance of Locarno in the context of international diplomacy in the 1920s. Within that assessment, the impact of the legacy of the First World War and the universal yearning for peace would both provide valuable perspectives to help your judgement. Each had a powerful influence, but to what extent was either responsible in any way for keeping the peace? Other alternative factors to consider would include:

- the diplomatic rehabilitation of Germany and its entry into the League (pages 115–16)
- the roles played by key statesmen of the era (Stresemann, Austen Chamberlain, Briand) (pages 112–14)
- the Kellogg–Briand Pact (page 129).

Further, you could might pick up 'major conflicts' from the question, and make it clear that the 1920s were not without conflict – pointing out disputes before 1925 that were settled by League of Nations' arbitration (pages 123–7). However you decide to argue on Locarno's impact, what matters is that you put together a clear case, backed up at each point with evidence. 'How far … ?' is a clear command that requires you to weigh the arguments. Do that and your essay will score in the top mark bands. Describe what Locarno did and your essay will be in one of the lowest bands.

Study Guide: A2 Question

In the style of Edexcel

Why were the attempts to secure international agreement on disarmament successful in 1922 and unsuccessful in 1932–3?

Exam tips

The question refers to the outcomes of the Washington Naval Conference of 1922 and the Geneva Disarmament Conference of 1932–3. The inclusion of both of them in the question requires not only discussion of the reasons for their separate outcomes, but also some exploration of why those outcomes were different.

In accounting for the outcome of 1922 you should examine:

- The role of the USA in the creation of the Four-Power Treaty of 1921 and the significance of the treaty.
- The positions of the signatories to the Washington Naval Convention, especially the USA's economic strength and Britain's desire to avoid a naval arms race.

In accounting for the outcome of 1932–3, you should note factors responsible for producing a different climate in the 1930s:

- The impact of the Manchurian crisis in weakening collective security.
- The fears engendered by the rise of nationalism in Germany.
- The impact of the Depression in reviving the isolationist tendencies of the USA.

7

The Democracies on the Defensive 1930–6

POINTS TO CONSIDER

This chapter analyses how the Depression unleashed forces that destroyed the peace settlement of 1919. It considers the following interlocking themes:

• The Great Depression 1929–33
• The rise to power of Hitler
• The reaction of the Great Powers to Nazi Germany 1933–5
• The Abyssinian crisis
• The remilitarisation of the Rhineland
• The Spanish Civil War
• The Rome–Berlin Axis and the Anti-Comintern Pact

A vital question to consider is why Britain and France were unable to contain Nazi Germany and Japan. The impact of the Depression is one reason, but as you read through the chapter, you may come to the conclusion that lack of unity among the former victorious powers in the years 1930–6 was also important, as was the disastrous mishandling of the Abyssinian crisis.

Key dates

1929	October	Wall Street Crash
1929–33		Great Depression
1932	July	Lausanne Conference – reparations virtually abolished
1933	January 30	Hitler appointed Chancellor of Germany
	October	Germany left both League of Nations and the Disarmament Conference
1934	January	German–Polish Non-aggression Pact
	July	Nazi uprising in Austria failed
1935	March	Hitler reintroduced conscription
	April	Stresa Conference
	May	Franco-Soviet Pact
	June	Anglo-German Naval Agreement
	October	Abyssinia invaded by Italy

1936	March	Rhineland remilitarised
	July	Spanish Civil War started
	October	Rome–Berlin Axis
	November	Anti-Comintern Pact

Key question
What impact did the Great Depression have on the international situation?

Key dates

Wall Street Crash: October 1929

Great Depression: 1929–33

1 | The Great Depression 1929–33

The Great Depression, triggered by the Wall Street Crash, marked a turning point in inter-war history. Not only did it weaken the economic and social stability of the world's major powers, but it also dealt a devastating blow to the progress made since 1924 towards creating a new framework for peaceful international co-operation. It has been called by historian Robert Boyce 'the third global catastrophe of the century' (along with the two world wars). It is hard to exaggerate its international impact. To a great extent the economic recovery in Europe after 1924 had been dependent on short-term US loans, of which $4 billion went to Germany. After the Wall Street stock exchange crash, US investors abruptly terminated these loans and no more were forthcoming. This was a devastating blow to the European and world economies. Between 1929 and 1932 the volume of world trade fell by 70 per cent. Unemployment rose to 13 million in the USA, to six million in Germany and to three million in Britain. Japan was particularly hard hit: some 50 per cent of its mining and heavy industrial capacity was forced to close and the collapse of the US market virtually destroyed its large and lucrative export trade in silk.

Inevitably an economic crisis on this scale had a decisive political impact:

- In Germany it helped to bring Hitler to power in January 1933.
- In Japan it strengthened the hand of an influential group of army officers who argued that only by seizing Manchuria could Japan recover from the slump.
- In Italy it prompted Mussolini to have plans drawn up for the conquest of Abyssinia.
- The Depression's long-term impact on the politics of the three democracies – Britain, France and USA – was equally disastrous. It delayed their rearmament programmes and created an international climate in which each of the three suspected the others of causing its financial and economic difficulties. It thus prevented any effective collaboration between them at a time when it was vital both to deter the aggressive nationalism of Japan and Germany and to deal with the global economic crisis.

As international trade collapsed, the Great Powers erected tariff barriers and attempted to make themselves economically self-sufficient. The British and the French with their huge empires had a decisive advantage over the Germans, Italians and Japanese, who increasingly began to assert their right to carve out their own empires, spheres of interest or *Lebensraum* as Hitler called it.

German soldiers serving out food from their soup kitchen to unemployed and destitute civilians in 1931.

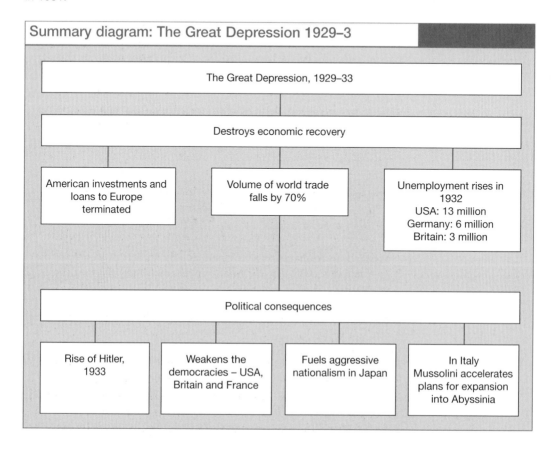

Summary diagram: The Great Depression 1929–3

The Great Depression, 1929–33

Destroys economic recovery

American investments and loans to Europe terminated

Volume of world trade falls by 70%

Unemployment rises in 1932
USA: 13 million
Germany: 6 million
Britain: 3 million

Political consequences

Rise of Hitler, 1933

Weakens the democracies – USA, Britain and France

Fuels aggressive nationalism in Japan

In Italy Mussolini accelerates plans for expansion into Abyssinia

2 | The Rise to Power of Hitler

The foreign policy of Hitler's predecessors 1930–3

Key question
What legacy in foreign policy did Brüning, Papen and Schleicher leave Hitler?

Key dates
Lausanne Conference – reparations virtually abolished: July 1932

Hitler appointed Chancellor of Germany: 30 January 1933

In March 1930 Heinrich Brüning (see page 116) was appointed Chancellor of a minority government supported by the German Nationalist Party (DNVP). Although he and his two successors, **Franz von Papen** and **General von Schleicher**, failed to revive the German economy and so prepared the way for Hitler's rise in power in January 1933, they achieved two great successes, which assisted Hitler.

The German government managed to persuade the Western democracies effectively to abolish reparations at the Lausanne Conference in July 1932. It also achieved another success at the World Disarmament Conference, which met in February 1932, when the Great Powers agreed to concede to Germany 'equality of rights' within a 'system which would provide security for all nations'. As a result of this concession, in November 1932 the German War Ministry finalised plans for large increases in military spending by 1938.

Hitler's long-term aims

Key question
What were the aims of Nazi foreign policy and what had Hitler achieved by 1935?

Key figures
Franz von Papen (1879–1969)
German Chancellor, May–November 1932; Vice-Chancellor 1933–4.

Kurt von Schleicher (1882–1934)
German Chancellor December 1932 to January 1933. Murdered by Hitler in 1934.

Key term
Programme school
Historians who believe that Hitler had a specific programme to carry out.

The tempo of the German campaign against Versailles quickened once Hitler came to power in 1933, although for two years, at least, he appeared to pursue the same policy as his three predecessors, albeit somewhat more vigorously and unconventionally. Was he, then, just following the traditional policy of making Germany 'the greatest power in Europe from her natural weight by exploiting every opportunity that presented itself', as the historian A.J.P. Taylor argued?

In his book *Mein Kampf* (*My Struggle*), written in 1924, Hitler was quite specific about the main thrust of Nazi foreign policy. Germany was to turn its 'gaze towards the land in the east', which meant above all Russia.

Was this still an aim in 1933 or was it just a pipe dream long since forgotten? Like Taylor, Hans Mommsen, a German historian, doubts whether Hitler had a consistent foreign policy of 'unchanging … priorities' and argues that it was usually determined by economic pressures and demands for action from within the Nazi Party itself. Other historians, particularly those of the '**programme school**', take a diametrically opposed line and argue on the strength of *Mein Kampf* and *Hitler's Secret Book* (published in 1928) that he had a definite programme. First of all he planned to defeat France and Russia, and then after building up a large navy, to make a determined bid for world power, even if it involved war against both Britain and the USA.

The history of Nazi foreign policy generates such controversy because Hitler's actions were so often ambiguous and contradictory. Despite this, there is currently a general consensus among historians that Hitler did intend to wage a series of wars which would ultimately culminate in a struggle for global hegemony. As the historian Alan Bullock has argued, the key to understanding Hitler's foreign policy is that he combined 'consistency of aim with complete **opportunism** in method and tactics'.

Hitler's immediate priorities

In 1933 Hitler's first priority was to consolidate the Nazi takeover of power and to rebuild Germany's military strength. This would eventually put him in a position to destroy what remained of the Versailles system. However, while rearming, he had to be careful not to provoke an international backlash. He therefore followed a cautious policy of avoiding risks and defusing potential opposition, while gradually withdrawing Germany from any **multilateral commitments**, such as being a member of the League of Nations, which might prevent him from pursuing an independent policy. He hoped particularly to isolate France by negotiating alliances with Britain and Italy.

Hitler's immediate aim was to extricate Germany from the World Disarmament Conference, but he was careful to wait until the autumn of 1933 before he risked withdrawing from both the conference and the League of Nations. He had first skilfully reassured Britain and Italy of his peaceful intentions by signing in June 1933 the Four Power Pact, proposed by Mussolini, which aimed at revising Versailles through joint agreement of the Great Powers. Although on the face of it this seemed to limit Germany's freedom of action, Hitler calculated, correctly as it turned out, that the French would never ratify it.

The German–Polish Non-aggression Pact

Hitler's first major initiative in foreign policy was the conclusion of the German–Polish **Non-aggression Pact**. He decided on this despite opposition from the German Foreign Office, which wanted to maintain good relations with Soviet Russia. The pact seriously weakened France's security system in eastern Europe (see page 118), as it had relied on its alliance with Poland to put pressure on Germany's eastern frontiers. Nevertheless, Germany still remained very vulnerable. Hitler was warned in August 1934 by a senior German diplomat, B.W. von Bülow, that:

> In judging the situation we should never overlook the fact that no kind of rearmament in the next few years could give us military security. Even apart from our isolation, we shall for a long time yet be hopelessly inferior to France in the military sphere. A particularly dangerous period will be 1934–5 on account of the re-organisation of the *Reichswehr*.

The attempted Nazi coup in Austria, July 1934

Hitler was certainly aware of Germany's vulnerability, but over Austria he adopted a more provocative line, possibly because he assumed that Austria was a domestic German affair. In June 1934 he met Mussolini, in Venice, and tried to convince him that

---

Key term

Opportunism
Seizing the opportunity when it occurs.

Key question
What were Hitler's immediate priorities?

Key date

Germany left both League of Nations and the Disarmament Conference: October 1933

Key terms

Multilateral commitments
Membership of international organisations.

Non-aggression pact
An agreement between two or more countries not to resort to force.

Key question
Why did the German–Polish Non-aggression Pact weaken France's security system?

Key dates

German–Polish Non-aggression Pact: 1934

Nazi uprising in Austria failed: July 1934

Key term

Reichswehr
The German army 1919–35.

Key question
Why did Hitler support the attempted Nazi coup in Austria?

Key terms

Buffer state
Small state
positioned between
two much larger
ones.

Luftwaffe
The German air
force.

Conscription
Compulsory
military service.

Key dates

Hitler reintroduced
conscription: March
1935

Stresa Conference:
April 1935

Anglo-German Naval
Agreement: June
1935

Austria should become a German satellite. When Mussolini
rejected this, Hitler gave the Austrian Nazis strong unofficial
encouragement to stage a month later what turned out to be a
disastrously unsuccessful uprising in Vienna. Mussolini,
determined to keep Austria as a **buffer state** between Italy and
Germany, immediately mobilised troops on the Brenner frontier
and forced Hitler to disown the coup. The incident brought about
a sharp deterioration in German–Italian relations and appeared
to rule out any prospect of an alliance.

German rearmament 1933–5

Germany did begin to rearm as soon as Hitler seized power. In
February, Hitler announced a long-term plan for increases in the
armed forces. Ultimately his intention was to mobilise the whole
German economy and society for war. In July 1933 the decision
was taken to create an independent *Luftwaffe* and a year later the
July programme was unveiled, which envisaged the construction
of some 17,000 airplanes. The majority of these were training
planes to familiarise future pilots with flying so that the
Luftwaffe could be greatly increased in size in the near future.
On 18 December 1933 the Defence Ministry unveiled a new
programme that aimed to create a peacetime army of 300,000
men. In March 1935 Hitler announced the reintroduction of
conscription, despite the fears of his advisers that this would lead
to French intervention.

Even though naval rearmament was not initially one of Hitler's
priorities, as he hoped for at least a temporary alliance with
Britain, a naval programme was drawn up which would produce a
moderate-sized German fleet of eight battleships, three aircraft
carriers, eight cruisers, 48 destroyers and 72 submarines by 1949.

Key question
Why was the Stresa
Conference called?

The Stresa Conference

In April the British, French and Italian heads of government met
at Stresa to discuss forming a common front against Germany in
view of Hitler's rejection of the clauses of Versailles limiting
Germany's armaments. They both condemned German
rearmament and resolved to maintain the peace settlements.

Hitler, however, quickly launched a diplomatic offensive to
reassure the powers of his peaceful intentions. In a speech that in
places appeared to echo the language of Stresemann and Briand
(see pages 115–16) he proposed a series of non-aggression pacts
with Germany's neighbours, and promised to observe Locarno
and accept an overall limitation on armaments. He also offered
Britain an agreement limiting the German fleet to 35 per cent of
the total strength of the Royal Navy.

Profile: Adolf Hitler 1889–1945

1889		– Born in Braunau, Austria
1914–18		– Served in the German army
1919		– Joined the German Workers' Party, which became the NSDAP (Nazi Party)
1921		– Chairman of the NSDAP
1923		– Played a key role in the Munich *putsch* for which he was imprisoned for a year
1925–9		– Rebuilt the Nazi Party
1930–3		– As a consequence of the Depression the Nazi Party became a mass movement
1933	January	– Chancellor of the German *Reich*
1935		– Reintroduced conscription
1936		– German troops reoccupied the Rhineland
		– Hitler launched the Four-Year Plan to prepare the German economy for war
1938	March	– Germany absorbed Austria
	October	– Annexed the Sudetenland
1939	September	– Germany invaded Poland and unleashed Second World War
1940	June	– Defeat of France
1941	June	– Invasion of Russia
1941	December	– Hitler declared war on the USA
1945	April	– Hitler shot himself in his bunker in Berlin

Adolf Hitler's father, Alois, was an Austrian customs official. Hitler left school without any qualifications in 1905, and, convinced of his artistic gifts, tried unsuccessfully to gain a place at the Academy of Fine Arts in Vienna. Up to 1914 he lived the life of an increasingly penniless artist in Vienna and Munich. He showed great interest in the current Social Darwinistic, nationalist and racist thinking, which was to form the basis of his future foreign policy.

In August 1914 Hitler joined a Bavarian regiment and fought for the next four years with considerable personal bravery, winning the Iron Cross (First Class). In 1919 he joined the German Workers' Party, which was subsequently renamed the NSDAP, the chairman of which Hitler became in July 1921. After the failure of the Munich *putsch* in November 1923 he was imprisoned at Landsberg, where he wrote *Mein Kampf*. On his release he rebuilt the Nazi Party.

The Depression made the NSDAP the largest party in the *Reichstag*. Hitler came to power in 1933 because the Conservative–Nationalist **élites** were convinced wrongly that they could control him. By August 1934 Hitler had destroyed all opposition and was able to combine the post of Chancellor and President and call himself '*Führer* of the German *Reich*'.

Key terms

Putsch
Takeover of power.

Élites
The ruling classes.

By 1937 Hitler had laid the foundations for 'rearmament in depth' and had dismantled the Versailles system. From 1938 onwards his foreign, domestic and racial policies became increasingly radical. He annexed Austria, Czechoslovakia and invaded Poland, which caused war with Britain and France. In June 1941 he made a major error of attacking the USSR and then in December of declaring war on the USA while leaving Britain undefeated in the west. Hitler committed suicide on 30 April 1945 when the Red Army had reached Berlin.

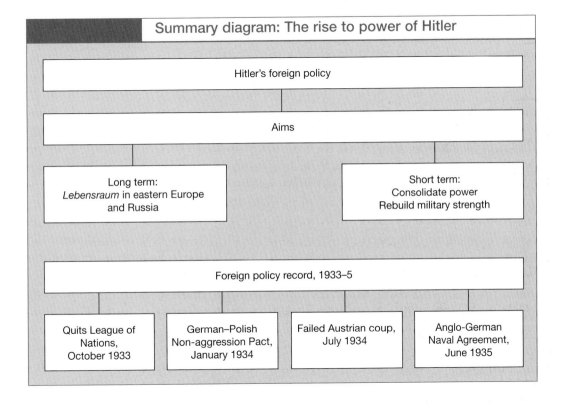

Summary diagram: The rise to power of Hitler

Hitler's foreign policy

Aims

Long term:
Lebensraum in eastern Europe and Russia

Short term:
Consolidate power
Rebuild military strength

Foreign policy record, 1933–5

Quits League of Nations, October 1933

German–Polish Non-aggression Pact, January 1934

Failed Austrian coup, July 1934

Anglo-German Naval Agreement, June 1935

3 | The Reaction of the Great Powers to Nazi Germany 1933–5

For the Great Powers 1933–5 was a period in which they had to come to terms with the reality of Nazi Germany. In 1933, even though Germany was only just beginning to rearm, its strength was potentially far greater than in 1914, as it was enhanced by a ring of weak states which had been created in 1919 out of the ruins of the Austrian and Russian Empires around its eastern and southern frontiers.

France

By 1934 France had long since lost the diplomatic leadership of Europe which it had exercised in the immediate post-war years. France's economy had been belatedly hit by the Depression and

Key question
How did France respond to the rise of Hitler 1933–5?

its **social cohesion** threatened by a wave of rioting sparked off in February 1934 by the exposure of a series of financial scandals. French society was deeply divided as the **right** wanted to negotiate with Hitler and Mussolini, while the **left** wanted to fight fascism and looked to Russia as an ally.

Even if France had still possessed the will to intervene militarily in Germany, the Locarno Treaties prevented it from reoccupying the Rhineland. Neither could it rely on Poland after the German–Polish Non-aggression Pact of January 1934. France's response to the new Nazi Germany was therefore hesitant and sometimes contradictory. The French sought to contain Germany, as they had done since 1919, through a network of alliances and pacts but, like the British, they also tried to negotiate with Hitler.

Although ultimately Britain remained France's major European partner, it was not ready in 1935 to commit itself to an alliance with France. The French therefore attempted to strengthen the Little *Entente* (see page 118) and negotiate agreements with Italy and Russia. However, this was by no means an easy task as in 1933 its relations with both powers were strained.

Franco-Italian negotiations and the Rome Agreement

In its attempts to negotiate an Italian alliance, France was greatly assisted by the abortive Nazi coup in Vienna, which more than anything convinced Mussolini that a military agreement with France was essential.

In January 1935 both countries signed the Rome Agreement by which they undertook not to meddle in the affairs of their Balkan neighbours and to act together in the event of unilateral German rearmament or another threat to Austrian independence. In June direct Franco-Italian military staff talks started to discuss joint action in the event of a German attack on Austria, Italy or France.

Franco-Russian negotiations

Parallel with these negotiations, talks were proceeding between the French and the Russians. Paris did not show the same enthusiasm for a Russian alliance as it did for one with Italy. This was partly because Soviet Russia had been regarded as scarcely less of a threat to the West than Germany and partly because it no longer had a common border with Germany.

The French intended to enmesh Soviet Russia in an elaborate treaty of regional assistance or, in other words, an eastern European version of the Locarno Treaty, which would be signed not only by Russia but also by Germany, Poland, Czechoslovakia and the Baltic States. This was to be strengthened by a separate Franco-Russian agreement which would associate Russia with the Locarno Agreements in western Europe (see page 113) and France with the proposed eastern pact.

But the whole plan came to nothing as both Germany and Poland refused to join. The Poles were more suspicious of the Russians than of the Germans. France had therefore little option but to pursue a mutual assistance pact with Soviet Russia alone. By May, the Franco-Soviet Treaty of Mutual Assistance had been

Key terms

Social cohesion
The social unity of a country.

Right
Term used to denote parties stretching from Conservative to Nazi or Fascist (extreme right).

Left
Term used to denote parties stretching from Social Democrat to Communist.

Key question
How successful were the Franco-Italian negotiations?

Key question
What did the French intend to achieve in the negotiations with the USSR?

Key date
Franco-Soviet Pact: May 1935

signed, but Paris refused to follow up the treaty with detailed military staff talks between the two armies. The main aim of the pact was to restrain Russia from moving closer to Germany, as it had done in 1922 with the signature of the Rapallo Agreement (see page 104).

Franco-German negotiations

Meanwhile the French government attempted to negotiate a settlement with Germany. Both in the winter of 1933–4 and in the summer of 1935, immediately after the signature of the Franco-Soviet Treaty, attempts were made to open up a Franco-German dialogue. These efforts were doomed as the French attempted to draw the Germans into negotiating agreements essentially aimed at preserving the Versailles system. Hitler was ready, when it suited him, to lower the political temperature through cordial diplomatic exchanges, but he was not ready to tolerate the restrictions with which French – and British – diplomacy was attempting to entangle him.

Key question
What was the main aim of British policy towards Germany?

Great Britain

Like France, Britain's reaction to Nazi Germany was conditioned by its military, economic and strategic vulnerability. In 1933 it faced a growing threat not only from Germany in Europe, but also from Japan in the Far East. Consequently, the main aim of British policy towards Germany was to blunt Hitler's aggression by continuing to modify the Treaty of Versailles peacefully while simultaneously drawing Germany back into the League where it could be tied down in multilateral agreements on security. Sir John Simon (1873–1954), the Foreign Secretary, summed up this policy in a letter to King George V in February 1935:

> The practical choice is between a Germany which continues to rearm without any regulation or agreement and a Germany which, through getting a recognition of its rights and some modification of the peace treaties, enters into the **comity** of nations and contributes, in this and other ways, to European stability.

Key term

Comity
Community.

Britain also worked hard for an overall settlement with Germany. Despite the reintroduction of German conscription in March, Simon went to Berlin later in the month to explore the possibility of a comprehensive settlement with Germany involving German recognition of Austrian independence, its participation in an 'eastern Locarno' and return to the League. British ministers attended the Stresa meeting on 8 April, but they were determined at that stage not to join any alliances or pacts directed against Germany as they was convinced that the pre-1914 alliance system (see page 55) had been a major cause of the very war it was aimed to prevent. In June this policy seemed to be rewarded with success when the Anglo-German Naval Agreement was signed (see above).

Italy

Mussolini, who had extensive territorial aims in the Balkans and
North Africa, at first attempted to maintain a special position as
mediator between Germany on the one hand and Britain and
France on the other, hoping that would in time bring him
concessions from both sides. However, the increasing German
threat to Austria began to convert Mussolini from a critic and

Key question
Why had Italy by the
spring of 1935 aligned
itself with Britain and
France in an attempt
to defend the
Versailles settlement?

Profile: Joseph Stalin 1879–1953

1879		– Born in Georgia in 1879 with family name of Djugashvili
1903		– Joined the Bolshevik Party
1913–17		– Exiled to Siberia
1917		– Assisted Lenin in the Russian Revolution
1922		– Secretary of the Communist Party
1929		– Effectively dictator of the USSR and introduced a policy of socialism in one country
1936–8		– Conducted the great purge of his enemies
1939	23 August	– Signed the Nazi–Soviet Pact
	17 September	– Ordered Soviet occupation of eastern Poland
	30 November	– Ordered invasion of Finland
1941–5		– Supreme Director of the Soviet war effort
1953		– Died

Stalin whose family name was Djugashvili, was born in Georgia as
the son of a cobbler. He was originally going to become a priest
but was expelled from the seminary for being a revolutionary in
1899. He was twice sent to Siberia but each time managed to
escape. At various times he was in exile in Paris and Vienna, and
in 1912 became the Bolshevik Party's expert on racial minorities.
He edited *Pravda* in 1917 and became Commissar for
Nationalities in the first Soviet government. In 1922 he became
Secretary of the Bolshevik Party. By 1929 he had defeated his
rivals for the control of the Bolshevik Party, and was in a position
to launch the first of the Five-Year Plans involving the
collectivisation of agriculture and the massive expansion of heavy
industry. He defended himself from the criticism which followed
the ruthless implementation of these policies through purges,
show trials and 'the terror'. In May 1941 he became Chairman of
the Council of Ministers, and during the Great Patriotic War (the
Second World War) against Germany took over supreme control
of the Soviet war effort. The Soviet victory in 1945 was celebrated
as his supreme achievement, and enabled the USSR to control
most of eastern Europe. After 1945, until his death in 1953,
Stalin's position in the USSR was unchallenged.

Key figure

Engelbert Dollfuss (1892–1934)
A devout Catholic who became Chancellor of Austria in 1932. He admired Fascist Italy and suspended the Austrian parliamentary constitution in 1933.

potential revisionist of the Treaty of Versailles to an upholder of the territorial status quo. As early as August 1933 Mussolini met **Engelbert Dollfuss**, the Austrian Chancellor, at Rimini and discussed arrangements for Italian military support in case of German intervention in Austria.

Mussolini's conversion to a defender of the existing territorial settlement was accelerated by the abortive Nazi *putsch* in Vienna in July 1934 and by the German announcement of conscription the following March. By the spring of 1935 Italy appeared to have aligned itself firmly with Britain and France in their desire to preserve what was left of the Versailles settlement.

Soviet Russia

Key question
What was Soviet Russia's reaction to the rise of Hitler?

Stalin, like the other European leaders, reacted cautiously to the Nazi takeover of power. His distrust of the West was at least as great as his fear of Nazi Germany. Consequently, even though he negotiated a defensive agreement with the French and sought collective security by joining the League of Nations in September 1934, he also attempted to maintain good relations with Germany despite such setbacks as the German–Polish Non-aggression Pact (see page 138).

The Soviet negotiations with the French in the spring of 1935 were also accompanied by a series of secret talks with the Germans, which mirrored the French tactics of trying for a settlement with Hitler in the summer of 1935 (see page 143) as an alternative to the Nazi–Soviet Pact. Soviet–Nazi talks continued intermittently right up to February 1936. Only with the ratification of the Franco-Soviet Treaty of Mutual Assistance by the French parliament were they broken off, but were renewed in the summer of 1939 (see page 172).

The USA

Key question
How isolationist was US foreign policy up to 1935?

In 1933 there was considerable sympathy in the USA for the economic hardships that Germany was suffering as a result of the Depression, while both Britain and France were viewed with some suspicion on account of their huge colonial empires. However, with the coming to power of Hitler and beginning of the persecution of the Jews, public opinion in the USA began to become more hostile to Germany, but nevertheless US foreign policy remained firmly isolationist.

Key figure

Franklin Roosevelt (1882–1945)
Democratic governor of New York in 1928 and then in 1932 President of the USA, a post he held until his death in 1945. He countered the Great Depression with a massive programme of public works.

In the Far East, the USA was alarmed by the Japanese occupation of Manchuria (see page 187), but did no more than make diplomatic protest. Indeed, the Temporary Neutrality Act of 1935, by empowering **President Roosevelt** to ban the supply of arms to all belligerents – whether aggressors or victims of aggression – in the event of the outbreak of war, strengthened the US policy of non-involvement.

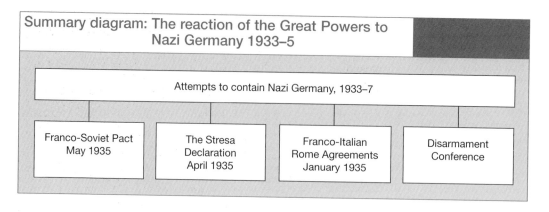

Summary diagram: The reaction of the Great Powers to Nazi Germany 1933–5

Attempts to contain Nazi Germany, 1933–7

Franco-Soviet Pact May 1935 | The Stresa Declaration April 1935 | Franco-Italian Rome Agreements January 1935 | Disarmament Conference

4 | The Abyssinian Crisis

Mussolini had for a long time wanted to build up a large empire in North Africa which would have the added advantage of distracting his people from the impact of the Depression on the Italian economy. By 1932 he had begun to plan in earnest the annexation of Abyssinia. Not only would Abyssinia provide land for Italian settlers, but it would also connect Eritrea with Italian Somaliland and thus put most of the Horn of Africa under Italian control (see map on page 147). In December 1934 a clash occurred between Italian and Abyssinian troops at the small oasis of Wal-Wal, some 50 miles on the Abyssinian side of the border with Italian Somaliland. The following October the long-expected invasion of Abyssinia began.

Key question
Why was the conquest of Abyssinia not stopped by Britain and France?

Key date
Abyssinia invaded by Italy: October 1935

The failure of Anglo-French attempts to compromise

Mussolini was convinced that neither Britain nor France would raise serious objections. In January 1935 Laval, the French Foreign Minister, had verbally promised him a free hand, while the British Foreign Office was desperate to avert the crisis either by offering Mussolini territorial compensation elsewhere or by helping to negotiate an arrangement, comparable to Britain's own position in Egypt, which would give Italy effective control of Abyssinia without **formally annexing** it. Sir Robert Vansittart, a senior British diplomat, forcefully pointed out that:

Key question
Why did attempts to find a compromise over Abyssinia fail?

> The position is as plain as a pikestaff. Italy will have to be bought off – let us use and face ugly words – in some form or other, or Abyssinia will eventually perish. That might in itself matter less, if it did not mean that the League would also perish (and that Italy would simultaneously perform another **volte-face** into the arms of Germany).

Why then could such a compromise not be negotiated? The scale and brutality of the Italian invasion confronted both the British and French governments with a considerable dilemma. The British government was facing an election in November 1935 and was under intense pressure from the electorate to support the League. In an unofficial peace ballot in June 1935 organised by

Key terms

Formal annexation
Taking over full control of a territory by another power.

Volte-face
An about turn; a sudden and complete change of policy.

The Hoare–Laval Plan for the partition of Abyssinia.

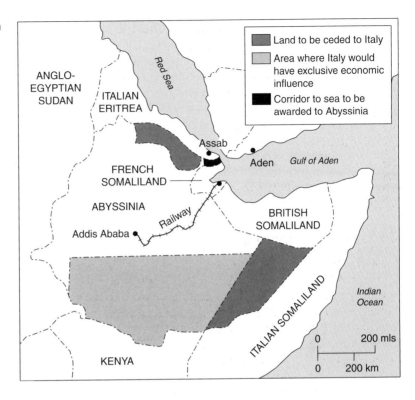

the League of Nations Union, which was formed in 1918 to win public support for the League, 10 million out of 11 million replies backed the use of economic sanctions by the League in a case of aggression. In France, public opinion was more divided, with the left supporting the League and the right supporting Italy. However, both powers feared the diplomatic consequences of alienating Italy over Abyssinia. In particular, Britain's persistent refusal to join France in guaranteeing the status quo in central and eastern Europe inevitably increased the importance for the French of their friendly relations with Italy.

On 18 October the League condemned the Italian invasion of Abyssinia, and voted for a gradually escalating programme of sanctions. In the meantime both Britain and France continued to search for a compromise settlement. In December **Laval** and the British Foreign Minister, Sir Samuel Hoare, produced a plan which involved placing some two-thirds of Abyssinia under Italian control. There was a strong possibility that it would have been acceptable to Mussolini, but it was leaked to the French press and an explosion of rage amongst the British public forced Hoare's resignation and the dropping of the plan.

The failure of diplomacy did not then ensure vigorous action against Mussolini. The League put no embargo on oil exports to Italy, and Britain refused to close the Suez Canal to Italian shipping on the grounds that this might lead to war. Mussolini was thus able to step up his campaign and by May 1936 had overrun Abyssinia.

Key figure

Pierre Laval (1883–1945)
French Socialist and Prime Minister 1931–2. He was Chief Minister in Vichy France and was executed in 1945.

The consequences of the Abyssinian War

The crisis was a crucial turning point in the 1930s. Not only did it irreparably weaken the League and provide Hitler with an ideal opportunity for the illegal remilitarisation of the Rhineland (see below), but it also effectively destroyed the Franco-Italian friendship and ultimately replaced it with the Rome–Berlin 'Axis' (see page 152). This eventually enabled Hitler in 1938 to absorb Austria without Italian opposition. The 'Axis' was also to threaten vital British and French lines of communication in the Mediterranean with the possibility of hostile naval action and thus seriously weaken their potential response to future German – or indeed Japanese – aggression.

Key question
What were the consequences of the Abyssinian War?

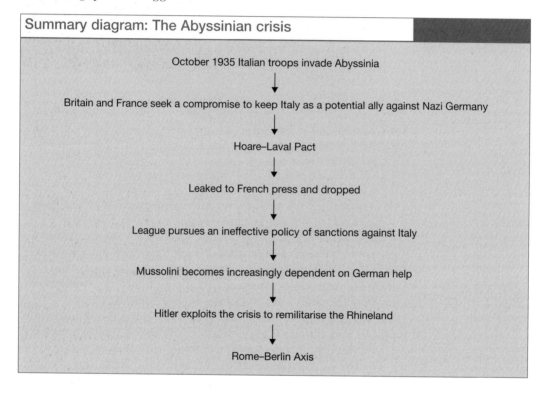

Summary diagram: The Abyssinian crisis

October 1935 Italian troops invade Abyssinia

↓

Britain and France seek a compromise to keep Italy as a potential ally against Nazi Germany

↓

Hoare–Laval Pact

↓

Leaked to French press and dropped

↓

League pursues an ineffective policy of sanctions against Italy

↓

Mussolini becomes increasingly dependent on German help

↓

Hitler exploits the crisis to remilitarise the Rhineland

↓

Rome–Berlin Axis

5 | The Remilitarisation of the Rhineland

The remilitarisation of the Rhineland marked an important stage in Hitler's plans for rebuilding German power. The construction of strong fortifications there would enable him to stop any French attempts to invade Germany. Hitler had originally planned to reoccupy the Rhineland in 1937, but a combination of the favourable diplomatic situation created by the Abyssinian crisis and the need to distract domestic attention from German economic problems brought about by the speed of the rearmament programme persuaded him to act in March 1936. In December 1935 the German army was ordered to start planning the reoccupation, while Hitler's diplomats began to manufacture a legal justification for such action by arguing that the Franco-Soviet Pact (see page 142) was contrary to the Locarno Agreement.

Key question
Why, despite the Locarno Agreements, was there no effective opposition when Hitler broke the Treaties of Versailles and Locarno and remilitarised the Rhineland?

Key date
Rhineland remilitarised: March 1936

German soldiers cross the Cologne Bridge during Germany's militarisation of the Rhineland in 1936, in direct violation of the Treaty of Versailles.

Key terms

Stresa Powers
The powers who attended the Stresa Conference in 1935.

Maginot line
A line of concrete fortifications, which France constructed along its borders with Germany. It was named after André Maginot, the French Minister of Defence.

Crucial to the success of his plan was the attitude of Italy. Mussolini, isolated from the other **Stresa Powers** because of his Abyssinian policy, had little option but to reassure Germany that he would not co-operate with the British and French to enforce Locarno if German troops entered the Rhineland.

German troops marched into the Rhineland on 7 March 1936. In order to reassure France that they did not intend to violate the Franco-German frontier they were initially, at any rate, few in number and lightly equipped. So why did the French army not immediately intervene? The French general staff, which since the late 1920s had been planning for a defensive war against Germany based on the fortifications of the **Maginot line** (see page 159) on France's eastern frontier, refused to invade the Rhineland unless they had full backing from the British.

The most the British government was ready to do was to promise France that, in the event of an unprovoked German attack on French territory, it would send two divisions of troops across the Channel. Essentially, British public opinion was convinced that Hitler was merely walking into 'his own back garden'.

The remilitarisation of the Rhineland was a triumph for Hitler, and, as an internal French Foreign Office memorandum of 12 March 1936 stressed, it marked a decisive shift in power from Paris to Berlin:

A German success would likewise not fail to encourage elements which, in Yugoslavia, look towards Berlin … In Romania this will be a victory of the elements of the right which have been stirred up by Hitlerite propaganda. All that will remain for Czechoslovakia is to come to terms with Germany. Austria does not conceal her anxiety. 'Next time it will be our turn' … Turkey, who has increasingly close economic relations with Germany, but who politically remains in the Franco-British axis, can be induced to modify her line. The Scandinavian countries … are alarmed.

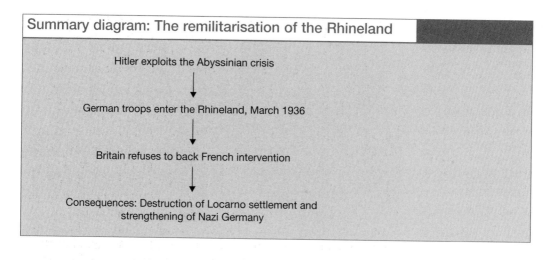

Summary diagram: The remilitarisation of the Rhineland

Hitler exploits the Abyssinian crisis

↓

German troops enter the Rhineland, March 1936

↓

Britain refuses to back French intervention

↓

Consequences: Destruction of Locarno settlement and strengthening of Nazi Germany

6 | The Spanish Civil War

Key question
How did the Great Powers react to the Spanish Civil War?

The civil war in Spain was essentially a domestic matter which rapidly became an international issue threatening to involve the major powers in a European conflict. It began in July 1936 with a Nationalist revolt led by the army against the Spanish Republican government. When the rebels were defeated in a number of cities by the workers, both sides appealed to the international community for help. The Nationalists, led by **General Franco**, looked to Germany and Italy, while the Republicans approached Britain, France and Soviet Russia.

Spanish Civil War started: July 1936

Key date

German and Italian intervention

Key question
Why did the Germans and Italians support General Franco?

Hitler quickly agreed to provide a fleet of transport aircraft to fly Franco's men across to Spain. He then followed this up with the dispatch of some 6000 troops. Hitler certainly wanted to stop Spain becoming communist but he also wanted to distract the Western Powers so that he could continue to rearm without fear of intervention. He was also aware of the advantages of having a friendly government in Madrid which would not only supply Germany with Spanish mineral resources but also in wartime possibly provide bases for German submarines.

Mussolini also agreed to assist Franco for the same mixture of ideological and strategic reasons: he hoped to defeat the left in Spain, gain a new ally in Franco, who might grant Italy a naval base on one of the Balearic islands, and 'strengthen' the Italian character by exposure to war.

Francisco Franco (1892–1975)
Spanish general, leader of the Spanish Nationalists and then ruler of Spain 1939–75.

Key figure

The non-intervention policy of Britain and France

Key question
Why did France and Britain propose to the European powers a non-intervention agreement?

With both Germany and Italy openly helping Franco there was a real danger of a European war, should France and Britain be drawn in on the Republican side. When the French Prime Minister, **Léon Blum** (see opposite page), whose power rested on a left-wing coalition, was first asked for help by the Republic, he was tempted to give it, if only to deny potential allies of Germany a victory in Spain. However, two factors forced him to have

Key figure

Léon Blum (1872–1950)
France's first Socialist Prime Minister. Led the Popular Front Government 1936–36. Imprisoned by the Vichy regime in 1940.

second thoughts. First, the actual dispatch of French military aid to the Republicans would have polarised French society, which was already deeply divided between right and left, and run the risk of plunging France into a civil war of its own; and secondly, the British government came out strongly against intervention. The British ambassador in Paris even threatened neutrality should French assistance to the Republicans lead to war with Germany. Despite the strategic dangers for Britain's position in the Mediterranean in the event of a Nationalist victory, the cabinet viewed the civil war as essentially a side issue which must not be allowed to prevent its continued search for a lasting settlement with Germany. In addition, there were powerful voices within the Conservative Party who actively sympathised with Franco.

In an attempt to prevent the war spreading, Britain and France proposed a non-intervention agreement. This was signed by the other European powers, but Germany and Italy ignored it and continued to assist Franco.

Soviet intervention

Key question
Why did Stalin decide to help the Republicans?

The Republican government therefore had little option but to approach Soviet Russia for help. In September 1936 Stalin sent hundreds of military advisers and large quantities of military equipment, while the **Comintern** was made responsible for recruiting brigades of international volunteers. Stalin, like Hitler, saw the civil war as a way of dividing his enemies.

Key term

Comintern
The Communist international movement set up in 1919 to organise worldwide revolution.

A conflict between the Western Powers and Germany would certainly have suited Stalin's policy, but he was also anxious to prevent a Nationalist victory in Spain since this would strengthen the forces of international fascism and make a German attack on the Soviet Union more likely. However, by early 1937, when he realised that the Republicans could not win, he reduced the flow of arms to a level that was just sufficient to prolong the conflict. In this he was successful, as it was not until March 1939 that Franco at last occupied Madrid.

The consequences of the civil war

Key question
What were the consequences of the civil war?

For the democracies the civil war could not have come at a worse time. It polarised public opinion between right and left, threatened France with encirclement and cemented the Italian–German *rapprochement*. It may also have helped to convince the Soviet Union of the weakness of the West and prepare the way for the Nazi–Soviet Pact of September 1939 (see page 172). As with the Abyssinian crisis, it was undoubtedly Germany who benefited most from the conflict since it diverted the attention of the powers during the crucial period 1936–7 from the Nazi rearmament programme.

Summary diagram: The Spanish Civil War

Reaction of the Great Powers to the Spanish Civil War

Germany	Italy	USSR	Britain	France
Sends troops Hopes to keep war going to distract Britain and France	Wants Franco as an ally against Britain and France	Assists Republicans	Proposes non-intervention	Backs British proposals

7 | The Rome–Berlin Axis and the Anti-Comintern Pact

Key question
Why and how did Japan, Germany and Italy draw closer to together in the period 1936–7?

The summer of 1936 saw increasingly cordial relations between Berlin and Rome. While Britain pointedly refused to recognise the King of Italy as the 'Emperor of Abyssinia', Germany rapidly did so. Hitler and Mussolini also co-operated in blocking a new British initiative to update the Locarno Treaty. Italy's growing hostility towards Britain, France and especially the USSR, with whom until the Spanish Civil War it had enjoyed good relations, also ensured that it had to be more tolerant of German influence in Austria. In January 1936 Mussolini assured the German ambassador in Rome that 'If Austria, as a formerly independent state, were … in practice to become a **German satellite**, he would have no objection.'

German satellite
A state completely dominated by Germany.

Key term

The October Protocols: the Rome–Berlin Axis

The understanding between Italy and Germany over Austria prepared the way for a German–Italian agreement, the October Protocols, which were signed in Berlin in October 1936. Mussolini announced this new alignment to the world at a mass meeting in Milan on 1 November:

Key question
Why did Mussolini call the October Protocols the Rome–Berlin Axis?

Rome–Berlin Axis: October 1936

Anti-Comintern Pact: November 1936

Key dates

> The Berlin conversations have resulted in an understanding between our two countries over certain problems which have been particularly acute. By these understandings … this Berlin–Rome line is … an axis around which can revolve all those European states with a will to collaboration and peace.

The Anti-Comintern Pact

Three weeks later Hitler overrode advice from his professional diplomats and signed the Anti-Comintern Pact with Japan (see page 192). This was more of symbolic than practical importance as it was aimed against the Comintern rather than the Soviet Union itself. For Hitler, coming so soon after the Rome–Berlin Axis, the pact trumpeted to the world that Germany was no longer isolated, as it had appeared to be in the spring of 1935. In November 1937 the pact was further strengthened by Italy's accession.

Key question
What was the value of the Anti-Comintern Pact with Japan?

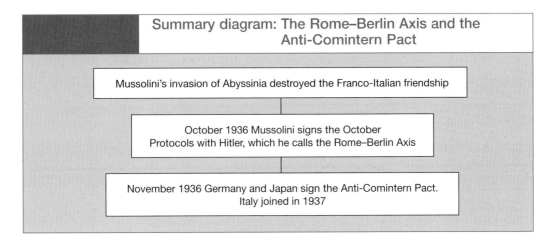

Summary diagram: The Rome–Berlin Axis and the Anti-Comintern Pact

Mussolini's invasion of Abyssinia destroyed the Franco-Italian friendship

October 1936 Mussolini signs the October Protocols with Hitler, which he calls the Rome–Berlin Axis

November 1936 Germany and Japan sign the Anti-Comintern Pact. Italy joined in 1937

8 | The Key Debate

> In what ways, and for what reasons, was the diplomatic situation in Europe transformed from 1930 to 1937?

In 1930 Britain and France, thanks to their victories in 1919, had still dominated Europe. Germany was committed to co-operation with Britain and France and was in many ways still dependent on them. Both the USSR and Italy remained marginal powers.

By 1937 all this had changed. Germany had begun to rearm and by reoccupying the Rhineland had made it virtually impossible for the Western Powers to threaten it with military sanctions again. Japan had broken free from US domination in the Far East (see page 188) and Italy had defied the League to occupy Abyssinia. Britain, France, Russia and even the USA would now have to come to terms with the fact that 'a new globe spanning alliance', as the historian Gerhard Weinberg has described it, was apparently being created which could threaten them simultaneously on both sides of the world. It was now the democracies and not Germany that were on the defensive.

Key books in the debate:
R. Bosworth, *Italy, the Least of the Great Powers* (CUP, 1980).
R. Boyce, 'World depression, world war: some economic origins of the Second World War' in R. Boyce and E.M. Robertson (eds), *Paths to War: New Essays on the Origins of the Second World War* (Macmillan, 1989).
A. Bullock, 'Hitler and the origins of the Second World War' in E. Robertson (ed.), *The Origins of the Second World War* (Macmillan, 1971).
M. Lamb and N. Tarling, *From Versailles to Pearl Harbor* (Palgrave, 2001).
G. Roberts, *The Soviet Union and the Origins of the Second World War, 1933–41* (Macmillan, 1995).
G. Weinberg, *The Foreign Policy of Hitler's Germany* (University of Chicago Press, 1983).

Study Guide: AS Question

In the style of OCR A

'The crises over Manchuria and Abyssinia fatally weakened the League of Nations.' How far do you agree with this judgement?

Exam tips

The page references are intended to take you straight to the material that will help you to answer the question.

This question asks you to evaluate the impact of two specific crises in undermining the effectiveness of the League. One approach would be to take the impact of each one separately. Another approach might consider the impact of the one crisis on the other – the degree to which the League in dealing with Italy (pages 146–8) was already weakened by Manchuria (Chapter 9, pages 187–8).

The attitudes of the major powers (especially Britain and France) will need to be discussed, along with their desire to construct other means of security (pages 146–8). The issue of whether the League was doomed from these crises onwards will add a powerful dimension to your assessment. To balance that line of thought, a strong essay will equally question the strength of the League in the first place, perhaps arguing that Manchuria and/or Abyssinia only confirmed a fatal weakness present since its foundation (for example, it had not stopped the Italian invasion of Corfu, pages 125–6; the Geneva Protocol, page 128, was never ratified so collective military action was impossible).

You can argue the case in several ways. What is crucial is that you assess the extent to which the League was 'fatally weakened' by these crises and argue a clear case. 'How far …?' is a command that you must obey, or lose marks heavily.

Study Guide: A2 Question

In the style of Edexcel

How far do you agree with the view that the impact of the world economic crisis accounts for the failure of the League of Nations in the 1930s? Explain your answer, using Sources 1–3 and your own knowledge of the issues related to this controversy.

Source 1

From: J.M. Roberts, Europe 1880–1945, *published in 1972.*

Britain and France were the two Stresa powers who saw Italy as a potential ally against Germany. Both wished for most of the time not to alienate Mussolini so violently that his troops would be unavailable on the Brenner. Mussolini did leave the League, and this alienation did take place, but this does not mean that the inconsistency at the heart of the British and French policy could have been recognised and eliminated at the start. Other complications made that difficult. One was timing: the Ethiopian [Abyssinian] crisis was not a major preoccupation of statesmen. Ethiopia's appeal to the League, for example, had to compete for attention with German reintroduction of conscription on the same day. In spite of these complications, it is difficult to envisage any outcome worse than that which actually resulted. The League was fatally damaged.

Source 2

From: D. Thomson, Europe Since Napoleon, *published in 1966.*

In the realm of international relations the world [economic] crisis reached its climax and its most devastating effects, for here it led directly to the Second World War. The keynote of the general world crisis was exclusiveness, its most important consequence, separatism. European nations huddled behind rising barriers of protective tariffs and defensive armaments, and demonstrated their reluctance to take effective collective action against powerful aggressors. The expanding world economy of 1914 had [in the 1930s] broken down into a contracting system of separate autarchic national economies; the universal structure of the League of Nations was abandoned by Japan and Germany.

Source 3

From: P. Johnson, Modern Times, *published in 1983.*

Britain and France were left [without US membership] with a League in a shape they did not want, and the man who had shaped it disavowed by his own country. An American presence in the League would have made it far more likely that during the 1920s Germany would have secured by due process of international law those adjustments which, in the 1930s, she sought by force and was granted by cowardice.

Exam tips

The page references are intended to take you straight to the material that will help you to answer the question.

This question provides you with sources which each contain a different view about the reasons for the failure of the League of Nations and asks you to use them, together with your own knowledge, to discuss the statement. It is important to treat questions of this type differently from the way you would plan an essay answer. If you ignore the sources, you will lose more than half the marks available. The sources raise issues for you. You can use them as the core of your plan since they will always contain points which relate to the claim stated in the question. Make sure you have identified all the issues raised by the sources, and then add in your own knowledge, both to make more of the issues in the sources (add depth to the coverage) and to add new points (extend the range covered). In the advice given below, links are made to the relevant pages where information can be found.

The claim in the question, that the League's failure resulted primarily from the impact of the world economic crisis, is contained in Source 2. In contrast, Source 3 emphasises the League's weaknesses from the beginning – shaped by Wilson and weakened by the absence of the US membership. Source 1 emphasises the significance of the Ethiopian crisis, and its mishandling by Britain and France in particular. You should use your own knowledge to discuss the significance of each of these. The sources also introduce other issues on which you should expand:

- the aggressive policies followed by Japan and Italy (pages 135, 146–8, 186–8, 190–4)
- the diplomatic situation in the 1930s (pages 141–8)
- the implications of German grievances not addressed in the 1920s (pages 103–5)
- the actions taken by Hitler to secure adjustments 'sought by force and granted by cowardice' (pages 148–9).

You should reach a clearly stated judgement on whether you see the impact of the world economic crisis as the most significant factor in the League's failure to 'take effective collective action against powerful aggressors'.

8

The Countdown to War in Europe 1937–41

POINTS TO CONSIDER

The core of this chapter covers the crucial period from March 1938 to September 1939. It begins with Hitler's plans for expansion and then looks at the succession of crises which start with the *Anschluss* and end with Britain's and France's declaration of war on Germany. It then briefly traces the spreading conflict in Europe up to June 1941.

In dealing with these events this chapter focuses on:

- Hitler considers his options
- The arms race: Britain, France and Germany 1936–9
- Britain, France and appeasement
- The *Anschluss* and the destruction of Czechoslovakia
- The Anglo-French guarantees and attempts to construct a peace front
- The race to gain the support of the USSR
- The outbreak of war
- The spreading conflict, June 1940 to June 1941

Key dates

1938	March 12	German occupation of Austria (*Anschluss*)
	May 20–22	Rumours that Germany was about to invade Czechoslovakia
	September 8	Sudeten Germans broke off negotiations with Prague
	September 15	Chamberlain visited Hitler at Berchtesgaden
	September 22–23	Chamberlain at Bad Godesberg
	September 28	Hitler accepted Mussolini's plan for four-power talks
	September 29–30	Four-Power Conference at Munich
1939	March 15	Germany occupied Bohemia and Moravia
	March 23	Lithuania handed over Memel to Germany
	March 31	Anglo-French guarantee of Poland

	April 7	Italian occupation of Albania
	April 13	Anglo-French guarantee of Greece and Romania
	April 14	Anglo-French negotiations with USSR started
	April 28	Hitler terminated Anglo-German Naval Agreement and Non-aggression Pact with Poland
	May 22	Pact of Steel signed in Berlin
	August 23	Nazi–Soviet Pact
	September 1	Germany invaded Poland
	September 3	Britain and France declared war on Germany
1940	June 10	Italy declared war on Britain and France
	June 22	Fall of France
	September 27	Tripartite Pact signed by Germany, Italy and Japan
1941	June 22	German invasion of Russia

1 | Hitler Considers his Options

By the autumn of 1937 Hitler had virtually dismantled the
Europe created by the Locarno and Versailles Treaties. The
Spanish Civil War (see page 150) and the Sino-Japanese War (see
page 190) distracted his potential enemies, while Italy was
drawing ever closer to Germany. In August 1936 he had initiated
the Four-Year Plan for preparing the German economy for war by
1940. He was thus in a favourable position to consider options for
a new and more aggressive phase of foreign policy.

The Hossbach Memorandum

On 5 November 1937 Hitler called a special meeting which was
attended by his Commanders-in-Chief and Foreign and War
Ministers. The account of the meeting was written down by
Hitler's adjutant, Colonel Hossbach. Hitler told them that what
he had to say was so important that it was to be regarded as 'his
last will and testament'. He stressed that his overriding aim was
to acquire *Lebensraum* within Europe rather than colonies in
Africa, at the latest by the period 1943–5, but indicated that
he would move against Czechoslovakia and Austria before this
date if France were distracted either by a civil war or by hostilities
with Italy.

At the **Nuremberg trials** after the war in 1946 the Allies
claimed that Hossbach's memorandum showed that Hitler had
drawn up a detailed timetable for war, but the historian A.J.P.
Taylor was more sceptical. He argued that the meeting was not
really about foreign policy but about the allocation of armaments
between the German armed services. Today few historians agree

Key question
What light does the
Hossbach
Memorandum shed
on the aims of Hitler's
foreign policy?

Nuremberg trials
The trials of
German war
criminals in
Nuremberg.

Key term

Key figure

Alfred Jodl (1890–1946)
Chief of the Operations Staff of the German Armed Forces High Command. At Nuremberg trials in 1946, sentenced to death and hanged as a war criminal.

with Taylor's conclusions that Hitler's exposition was for the most part 'day dreaming unrelated to what followed in real life' and that he was in fact 'at a loss what to do next even after he had the power to do it'. The consensus of research still favours the historian William Carr's view that Hitler was warning his generals 'that a more adventurous and dangerous foreign policy was imminent'. It was significant, for instance, that a month later **General Jodl**, the Chief of the Operations Staff, drew up plans for an offensive rather than defensive war against Czechoslovakia.

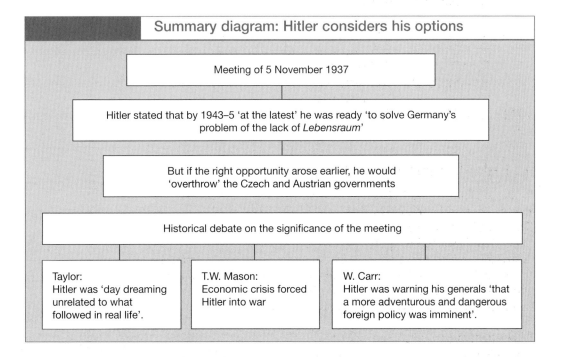

Summary diagram: Hitler considers his options

Meeting of 5 November 1937

Hitler stated that by 1943–5 'at the latest' he was ready 'to solve Germany's problem of the lack of *Lebensraum*'

But if the right opportunity arose earlier, he would 'overthrow' the Czech and Austrian governments

Historical debate on the significance of the meeting

Taylor:
Hitler was 'day dreaming unrelated to what followed in real life'.

T.W. Mason:
Economic crisis forced Hitler into war

W. Carr:
Hitler was warning his generals 'that a more adventurous and dangerous foreign policy was imminent'.

Key question
In what ways did the experiences of the First World War influence the arms race of the period 1936–9?

2 | The Arms Race: Britain, France and Germany 1936–9

It was not until 1935 that the scale of German rearmament became clear. Inevitably this triggered an arms race with Britain and France. Unlike in 1914, there was no calm assumption that the next war would be soon over. All three countries, learning from the First World War, expected a long struggle. Even though the tank and aeroplane had restored mobility to the battlefield, most military experts still thought in terms of First World War tactics. The French built the Maginot line, which was an enormous series of concrete fortifications along their frontier with Germany, while the Germans built the *Westwall* along the east bank of the Rhine.

An important lesson from the First World War was that the armed forces needed so much equipment that the economy and the workforce had to be totally mobilised in order to supply them.

The nation which could most efficiently supply and finance its armed forces in a long, protracted struggle would in all probability win the war. In all three countries rearmament caused major financial problems.

Germany

By 1936 Germany was already finding it difficult to finance rearmament. Hitler, however, brushed aside complaints from **Hjalmar Schacht**, his Economics Minister, and appointed **Göring** to implement the Four-Year Plan which was to prepare Germany for war by 1940. Through raising taxes, government loans and cutting consumer expenditure, military expenditure nearly quadrupled between 1937 and 1939. An ambitious programme for the production of **synthetic materials** was also started to beat the impact of a British blockade. By August 1939 the *Luftwaffe* had 4000 frontline aircraft and the strength of the army had risen to 2,758,000 men. In January 1939 Hitler also announced plans for the construction of a major battle fleet to challenge Britain.

Despite the initial target of 1940 set by the Four-Year Plan, the German rearmament programme was planned to be ready by the mid-1940s. In the meantime, as the historian Richard Overy observes, 'Hitler pursued a policy of putting as much as possible in the "shop window" to give the impression that Germany was armed in greater depth than was in fact the case'.

The pace of German military expansion created concern in both France and Britain, which in turn both embarked on major rearmament programmes.

France and Britain

France

In France rearmament caused considerable economic and social problems. Between 1936 and 1938 the franc had to be **devalued** three times to help pay for rearmament. In November 1938 a general strike was called in Paris in protest against wage cuts and the decline in living standards caused by diverting resources to rearmament. The pace of French rearmament was slowed by the weakness of their economy, but even so military expenditure had increased six times between 1936 and 1939.

Britain

In Britain too rearmament caused considerable financial strain, which Neville Chamberlain (see page 162) feared might 'break our backs'. Nevertheless in 1936 a Four-Year Plan for rearmament was unveiled in which priority was given to the navy and air force. A key part of the programme was the construction of a bomber striking force. The programme was accelerated when Chamberlain became Prime Minister in 1937 and increased funds were also made available for the army. Between 1936 and 1939 expenditure on armaments increased from £185.9 million to £719 million. On 22 February 1939 the government authorised aircraft production 'to the limit' regardless of cost.

Key question
How did Germany prepare for war 1936–9?

Key figure

Hjalmar Schacht (1877–1970)
As President of the *Reichsbank* and Economics Minister he played an important part in financing German rearmament 1933–5. After disagreements about the pace of rearmament he was dismissed in 1937.

Key question
What problems did the French and British rearmament programmes face 1936–9?

Key figure

Hermann Göring (1893–1946)
Nazi leader and First World War air ace. In charge of the *Luftwaffe* and the Four-Year Plan. Committed suicide in May 1945.

Key terms

Synthetic materials
Objects imitating a natural product but made chemically.

Devalue
Reduce the value of.

Key question
What was the impact of the arms race on the diplomatic situation?

The impact of the arms race on the diplomatic situation

The German rearmament programme would not be completed until the mid-1940s. This would not, however, stop Hitler from waging a limited war against Czechoslovakia or Poland if he believed that Britain and France would stand aside.

The British and French programmes, on the other hand, were planned to be ready by 1939–40. Neither Britain nor France wanted war, and both were ready to seek agreement with Nazi Germany to prevent it, but if there was no option but war, then 1939–40 was the best possible date for it to occur. Beyond that date both countries would find it increasingly difficult to maintain the high level of spending that their armament programmes demanded.

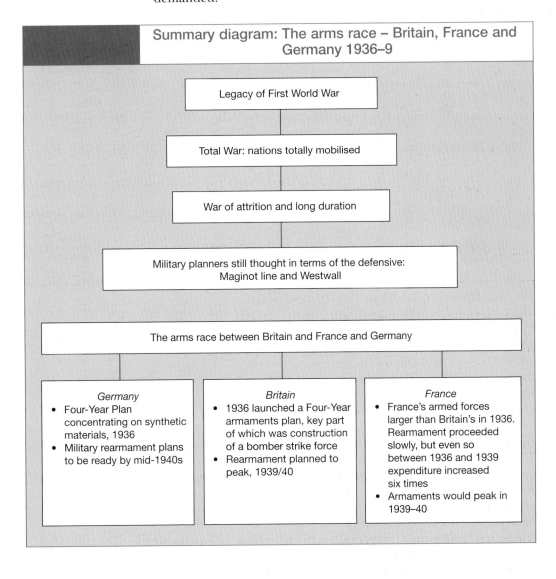

Summary diagram: The arms race – Britain, France and Germany 1936–9

Legacy of First World War

Total War: nations totally mobilised

War of attrition and long duration

Military planners still thought in terms of the defensive: Maginot line and Westwall

The arms race between Britain and France and Germany

Germany	Britain	France
• Four-Year Plan concentrating on synthetic materials, 1936 • Military rearmament plans to be ready by mid-1940s	• 1936 launched a Four-Year armaments plan, key part of which was construction of a bomber strike force • Rearmament planned to peak, 1939/40	• France's armed forces larger than Britain's in 1936. Rearmament proceeded slowly, but even so between 1936 and 1939 expenditure increased six times • Armaments would peak in 1939–40

3 | Britain, France and Appeasement

Appeasement: the historical debate

Essentially appeasement was a realistic policy for the rulers of the large and vulnerable British Empire. It was based on the assumption that a willingness to compromise would avert conflict and protect the essential interests of the empire (see page 8). With Hitler, however, it completely failed to achieve any lasting settlement and appeared in retrospect to be a cowardly policy of surrender.

In the first 20 years after the defeat of Hitler, historians on both the right and left scornfully dismissed Chamberlain's appeasement policy. They were heavily influenced not only by Winston Churchill's memoirs, but also by a brilliant pamphlet, *Guilty Men*, which was written by three left-wing journalists, including Michael Foot, later a leader of the Labour Party. It was published in July 1940, just a few weeks after the fall of France and the evacuations from **Dunkirk**. It bitterly accused Chamberlain of pursuing a disastrous policy that had left Britain unprepared militarily to face the dictators. In the eyes of the general public and for historians on both the left and right, Neville Chamberlain rapidly became the scapegoat – and not only for his own countrymen. French historians and politicians claimed that he bullied them into appeasement, while some Germans were tempted to excuse their own support for Hitler by blaming Chamberlain for not standing up to the Nazis.

Only with the opening up of the British and French archives in the 1960s and 1970s did it gradually become possible to reassess the whole policy of appeasement and place Chamberlain's policy of appeasement in the context of Britain's slow economic decline as well as the global challenges facing the British Empire.

Key questions
Why and how did Chamberlain launch a policy of appeasement in the autumn of 1937?

What are the historical arguments about appeasement?

Key term

Dunkirk
In May 1940 the British Expeditionary Force in France was forced to retreat to Dunkirk and was only rescued by a risky sea evacuation.

Profile: Neville Chamberlain 1869–1940

1915–18	–	Lord Mayor of Birmingham
1918	–	Entered parliament
1923–9	–	Minister of Health
1931–7	–	Chancellor of the Exchequer
1939–40	–	Prime Minister
1940	–	Died

Chamberlain was an energetic politician, who had been a very successful Minister of Health and Chancellor of the Exchequer. When he became Prime Minister he was determined to solve the German problem and avoid plunging Europe into war. He took control of British foreign policy and marginalised the Foreign Office. He believed that he would be able to come to an agreement by a direct man-to-man discussion with Hitler. He was convinced that German grievances could be met through a policy of appeasement. Even though he reluctantly realised that war was probable after Hitler's seizure of Bohemia in March 1939, he never completely abandoned appeasement.

R.P. Shay, in his study of British rearmament in the 1930s, argues that Chamberlain had to maintain a balance between rearming and balancing the budget, so that if war came Britain would have enough money to buy vital materials and equipment from the USA. By the end of the 1980s revisionist historians were arguing that Chamberlain's policy was essentially determined by Britain's economic weakness and that he had no other option but to attempt to appease Germany, if the Empire was to be preserved. John Charmley even argued that Churchill was the real 'guilty man' by fighting a war that could only end in the dissolution of the Empire and bankruptcy. This revisionist line was, however, strongly challenged by R.A.C. Parker who insisted that 'after the *Anschluss* [see page 164] in March 1938 Chamberlain could … have secured sufficient support in Britain for a close alliance with France, and a policy of containing and encircling Germany, more or less shrouded under the League of Nations covenant'.

Chamberlain and appeasement

Key question
What did Chamberlain hope that his appeasement policies would achieve?

In the autumn of 1937 Chamberlain launched a major initiative aimed at achieving a settlement with Hitler. He hoped to divert German expansion in eastern Europe by offering Germany colonies in Africa. In late November an Anglo-French summit was held in London where this policy was more fully explored. Chamberlain won over the French to this policy and by March 1938 he was ready to negotiate a package of colonial concessions with Berlin, but the gathering pace of German expansion signalled first by the *Anschluss* and then by the destruction of Czechoslovakia made this approach irrelevant.

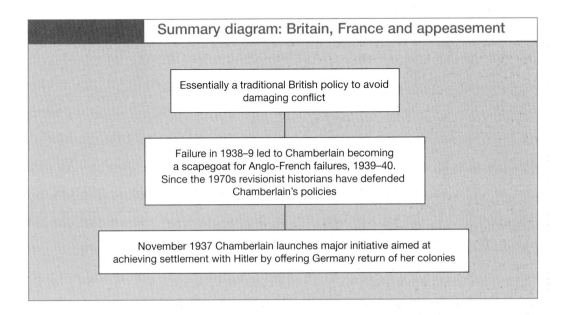

Summary diagram: Britain, France and appeasement

Essentially a traditional British policy to avoid damaging conflict

Failure in 1938–9 led to Chamberlain becoming a scapegoat for Anglo-French failures, 1939–40. Since the 1970s revisionist historians have defended Chamberlain's policies

November 1937 Chamberlain launches major initiative aimed at achieving settlement with Hitler by offering Germany return of her colonies

4 | The *Anschluss* and the Destruction of Czechoslovakia

In November 1937 Hitler had outlined a possible scenario involving civil war in France or a Franco-Italian war (see page 158), which would enable him to annex Austria and dismember Czechoslovakia without fear of international intervention. He was able to achieve these aims in 1938–9, even though the circumstances that he had predicted never in fact came about. Both the *Anschluss*, and the eventual destruction of Czechoslovakia do indeed show Hitler's ability to adapt his tactics to the prevailing circumstances while steadily pursuing his overall aims.

The *Anschluss*

The annexation of Austria had long been a key aim of Nazi foreign policy, but Hitler did not plan the actual events that enabled him to achieve it. The crisis was ultimately triggered when **Schuschnigg**, the Austrian Chancellor, alarmed by the activities of the Austrian Nazis, requested an interview with Hitler. Hitler welcomed the chance to achieve an easy diplomatic success by imposing on Schuschnigg an agreement which would not only have subordinated Austrian foreign policy to Berlin but also have given the Austrian Nazi Party complete freedom. However, Schuschnigg then decided unexpectedly to regain some room for manoeuvre by asking his countrymen to vote in a referendum, which he planned to hold on Sunday 14 March, for a 'free and German, independent and social, Christian and united Austria'.

Key question
What did Hitler initially hope to achieve in his talks with Schuschnigg?

Key figure

Kurt von Schuschnigg (1897–1977)
Chancellor of Austria 1934–8. He was imprisoned by the Nazis after the *Anschluss*.

The German army occupies Austria

The immediate danger for the German government was that if Schuschnigg's appeal was endorsed by a large majority, he would be able to renounce his agreement with Hitler. Confronted by this challenge, Hitler rapidly dropped his policy of gradual absorption of Austria and not only forced Schuschnigg to cancel the referendum but on 12 March ordered the German army to occupy Austria. Then Hitler decided, apparently on the spur of the moment after a highly successful visit to the Austrian city of Linz where he had attended secondary school as a boy, to incorporate Austria into the *Reich* rather than install a satellite Nazi government in Vienna.

Key question
Why did Hitler decide to invade Austria?

Key date

German occupation of Austria (*Anschluss*): 12 March 1938

The reaction of Italy, Britain and France

Besides violating the Treaty of Versailles, which specifically forbade the union of Germany and Austria (see page 96), Hitler had for the first time invaded an independent state, even though the Austrian army did not oppose him, and put himself in a position from which to threaten Czechoslovakia. Why then did this not bring about a repetition of the Stresa Front that was briefly formed in 1934 against German aggression (see page 139)? Although Chamberlain was in contact with the Italian government, and in April concluded an agreement aimed at

Key question
What was the reaction of Italy, Britain and France to the *Anschluss*?

Central Europe
showing German
expansion from 1935
to August 1939.

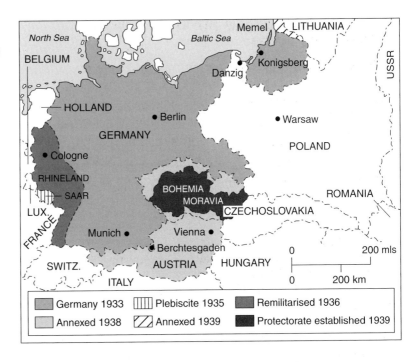

North Sea

Baltic Sea

Memel

LITHUANIA

BELGIUM

Danzig

Königsberg

USSR

HOLLAND

Berlin

Warsaw

GERMANY

POLAND

Cologne

RHINELAND

BOHEMIA

ROMANIA

SAAR

MORAVIA

CZECHOSLOVAKIA

LUX.

FRANCE

Munich

Vienna

0   200 mls

Berchtesgaden

SWITZ.

AUSTRIA

HUNGARY

0   200 km

ITALY

Germany 1933	Plebiscite 1935	Remilitarised 1936
Annexed 1938	Annexed 1939	Protectorate established 1939

Key figure

Camille Chautemps
(1885–1963)
Served in several
French
governments and
was Prime Minister
three times.

lowering the tension in the Mediterranean, essentially Mussolini
had decided as long ago as 1936 that Austria was a German
sphere of interest. Not surprisingly therefore, on 11 March, he
backed Hitler's decision to invade Austria. Both Britain and
France protested to Berlin but neither had any intention of going
to war over Austria. Indeed, the French were paralysed by an
internal political crisis caused by the resignation of **Camille**
Chautemps' ministry, and between 10 and 13 March did not even
have a government.

The initial reaction of the British government was to hope that
the storm would blow over and that talks could resume with
Berlin on a package of possible colonial concessions (see
page 163), which had already been handed to the German
government on 3 March. These concessions were, after all, aimed
at distracting Berlin from pursuing its ambitions in central
Europe. Whether Chamberlain really believed that Hitler could
be bought off is hard to say. Privately he wrote that 'it was now
clear' that force was the only argument that Germany understood,
but publicly he was not yet ready to draw the logical conclusion
from this and confront Hitler. Was he gaining time for his country
to rearm or was he seriously giving peace one more chance?

Key question
What did Hitler hope
to achieve by
exploiting the
nationalism of the
Sudeten Germans?

The Sudeten crisis
The annexation of Austria with the minimum of international
protest greatly increased the vulnerability of Czechoslovakia to
Nazi pressure, as it was now surrounded on three sides by
German territory. Hitler had long regarded Czechoslovakia, with
its alliances with both France and Russia, as a strategic threat to
Germany which would eventually have to be eliminated. It is,

however, arguable that in April 1938 Hitler was by no means sure how he was to carry out this aim. He certainly played with the idea of launching a sudden attack on Czechoslovakia if a major crisis were to be triggered, for instance by the assassination of the German ambassador in Prague. An easier and safer way to bring about the disintegration of Czechoslovakia was to inflame the nationalism of the **Sudeten Germans**. Czechoslovakia was a fragile state undermined by an ethnically divided population. Its unity was particularly threatened by the three million Sudeten Germans and the two million Slovaks. Hitler therefore specifically instructed **Konrad Henlein**, the Sudeten German leader, to keep making demands for concessions which the Prague government could not possibly grant if it wanted to preserve the unity of Czechoslovakia.

In the aftermath of the *Anschluss* both Britain and France were acutely aware of the growing threat to Czechoslovakia. Britain was unwilling to guarantee Czechoslovakia and yet realised that it might well not be able to stand aloof from the consequences of a German attack on it. Chamberlain told the Commons on 24 March that if fighting occurred:

> it would be well within the bounds of possibility that other countries, besides those which were parties to the original dispute, would almost immediately become involved. This is especially true in the case of two countries like Great Britain and France, with long associations of friendship, with interests closely interwoven, devoted to the same ideals of democratic liberty and determined to uphold them.

The French, unlike the British, were pledged by two treaties signed in 1924 and 1925 to consult and assist Czechoslovakia in the event of a threat to their common interests (see page 118). In reality the French were in no position to help the Czechs. The Chief of the French Air Staff, who was in charge of operational planning, made no secret of his fears that the French air force would be wiped out within 15 days after the outbreak of war with Germany. The French government was therefore ready to follow the British lead in seeking a way of defusing the Sudeten crisis before it could lead to war.

The May crisis

The urgency of this was underlined by the war scare of the weekend of 20–21 May 1938, when the Czech government suddenly partially mobilised its army in response to false rumours that a German attack was imminent. Hitler, warned by both Britain and France of the dangerous consequences of any military action, rapidly proclaimed the absence of any mobilisation plans. Yet far from making Hitler more reasonable, this incident appears to have had the opposite effect, as he immediately stepped up military preparations for an invasion and set 1 October as a deadline for 'smashing Czechoslovakia'. Taylor sees this as bluff and argues that 'Hitler did not need to act. Others would do his

Key term

Sudeten Germans
Ethnic Germans who had been settled in the Sudetenland since the thirteenth century.

Key figure

Konrad Henlein (1898–1945)
Leader of the Sudeten German Nazis and later Nazi *Gauleiter* of the Sudetenland.

Key dates

Rumours that Germany was about to invade Czechoslovakia: 20–22 May 1938

Sudeten Germans broke off negotiations with Prague: 8 September 1938

Key question
What was the significance of the May crisis?

work for him.' There were certainly, as we have seen, powerful forces working for the disintegration of the Czech state, but most historians do not dismiss Hitler's plans so lightly. It is more likely that he was just keeping his options open, as Bullock argues, to the 'very last possible moment'.

Meanwhile, France and Britain were redoubling their efforts to find a peaceful solution. The Anglo-French peace strategy aimed to put pressure on both the Czechs and the Sudeten Germans to make concessions, while continuing to warn Hitler of the dangers of a general war. In early September, **Beneš**, the Czech Prime Minister, responded to this pressure by granting almost all Henlein's demands. As this threatened the justification for Hitler's campaign against Czechoslovakia, Hitler immediately instructed Henlein to provoke a series of incidents which would enable him to break off the talks with Beneš.

Chamberlain intervenes

On 12 September 1938 Hitler's campaign moved into a new phase when, in a speech at the Nuremberg rally, he violently attacked the Czechs and assured the Sudetens of his support. Both Britain and France desperately attempted to avoid war. **Daladier**, the French Prime Minister, suggested that he and Chamberlain should meet Hitler, but Chamberlain seized the initiative and flew to see Hitler on 15 September at Berchtesgaden. There he agreed, subject to consultation with the French, that Czechoslovakia should cede to Germany all areas which contained a German population of 50 per cent or over. This would be supervised by an international commission. Hitler also demanded that Czechoslovakia should renounce its pact with Soviet Russia. When Chamberlain again met Hitler at Bad Godesberg on 22 September, after winning French backing for his plan, Hitler demanded that the German occupation of the Sudetenland should be speeded up so that it would be completed by 28 September. Nor was it to be supervised by any international commission. Why Hitler should suddenly have changed his mind has puzzled historians. Taylor argued that Hitler was anxious to avoid accepting Chamberlain's plan in the hope that the Hungarians and Poles would formulate their own demands for Czechoslovakian territory and that he would then be able to move in and occupy the whole state under the pretext of being 'a peacemaker creating a new order'. On the other hand it is possible that Hitler had no such elaborate plan in mind and merely wanted to eliminate Czechoslovakia once and for all through war. At this stage Chamberlain's peace initiative seemed to have failed. France and Britain reluctantly began to mobilise, although both powers still continued to seek a negotiated settlement.

Key figure

Edvard Beneš (1884–1948)
A leader of the Czechoslovak independence movement before 1918, then Minister of Foreign Affairs and President 1935–8 and 1945–8.

Key question
Why did it appear that Chamberlain's peace initiative had failed after the Bad Godesberg meeting of 22–23 September 1938?

Key dates

Chamberlain visited Hitler at Berchtesgaden: 15 September 1938

Chamberlain at Bad Godesberg: 22–23 September 1938

Key figure

Édouard Daladier (1884–1970)
A radical French politician and Prime Minister 1938–41.

The Munich Agreement

In retrospect it is often argued that the French and British should have gone to war and called Hitler's bluff. Chamberlain's critics particularly stress that Russia was ready to come to the help of Czechoslovakia, but at the time offers of Russian help seemed to the British, French and even the Czechs to be unconvincing. As neither Poland nor Romania would allow Russian troops through their territory, how could they help Czechoslovakia? It is thus not surprising that Chamberlain and Daladier warmly welcomed Mussolini's last-minute proposal on 28 September for a four-power conference in Munich.

The next day, under pressure from his generals and from Mussolini, who both dreaded a premature war, Hitler reluctantly agreed to delay the occupation of the Sudetenland until 10 October and to allow an international commission to map the boundary line. He also consented, together with Britain, France and Italy, to guarantee what remained of the independence of Czechoslovakia and signed a declaration which affirmed the desire of Britain and Germany 'never to go to war with one another again'. This was supplemented by a similar declaration signed by Ribbentrop, Hitler's Foreign Minister, in Paris in December.

It is too simple to call Munich a triumph for Hitler. He had, it is true, secured the Sudetenland, but arguably he had been cheated of his real aim, the destruction of Czechoslovakia, which apparently was now about to be protected by an international guarantee. Germany seemed to be in danger of being enmeshed in just the sort of international agreement Hitler had always hoped to avoid. However, even the most revisionist of historians would be hard put to call Munich a great victory for Chamberlain. Arguably he did buy more time for rearmament, but to the outside world Munich seemed to be a major defeat for Britain and France. The British ambassador in Tokyo reported that 'the Japanese reaction … is that we are prepared to put up with almost any indignity rather than fight. The result is that, all in all, our prestige is at a low ebb in the East … .'

The destruction of Czechoslovakia

The argument that Hitler merely responded to events is hard to sustain when his foreign policy from October 1938 to March 1939 is analysed. His main priority remained the destruction of Czechoslovakia. On 21 October 1938 the German army was ordered to draw up fresh plans for military action. Simultaneously Hitler dangled the bait of territorial gains at the expense of the Czechs in front of the Hungarians, Poles and Romanians in order to enlist their support. German agents were also sent into Slovakia to fuel agitation against Prague. In practice Britain and France were already beginning to recognise Czechoslovakia as a German sphere of influence. The German representatives were allowed to dominate the international commission that was to map out the new frontiers after the secession of the Sudetenland

Key dates

Key question
Was the Munich Agreement a triumph for Hitler?

Hitler accepted Mussolini's plan for four-power talks: 28 September 1938

Four-Power Conference at Munich: 29–30 September 1938

Key question
Why was Hitler allowed by Britain and France to destroy Czechoslovakia?

and neither power protested when Germany refused to participate in finalising the terms of the joint guarantee of Czechoslovakia in February 1939.

On 6 March 1939 the Germans were given the opportunity finally to dismember Czechoslovakia. When the Czechs suddenly moved troops into Slovakia to crush local demands for independence, which the Nazis of course had helped to stir up, Hitler persuaded the Slovaks to appeal to Berlin for assistance. On 14 March 1939 the Czech President, Emil Hácha, was ordered to travel to Berlin where he was ruthlessly bullied into resigning the fate of his country into 'the hands of the *Führer*'. The next day German troops occupied Prague, and Slovakia was turned into a German protectorate. This action was to precipitate a major diplomatic revolution in Europe.

Key date

Germany occupied Bohemia and Moravia: 15 March 1939

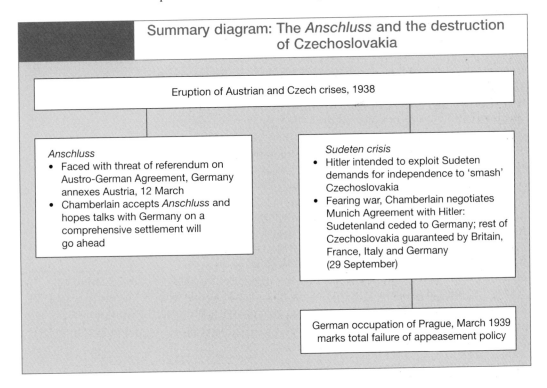

Summary diagram: The *Anschluss* and the destruction of Czechoslovakia

Eruption of Austrian and Czech crises, 1938

Anschluss
- Faced with threat of referendum on Austro-German Agreement, Germany annexes Austria, 12 March
- Chamberlain accepts *Anschluss* and hopes talks with Germany on a comprehensive settlement will go ahead

Sudeten crisis
- Hitler intended to exploit Sudeten demands for independence to 'smash' Czechoslovakia
- Fearing war, Chamberlain negotiates Munich Agreement with Hitler: Sudetenland ceded to Germany; rest of Czechoslovakia guaranteed by Britain, France, Italy and Germany (29 September)

German occupation of Prague, March 1939 marks total failure of appeasement policy

Key question

Why did Britain and France guarantee Poland, Greece and Romania?

5 | The Anglo-French Guarantees and Attempts to Construct a Peace Front

In 1925 the British Foreign Minister had declared that the defence of the Polish corridor was not worth the bones of one British grenadier (see page 112), yet on 31 March 1939 Britain broke decisively with its traditional foreign policy of avoiding a Continental commitment, and, together with France, guaranteed Poland against a German attack. In many ways it appeared a foolhardy and contradictory gesture as both Britain and France lacked the military power to defend Poland and had already tacitly written off eastern Europe as a German sphere of influence. What caused this U-turn was the speed and brutality of the German occupation of the Czech province of Bohemia, which clearly indicated that Hitler could no longer be trusted to respect treaties and guarantees. It is also important to stress that, in the spring of 1939, the French economy and with it French self-confidence had made a strong recovery. Thus a tougher policy towards Hitler increasingly appeared to the French government to be a realistic option.

Britain was initially stampeded into this revolutionary new policy by panic-stricken rumours on 17 March that Hitler was about to occupy Romania and seize the oil wells there. Access to these would greatly strengthen the German war industry and enable it to survive any future British naval blockade. At first Britain aimed to contain Germany by negotiating a four-power pact with France, Russia and Poland, but given the intense suspicion with which Russia was viewed by Poland and the other eastern European states this was not a practical policy. Yet when Hitler went on to force Lithuania to hand back the former German city of Memel to the *Reich* on 23 March, it became even more vital to deter Hitler by any means possible. Thus, Chamberlain and Daladier had little option but to announce on 31 March 1939 an immediate Anglo-French guarantee of Poland against external attack. The Polish guarantee was, however, seen as merely the first step towards constructing a comprehensive security system in eastern Europe. Chamberlain hoped to buttress it with a series of interlocking security pacts with other eastern European and Baltic states.

When, on 7 April, Mussolini invaded Albania a similar wave of panic among the eastern Mediterranean states galvanised Britain and France to guarantee both Greece and Romania. In May, Britain considerably strengthened its position in the eastern Mediterranean by negotiating a preliminary agreement with Turkey for mutual assistance 'in the event of an act of aggression leading to war in the Mediterranean area'. By July both Bulgaria and Yugoslavia were beginning to gravitate towards the Anglo-French '**peace bloc**'.

The German reaction to the British guarantee

In October 1938, and then again in January and March 1939, Hitler unsuccessfully sounded out the Poles about the return of Danzig, the construction of a road and rail link through the corridor and about joining the Anti-Comintern Pact. In return the Poles were offered the eventual prospect of acquiring land in the Ukraine. Essentially Hitler wanted to turn Poland into a reliable satellite, but given the fate of Czechoslovakia it was precisely this status that the Poles finally rejected in March 1939. The Anglo-French guarantee of Poland, far from deterring Hitler, convinced him that Poland would have to be eliminated, even if this meant war with Britain and France. On 23 May Hitler told his generals:

Key dates

Lithuania handed over Memel to Germany: 23 March 1939

Anglo-French guarantee of Poland: 31 March 1939

Italian occupation of Albania: 7 April 1939

Anglo-French guarantee of Greece and Romania: 13 April 1939

Hitler terminated Anglo-German Naval Agreement and Non-Aggression Pact with Poland: 28 April 1939

Key term

Peace bloc
A group of states committed to opposing aggressor powers.

Key question
Why did Hitler decide that Poland had to be destroyed?

Poland will always be on the side of our adversaries ... Danzig is not the objective. It is a matter of expanding our living space in the east ... We cannot expect a repetition of Czechoslovakia. There will be fighting. The task is to isolate Poland ... Basic principle: conflict with Poland, beginning with the attack on Poland, will be successful only if the West keeps out. If that is impossible, then it is better to attack the West and finish off Poland at the same time. It will be a task of dexterous diplomacy to isolate Poland ...

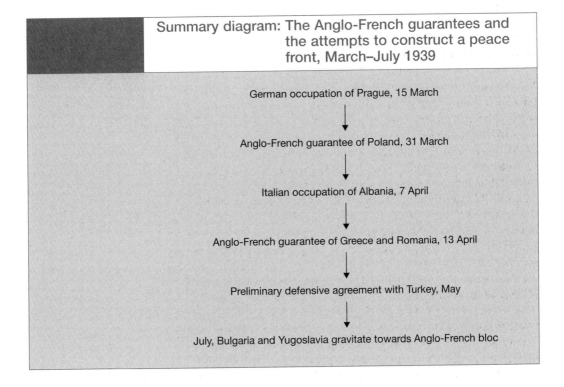

Summary diagram: The Anglo-French guarantees and the attempts to construct a peace front, March–July 1939

German occupation of Prague, 15 March

↓

Anglo-French guarantee of Poland, 31 March

↓

Italian occupation of Albania, 7 April

↓

Anglo-French guarantee of Greece and Romania, 13 April

↓

Preliminary defensive agreement with Turkey, May

↓

July, Bulgaria and Yugoslavia gravitate towards Anglo-French bloc

Key questions
Why did Britain, France and Germany begin negotiations with the USSR in the summer of 1939?

Why did Germany want an alliance with the Soviet Union?

Key date
Anglo-French negotiations with USSR started: 14 April 1939

6 | The Race to Gain the Support of the USSR

Origins of the Nazi–Soviet Pact

Once war against Poland seemed inevitable, it made good sense for Hitler to ensure the support or at least neutrality of the USSR. As soon as victory was assured over Poland and the Western democracies, Soviet Russia could in due course be dealt with. Britain and France also needed a pact with Russia to build up their 'peace front'. Stalin was now in the enviable position of being able to play off Hitler against Chamberlain and Daladier.

Protracted negotiations between Russia, Britain and France began in April 1939, but both sides deeply mistrusted each other. Stalin's demand that Russia should have the right militarily to intervene in the affairs of the small states on its western borders if they were threatened with internal subversion by the Nazis, as Austria and Czechoslovakia had been in 1938, was rejected outright by the British. They feared that the Russians would use the threat of Nazi indirect aggression as an excuse to seize the territories for themselves. Stalin, on the other hand, was equally suspicious that the democracies were attempting to manoeuvre the Russians into a position where they would have to do most of the fighting against Germany. The British delegate, William Strang (1893–1978), reported:

> ... if we do not trust them, they equally do not trust us. They are not, fundamentally, a friendly power; but they, like us, are driven to this course by force of necessity. If we are of two minds about the wisdom of what we are doing, so are they.

The Nazi–Soviet Pact

The Russians thus had ample time to explore the possibility of a pact with Germany, which became genuinely interested in negotiations once the decision was taken on 23 May to prepare for war against Poland. Right through to the middle of August Moscow continued to keep both options open, but by then the slow pace of the military discussions with Britain and France seems finally to have convinced Stalin that an agreement with Hitler would be preferable. With only days to go before the start of the military campaign against Poland, Hitler was ready to accept Stalin's terms and the Nazi–Soviet Pact was signed on 23 August.

Not only did the pact commit both powers to benevolent neutrality towards each other, but in a secret protocol it outlined the German and Russian spheres of interest in eastern Europe: the Baltic states and Bessarabia in Romania fell within the Russian sphere, while Poland was to be divided between the two. Above all, by neutralising Soviet Russia, the pact made an attack on Poland a much less risky policy for Hitler, even if Britain and France did try to come to its rescue.

Given the deep and often justified suspicions of Soviet Russia in Britain, France and the eastern European states, the Nazi–Soviet Pact was the most likely outcome from the tangle of negotiations that took place in the summer of 1939. It did, however, make a German attack on Poland almost inevitable.

Key question
Why was the Nazi–Soviet Pact signed?

Nazi–Soviet Pact: 23 August 1939

Key date

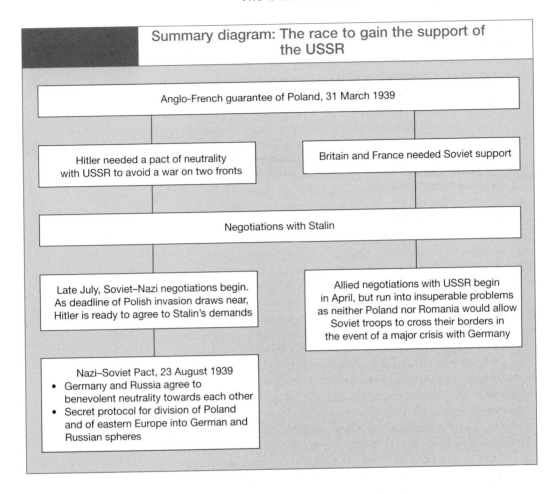

Summary diagram: The race to gain the support of the USSR

Anglo-French guarantee of Poland, 31 March 1939

Hitler needed a pact of neutrality with USSR to avoid a war on two fronts

Britain and France needed Soviet support

Negotiations with Stalin

Late July, Soviet–Nazi negotiations begin. As deadline of Polish invasion draws near, Hitler is ready to agree to Stalin's demands

Allied negotiations with USSR begin in April, but run into insuperable problems as neither Poland nor Romania would allow Soviet troops to cross their borders in the event of a major crisis with Germany

Nazi–Soviet Pact, 23 August 1939
- Germany and Russia agree to benevolent neutrality towards each other
- Secret protocol for division of Poland and of eastern Europe into German and Russian spheres

Key question
What signs were there that appeasement was not yet dead?

Key term

Autarchy
Economic self-sufficiency.

Key date

Pact of Steel signed in Berlin: 22 May 1939

7 | The Outbreak of War

On 22 August 1939, on the eve of the signature of the Nazi–Soviet Pact, Hitler boasted that:

To be sure a new situation has arisen. I experienced those poor worms, Daladier and Chamberlain, in Munich. They will be too cowardly to attack. They won't go beyond a blockade. Against that we have **autarchy** and the Russian raw materials. Poland will be depopulated and settled with Germans. My pact with the Poles was merely conceived of as a gaining of time ... After Stalin's death – he is a very sick man – we will break the Soviet Union. Then there will begin the dawn of German rule of the earth.

The omens did indeed look good for Hitler. Although he had failed to convert the Anti-Comintern Pact (see page 152) into a military alliance against Britain and France, he had in May concluded the Pact of Steel with Italy by which Mussolini rashly agreed to support Germany militarily. Privately Mussolini had been assured that Hitler had no intention of going to war for at least three years!

Neither did it appear that appeasement in Britain and France was dead. In June, **Lord Halifax**, the British Foreign Secretary, stressed that while Britain would defend Poland against any threat to its independence, this did not necessarily mean that its existing frontiers could not be altered or the status of Danzig changed. He went on to repeat a message that was frequently to come out of London in the summer of 1939; namely that once trust was re-established 'any of Germany's claims are open to consideration round a table'. In June and July there were also sporadic talks between British and German officials on economic collaboration in Europe and Africa. In France, too, the mood seemed increasingly defeatist, and **Bonnet**, the French Foreign Minister, was suggesting that France should 'push Warsaw into a compromise'.

War delayed by a week

Overall then Hitler had good grounds to be confident. On 23 August he ordered the army to prepare to attack Poland on the 26th, but then two days later on the 25th these orders were cancelled because, contrary to his expectations, Britain had reacted to the news of the Nazi–Soviet Pact by ratifying its guarantee of Poland. Mussolini also announced that he could not fight without impossibly large deliveries of German armaments and equipment. Was there now a chance for a compromise? Superficially it might seem that there was. During the next few days the British and French utilised all the diplomatic channels they could to avoid war. Theoretically some sort of compromise on Poland might eventually be possible, but in the final analysis they were not ready to sacrifice Poland's independence to achieve it. They were unwilling to repeat Munich. They wanted, as the historian A.P. Adamthwaite has stressed, '*détente*, but negotiated from strength'.

Hitler's position was diametrically opposed to this. He was insistent on first destroying Poland and only then negotiating with Britain and France. On 25 August he even offered Britain an alliance and a guarantee of its empire provided it consented to the destruction of Poland and German supremacy in eastern Europe. The response from London continued to be that only after a freely negotiated Polish–German agreement could the future of Anglo-German relations be discussed.

Belatedly it looked as if Hitler was making some concession to this position when, on 29 August, he suddenly demanded that the British should instruct the Poles to send a minister with full negotiating powers to Berlin by the following day. Fearing that Hitler would treat him as he had Schuschnigg and Hácha (see pages 164 and 169), the British government refused to press the Poles to send a negotiator to Berlin, and instead argued that such a deadline was impracticable since time was needed to prepare for negotiations. Was a last-minute chance to save the peace lost? Taylor argues that war began simply because Hitler launched 'on 29 August a diplomatic manoeuvre which he ought to have

Key question
Why did Hitler cancel his invasion plans for Poland on 25 August 1939?

Key figures

Lord Halifax (1881–1959)
Viceroy of India 1926–31 and British Foreign Minister 1938–40.

Georges Bonnet (1889–1973)
French Foreign Minister 1938–9, and a leading spokesmen for French appeasement.

German troops demolish a Polish frontier barrier during the invasion of Poland which began in September 1939.

launched on 28 August'. It is more likely, however, that Hitler was aiming to isolate the Poles and to manoeuvre them into a position where their 'stubbornness' could be blamed for starting the war, and so give Britain and France an excuse not to back them.

War breaks out

Even when, on 1 September 1939, Germany at last invaded Poland, frantic efforts to avert war still continued. Mussolini urged a Four-Power European Conference, and only when it was absolutely clear that Hitler would not withdraw his troops from Poland did Britain and France declare war on Germany on 3 September. Italy, despite the Pact of Steel, remained neutral, until France was defeated in June 1940, as Mussolini was initially unsure of a speedy German victory and wanted to hedge his bets.

Key question
Why was Mussolini unable to avert the war?

Key dates

Germany invaded Poland: 1 September 1939

Britain and France declared war on Germany: 3 September 1939

Summary diagram: The outbreak of war

Hitler's position strengthened through Pact of Steel (23 May) and the Nazi–Soviet Pact (23 August)

↓

23 August Hitler orders German army to prepare to invade Poland on 26 August

↓

Cancelled on 25 August because Britain reacted to Nazi–Soviet Pact by ratifying Polish guarantee. Mussolini also informed Hitler that Italy was not ready for war

↓

25 August Hitler attempts to bribe Britain to give up Polish guarantee by offering German support for the British Empire and an alliance

↓

29 August Hitler sends demand to Britain that Poland should send a negotiator to Berlin with full powers. London refuses to press the Poles and demands more time

↓

31 August German army given orders to attack at 04.45 hours on 1 September

↓

German troops invade Poland 1 September

↓

3 September Britain and France declare war

8 | The Spreading Conflict, October 1940 to June 1941

Stalin exploits the 'phoney war', October 1939 to March 1940

German troops completed the occupation of Poland within six weeks and Soviet forces rapidly moved into the areas allocated to them by the Nazi–Soviet Pact. Hitler offered Britain and France, who had made hardly any effort to assist Poland, peace on the basis of setting up a small Polish state, which would in reality be a German satellite. When both states rejected this offer, Hitler had little option but to prepare to extend the war westwards. Inevitably he became more dependent on Soviet neutrality and supplies of raw materials to defeat the British blockade.

Stalin was not slow to exploit Russia's favourable position during this **'phoney war'**. He persuaded Hitler to transfer Lithuania, which by the Nazi–Soviet Pact of August (see page 172) had originally been assigned to the German sphere of influence, to the Soviet sphere. He also rapidly negotiated pacts with the Baltic states, which reduced them to the status of satellites. When Finland refused to cede Russia a naval base and agree to the revision of its frontier, the Soviet army invaded in November 1939 and by March 1940 had forced the Finns to comply with Stalin's demands.

Key question
How did Stalin exploit the 'phoney war' to achieve his aims?

Phoney war
The period October 1939 to March 1940 when there was no fighting in western Europe.

Key term

Key question
What were the immediate consequences for continental Europe of Hitler's victories in 1940?

Key dates

Italy declared war on Britain and France: 10 June 1940

Fall of France: 22 June 1940

German victory in the west

In April German troops rapidly occupied both Norway and Denmark to prevent a British attempt to interrupt the flow of iron ore from Sweden to Germany by seizing the Norwegian ports and mining the waters around Narvik. Then on 10 May the Germans turned west and within six weeks Belgium, France and Holland were defeated and Britain was driven from the continent.

The sheer scale of these victories in May 1940 at last persuaded Mussolini in June to take the plunge and declare war on Britain and France. The defeat of France radically changed the balance of power on a global scale. British and American assumptions that France would be able to hold the line against Germany while they would have time to build up their armaments were now destroyed, as was Stalin's calculation that Germany and the Western Powers would fatally weaken themselves in a replay of the most bloody campaigns of the First World War.

Key question
What problems did Britain's refusal to make peace create for Hitler?

Britain's refusal to make peace

By defeating France, Hitler had removed the most immediate threat to his continental policies. Hitler's next step was to attempt to negotiate a peace with Britain. On 25 June he optimistically declared:

German troops parade down the Champs-Elysées in Paris after the fall of France in 1940.

The war in the west has ended, France has been conquered, and I shall come, in the shortest possible time, to an understanding with England. There still remains the conflict with the east. That, however, is a task which throws up worldwide problems, like the relationship with Japan and the distribution of power in the Pacific; one might perhaps tackle it in 10 years' time, perhaps I shall leave it to my successor. Now we have our hands full for years to come to digest and to consolidate what we have obtained in Europe.

Yet despite this relaxed, almost statesman-like view of the future, within a year Hitler had attacked Russia. Why did he do so? Historians disagree as to whether Hitler was carrying out a long-term ideological programme or whether in H.W. Koch's words 'Hitler could only act and react within the context of the changing political constellation.'

The biggest blow to Hitler's plans came when Churchill (see page 65), convinced that with American aid Britain could still wage a war that would eventually wear down the German economy through, to quote the historian David Reynolds, 'the **triad** of blockade, bombing and propaganda', refused to react to Hitler's peace feelers in June 1940.

This was totally unexpected and forced Hitler to consider several options for bringing Britain to the conference table. In September 1940 pressure on Britain was intensified when a new Tripartite Pact was signed by Italy, Japan and Germany. In a key clause that was aimed at the USA they agreed 'to assist one another with all political, economic and military means' should one of them be attacked by a power not yet at war in Europe or China. In November, Hungary, Romania and Slovakia signed the pact, but significantly attempts to bring in Russia failed. The Russian price for membership was too high, as Stalin demanded not only that Bulgaria should be recognised as a Russian satellite, but that he should receive German backing for setting up a chain of bases in the Dardanelles and the Persian Gulf.

It is therefore possible to argue that a combination of British intransigence and mounting Russian ambitions forced Hitler to bring forward his plans for war against Russia. The historian G.L. Weinberg argues, for instance, that the 'decision to attack the Soviet Union was Hitler's answer to the challenge of England – as it had been Napoleon's'. This interpretation would certainly seem to be supported by Hitler's assessment of the military and diplomatic situation delivered to his generals at a conference on 31 July 1940. After stressing the difficulties involved in the invasion of the British Isles at a time when 'our small navy is only 15 per cent of [the] enemy's', Hitler went on to argue that:

Russia is the Far Eastern sword of Britain and the United States pointed at Japan … Japan, like Russia has her programme which she wants to carry through before the end of the war … With Russia smashed, Britain's last hope would be shattered. Germany will then be master of Europe and the Balkans. Decision: Russia's destruction must therefore be made part of this struggle. Spring 1941. The sooner Russia is crushed, the better.

Key dates

Tripartite Pact signed by Germany, Italy and Japan: 27 September 1940

German invasion of Russia: 22 June 1941

Key term

Triad
A group of three.

On the other hand, many historians remain unconvinced that Hitler attacked Russia merely as an extension of the war against Britain. They point out that if the defeat of Britain had really been Hitler's chief priority, then he would surely have concentrated on building up sufficient naval forces and on weakening Britain in the Mediterranean. The Nazi–Soviet Pact was, of course, fragile and likely to break down when the balance of advantages favoured either of the parties sufficiently, but in June 1941 there is absolutely no evidence that Stalin was planning an imminent war against Germany. On balance it seems more likely that Hitler's long-term ideological hatred of Bolshevism and his determination to gain *Lebensraum*, both of which are amply documented, played the key role in his decision to attack Russia in June 1941.

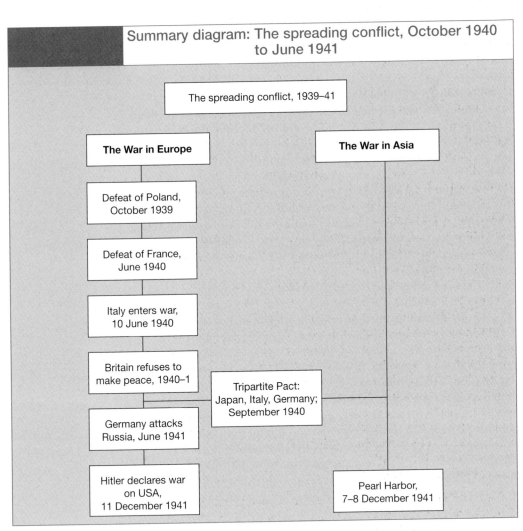

Summary diagram: The spreading conflict, October 1940 to June 1941

The spreading conflict, 1939–41

The War in Europe

Defeat of Poland, October 1939

Defeat of France, June 1940

Italy enters war, 10 June 1940

Britain refuses to make peace, 1940–1

Germany attacks Russia, June 1941

Hitler declares war on USA, 11 December 1941

The War in Asia

Tripartite Pact: Japan, Italy, Germany; September 1940

Pearl Harbor, 7–8 December 1941

9 | The Key Debate

What were the causes of the Second World War?

Was the Second World War inevitable? Was it essentially a continuation of the First World War or an entirely different conflict which competent diplomacy could have prevented? In 1918 the Germans were defeated but not destroyed. Germany still remained potentially strong and ultimately capable of making a second attempt at dominating Europe. In that sense the Treaty of Versailles, which humiliated but did not permanently weaken Germany, could well be seen as the 'seed bed' of the Second World War. Arguably, the chain of crises that started with the German remilitarisation of the Rhineland and ended in the German attack on Poland owed its origins to the Versailles settlement. Does it therefore follow that Versailles made the Second World War inevitable?

Stresemann, Briand and Austen Chamberlain appeared for a time to be able to make the settlement work after modifying the reparation clauses. Nevertheless, it was clear that a revived Germany would still demand its drastic revision, as indeed Stresemann was already beginning to do by the late 1920s. In that sense, there was a natural continuity of aims between the Weimar Republic and the Third Reich. Yet despite Taylor's attempts to portray Hitler as a normal politician, his coming to power in January 1933, which was made possible by the catastrophe of the Great Depression, did make a crucial difference. He gave a new and powerful impetus not only to German revisionism but to German demands for *Lebensraum* in eastern Europe based on the doctrine of racial superiority. It was this that prompted him to invade Russia in 1941 leaving an undefeated Britain supplied by the USA on his other front.

To a certain extent the horrendous figure of Adolf Hitler obscures the fact that the British and French governments went to war to maintain their position as great powers rather than to wage a crusade against the evil force of Nazism. There is no doubt that Hitler's successes in eastern Europe in 1938–9 did threaten to destabilise the whole continent. After the German occupation of Bohemia, the British and French governments believed that they had no choice but to oppose Hitler if they wished to maintain any influence in Europe. Of course, they still kept the door open to negotiations, and pursued the increasingly vain hope of a general settlement with Germany, but essentially Britain and France were ready to risk war in 1939. Indeed the British Treasury was beginning to argue that Britain's financial position would decline after 1939, and that if war had to come, it was preferable sooner rather than later. In France, Daladier had steadied the economy and the aeronautical industry was rapidly expanding in early 1939.

It does seem, therefore, that Britain and France went to war in 1939, as they did in 1914, to contain Germany and safeguard their own Great Power status. Arguably, then it was a continuation of the same struggle, even though Italy and Japan were later to join Germany, and the USSR only became an ally of Britain after the German invasion of June 1941. As in 1917, the USA again became Britain's key ally, but only entered the war as a result of the Japanese attack on Pearl Harbor in December 1941 (see page 194).

Some key books in the debate

A. Adamthwaite, *France and the Coming of the Second World War* (Cass, 1977).

W.M. Carr, *Arms, Autarky and Aggression* (Arnold, 1972).

'Cato', *Guilty Men*, London, 1940 (reprinted Penguin, 1998).

J. Charmley, *Churchill: The End of Glory* (Hodder & Stoughton, 1993).

M. Cowling, *The Impact of Hitler* (CUP, 1975).

T.W. Mason, 'Some origins of the Second World War' in E.M. Robertson (ed.), *The Origins of the Second World War* (Macmillan, 1971).

R.J. Overy, *The Origins of the Second World War* (Longman, 1987).

R.A.C. Parker, *Chamberlain and Appeasement: British Policy and the Coming of the Second World War* (Macmillan, 1993).

R.A.C. Parker, *Churchill and Appeasement* (Palgrave, 2000).

R. Self, *Neville Chamberlain: A Biography* (CUP, 2006).

R. Shay, *British Rearmament in the Thirties: Politics and Profits* (Princeton University Press, 1977).

A.J.P. Taylor, *The Origins of the Second World War* (Arnold, 1961).

Study Guide: AS Question

In the style of OCR A

How far was British foreign policy to blame for the outbreak of war in Europe in 1939?

Exam tips

The page references are intended to take you straight to the material that will help you to answer the question.

The instruction 'How far … ?' tells you how to approach this question. The task here is to examine the reasons for the outbreak of European war and put them in a hierarchy of importance so you can judge the relative importance of British foreign policy among those causes. You need to consider a variety of the elements that made up British policy, for example:

- the development of post-First World War planning (including disarmament) (page 128)
- the focus on imperial rather than continental concerns (page 102)
- the Ten-Year Rule (page 128)
- attitudes to the USSR (pages 117–18)
- appeasement under Chamberlain, perhaps set in the larger context of British policy from 1919 and the feeling that Germany had legitimate demands after Versailles (pages 162–3).

If you stop there, you will not have answered the question because you will only have examined British policy, not weighed up its importance among all the causes of war in 1939. Assessment thus needs to move on to consider other causal factors, for example:

- the rise of aggressive nationalism in Germany and Italy (pages 146–9)
- the weakness of French policy (page 65)
- the legacy of Versailles (pages 105–6).

Note that the question specifies a date. The question does not just ask you to explain why war began, but why it began when it did. That means you must weigh up short-term causes as well as longer-term factors. Some focus in this needs to be given to the Polish crisis (pages 169–71 and 173–5) and the behaviour of the Soviet Union in 1939 (pages 171–2).

Study Guide: A2 Question

In the style of Edexcel

How far do you agree with the view that the Second World War developed primarily because of the determination of the British and French governments to maintain their position as Great Powers? Explain your answer, using Sources 1–3 and your own knowledge of the issues related to this controversy.

Source 1

From: T. Baycroft, Nationalism in Europe, *published in 1998.*

The interwar period can be seen as a time when the idea of the nation was more widely accepted than it had ever been in history. It was the official doctrine of the majority of states and was widely popular among their populations. The right-wing nationalists were able to take a leading position in several European nations through the kind of rhetoric we find in the speeches of Mussolini and Goebbels. Their influence was strong enough to enable them to use the patriotic and national myths which were already popular in order to support their policies of violence, aggression and expansion. These policies ultimately brought most of Europe and the world back into a war of nations between 1939 and 1945.

Source 2

From: D.G. Williamson, Access to History. War and Peace: International Relations 1878–1941, *published in 2009.*

To a certain extent the horrendous figure of Adolf Hitler obscures the fact that the British and French governments went to war to maintain their position as great powers rather than to wage a crusade against the evil force of Nazism. There is no doubt that Hitler's successes in eastern Europe in 1938–9 did threaten to destabilise the whole continent. After the German occupation of Bohemia, the British and French governments believed that they had no choice but to oppose Hitler if they wished to maintain any influence in Europe. Of course, they still kept the door open to negotiations, and pursued the increasingly vain hope of a general settlement with Germany, but essentially Britain and France were ready to risk war in 1939. Indeed the British Treasury was beginning to argue that Britain's financial position would decline after 1939, and that if war had to come, it was preferable sooner rather than later. In France, Daladier had steadied the economy and the aeronautical industry was rapidly expanding in early 1939.

It does seem, therefore, that Britain and France went to war in 1939, as they did in 1914, to contain Germany and safeguard their own Great Power status. Arguably, then it was a continuation of the same struggle … .

Source 3

From: Douglas Hurd, The Search for Peace, *published in 1997.*

The Versailles settlement was fundamentally defective. This was not because it was a compromise between idealism and reality. Every peace settlement contains such a compromise. But the Versailles compromise was particularly perverse. The ingenious diplomatic tinkering in the 1920s did not tackle its real deficiencies. The settlement could have deteriorated into untidy confusion and occasionally minor conflict. Thanks to the demonic ruthlessness of Adolf Hitler, it collapsed instead into a new cataclysmic world war.

Exam tips

The page references are intended to take you straight to the material that will help you to answer the question.

The question requires you to account for the outbreak of the Second World War. Why did German expansion in eastern Europe result in a broader conflict which negotiation in 1939 failed to prevent? The sources raise issues for you and can be used as the core of your plan. They contain points for and against the stated claim. Make sure you have identified all the issues raised by the sources, and also add in your own knowledge, both to make more of the issues in the sources (add depth to the coverage) and to add new points (extend the range covered).

Your answers will be stronger if you cross-refer between the sources rather than treating them separately. Note, for example, the scope to link the views of right-wing nationalists (Source 1) with the direct reference to Hitler's ruthlessness (Source 3) in challenging the Versailles settlement. There is also scope to link and contrast this with the observations in Source 2 which suggest that, in accounting for conflict, too much weight has been given to the 'horrendous figure of Adolf Hitler' and the 'crusade against the evil force of Nazism'.

There are differences of emphasis between the sources:

- Source 1 emphasises the influence of nationalism in promoting policies of 'aggression and expansion'.
- Source 3 refers to the 'demonic ruthlessness' of Hitler, but also sees a contribution to conflict in the fundamental deficiencies of the Versailles settlement.
- Source 2 gives weight to the motives of Britain and France in seeking to maintain their Great Power status, going so far as to observe that 'arguably it was a continuation of the same struggle' as in 1914. Source 2 also introduces the issue, of timing that Britain and France were 'ready to risk a war in 1939'.

You should integrate your own knowledge into a discussion of the significance of these factors. From your own knowledge you should explore:

- the significance of the economic and military strength of the powers in 1939 and the perception that 'if war had to come it was preferable sooner rather than later' (pages 180–1)
- the impact of the arms race (page 161)
- the parts played by Mussolini and Stalin (pages 170 and 171–2)
- the reasons for the failure of diplomacy in the immediate pre-war period (pages 166–7).

Remember to conclude by reaching a clearly stated judgement in relation to the claim in the question.

9 The Countdown to War in Asia 1931–41

POINTS TO CONSIDER

Japanese expansion into Manchuria and China had a major impact on the situation in Europe during the decade after 1941. Ultimately through the attack on Pearl Harbor the Japanese turned a predominantly European war into a global war. The nature of this impact, from 1931 to 1941, is studied under the following headings:

- The Manchurian crisis
- The outbreak of the Sino-Japanese War
- Japan and the Anti-Comintern Pacts 1936–9
- The road to Pearl Harbor 1940–1

Key dates

1931	September	Mukden incident
1933	February	Japan left the League of Nations
1936	November	Anti-Comintern Pact signed
1937	July	Japan attacked China
1940	September 27	Tripartite Pact signed by Germany, Italy and Japan
1941	July	Japan occupied southern Indo-China
	December 7–8	Japan attacked Pearl Harbor
	December 8	USA declared war on Japan
	December 11	Germany declared war on the USA

1 | The Manchurian Crisis

Arguably, the Japanese occupation of Manchuria in 1931 was a continuation of policies followed by Japanese governments since the defeat of Russia in 1905 (see page 37) when Japan had been awarded the lease of the South Manchurian Railway and the right to protect it with some 15,000 troops. In the late 1920s these concessions were threatened by the turmoil caused by the Chinese Civil War, which broke out in 1927 and was fought between the Nationalists and Communists.

Key question
Why did Japan occupy Manchuria?

Key date

Mukden incident: September 1931

Key figure

Lord Lytton (1876–1947)
British Governor of Bengal 1922–7. In 1931 he chaired the Lytton Commission in Manchuria.

Key question
What was the League's initial response to the occupation of Manchuria by Japan?

Key question
Why were both Britain and USA not ready to use force in the Manchurian crisis?

Key term

Gold standard
A system by which the value of a currency is defined in terms of gold. The value of the pound was linked to gold. On 20 September 1931 the pound was forced off the gold standard and its value fell from $4.86 to $3.49.

The Japanese occupation of Manchuria 1931

The failure of the Japanese government to deal with the impact of the Depression on the economy convinced the Japanese officer corps that it would have to act decisively and occupy the whole of Manchuria. This would then enable Japan to control the region's valuable coal and iron resources at a time when economic nationalism was already making it difficult for it to purchase these vital raw materials elsewhere. Consequently, Japanese officers in Manchuria decided to devise an incident which would provide the pretext for intervention. On 18 September 1931 a bomb exploded on the railway line just outside Mukden where both Chinese and Japanese troops were stationed. This was immediately blamed on the Chinese and provided the Japanese forces with the desired excuse to occupy not only Mukden but the whole of southern Manchuria.

The response of the League of Nations

China immediately appealed to the League of Nations, but the council responded cautiously. It first asked Japan to withdraw its troops back into the railway zone and, when this was ignored, sent a commission of inquiry under the chairmanship of **Lord Lytton**. The Japanese were able to complete the occupation of Manchuria and turned it into the satellite state of Manchukuo while the Lytton Commission was conducting a leisurely fact-finding operation in the spring of 1932.

Refusal of Britain and the USA to use force

It is easy to criticise the League for not acting more decisively, but without the commitment of the Great Powers it was not in the position to take effective action. Neither of the two most important naval powers, Britain and the USA, was ready to use force against Japan. From the Japanese point of view, the timing of the Mukden incident could not have been better. On 15 September a minor mutiny at the naval base at Invergordon, which was caused by a cut in the sailors' wages, threatened temporarily to paralyse the Royal Navy; and five days later Britain was forced off the **gold standard**. The USA, shell-shocked by the Depression, was unwilling to do more than denounce Japanese aggression. President Hoover, for instance, argued that economic sanctions would be like 'sticking pins in tigers' and would run the risk of leading to war.

It is sometimes argued that the British government and powerful financial interests in the City of London secretly supported Japan. It is true that Britain did have some sympathy with Japanese action in Manchuria. Like Japan it had commercial interests in China, which it felt were threatened by the chaos and civil war there. Britain also appreciated Japan's potential role in providing a barrier against the spread of Bolshevism from the USSR into northern China. Nevertheless, the real reason why Britain was not ready to urge more decisive action against Japan was that neither the government nor the people desired to fight a war on an issue that was not central to British interests. In February 1933 Sir John Simon, the Foreign Minister, told the House of Commons:

> I think I am myself enough of a pacifist to take the view that however we handle the matter, I do not intend my own country to get into trouble about it … There is one great difference between 1914 and now and it is this: in no circumstances will this government authorise this country to be party to this struggle.

The report of the Lytton Commission

It was not until September 1932 that the League received the Commission's report. Although it conceded that the treaty rights, which Japan had enjoyed in Manchuria since 1905, had made Sino-Japanese friction unavoidable, it nevertheless observed that 'without a declaration of war a large area of what was indisputably Chinese territory had been forcibly seized and occupied by the armed forces of Japan and has in consequence of this operation been separated from and declared independent of the rest of China'. It proposed that Japanese troops should withdraw back into the railway zone, and then both China and Japan should negotiate not only a treaty guaranteeing Japan's rights in Manchuria but also a non-aggression pact and a trade agreement.

Essentially the report was mistakenly based on the assumption that the Japanese had no territorial designs in China and were ready to compromise over Manchuria. When it was adopted unanimously, with the single exception of Japan, by the League Assembly on 24 February 1933, Japan withdrew from the League in protest. It was obvious that only armed intervention by the Great Powers would now be able to force Japan out of Manchuria, and that option was not politically realistic in 1933.

Key question
What were the recommendations of the Lytton report?

Key date

Japan left the League of Nations: February 1933

The consequences of the occupation

The Japanese occupation of Manchuria changed the balance of power in the Pacific. Japan had broken free from the restraints that had been imposed on it at the Washington Conference in 1922 by Britain and the USA (see page 128) and had guaranteed it access to valuable coal and iron ore resources. Above all, Japan was now in a favourable strategic position to plan a large-scale military invasion of China. The Manchurian incident is often seen as the first link in a chain of events that led to the Second World War. Later, a Liberal British MP, Sir Geoffrey Mander (1882–1962), argued that the 'pathway to the beaches of Dunkirk lay through the waste of Manchuria'.

Key question
What were the consequences of the Japanese occupation of Manchuria?

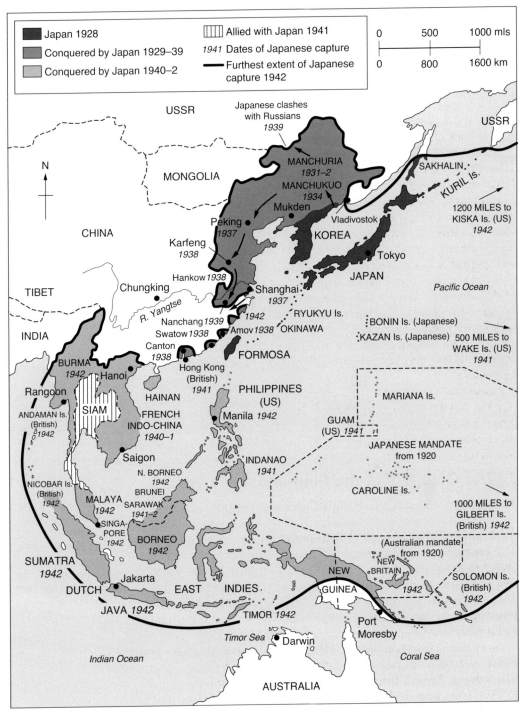

Manchuria, East Asia and the Pacific 1931–42.

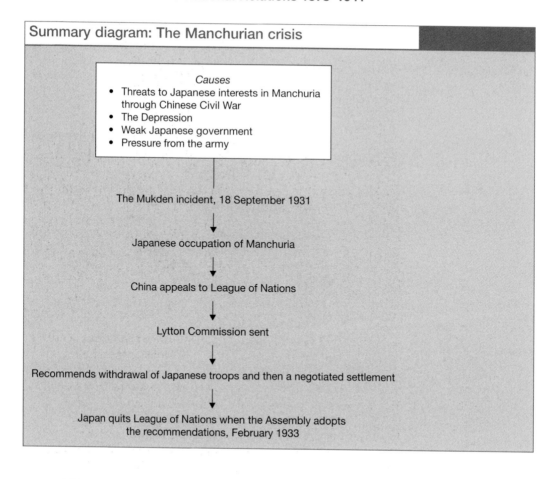

Summary diagram: The Manchurian crisis

Causes
- Threats to Japanese interests in Manchuria through Chinese Civil War
- The Depression
- Weak Japanese government
- Pressure from the army

↓

The Mukden incident, 18 September 1931

↓

Japanese occupation of Manchuria

↓

China appeals to League of Nations

↓

Lytton Commission sent

↓

Recommends withdrawal of Japanese troops and then a negotiated settlement

↓

Japan quits League of Nations when the Assembly adopts the recommendations, February 1933

2 | The Outbreak of the Sino-Japanese War

Key question
What impact did the Sino-Japanese War have on Britain, France and the USA?

The war in the Pacific, which ended with the dropping of atom bombs on Hiroshima and Nagasaki in 1945, began when a minor incident involving Japanese and Nationalist Chinese troops occurred at the Marco-Polo bridge near Beijing on 7 July 1937, and then rapidly escalated into full-scale hostilities. Japan was determined to turn northern China into an economic and political satellite and progressively to extend its influence throughout the whole of South-east Asia at the cost of the US and European colonial empires.

Japan attacked China: July 1937

Key date

Inevitably, the war emphasised the fragility of British and French power as neither country could afford simultaneous hostilities in Europe and the Far East. Thus, as tension mounted in Europe, both governments in practice avoided confrontation with the Japanese. In 1937 a senior French diplomat bluntly informed the US ambassador in Paris that:

> ... as long as the present tension existed in Europe it would be impossible for France to take part in any common action in the Far East, which might imply at some stage the **furnishing** of armed forces ... It was regrettable that this situation existed ... but the situation was a fact and had to be faced.

Furnishing
Provision.

Key term

Japanese infantry advance while displaying their rising sun flag in China, 1938.

Although the USA was equally reluctant to take military measures against Japan, the spreading conflict did enable President Roosevelt to begin the slow process of realigning the USA with the democracies against the Axis powers and Japan. In December 1937, when British and US ships on the Yangtze river were attacked by Japanese planes, Roosevelt, despite immediate Japanese apologies and offers of compensation, took the potentially important step of sending a US naval officer to discuss possible future co-operation between the British and US fleets; but when Congress found out, there was an explosion of anger and Roosevelt was severely criticised for compromising US neutrality. No wonder that Chamberlain observed that 'It is always best and safest to count on nothing from the Americans but words.'

Summary diagram: The outbreak of the Sino-Japanese War

Japan determined to bring northern China under her control and extend her influence throughout S.E. Asia

↓

Incident at Marco Polo Bridge, 7 July 1937

↓

Escalating conflict puts pressure on British and French colonial possessions

↓

Italy joins the Anti-Comintern Pact, 1937

↓

American Congress enforces strict neutrality despite Roosevelt's attempt to draw closer to Britain and France

3 | Japan and the Anti-Comintern Pacts 1936–9

While the Far Eastern war increased the pressure on Britain and France, it did not automatically follow that Japan, Italy and Germany would find it easy to form a common front against the democracies. In December 1936, Germany and Japan had signed the Anti-Comintern Pact. Its value for Japan was that it could be seen as a counter-thrust to increasing Soviet penetration of Mongolia and to the activities of the Comintern in China. Tokyo could signal to Moscow that it was no longer isolated.

A year later Italy joined the pact. Again, the advantage for Japan was that it associated Japan with the two Axis powers in a vague and symbolic pact that was primarily anti-communist (see page 152), but which potentially could also be directed against the Western Powers as well.

4 | The Road to Pearl Harbor 1940–1

One historian, J.G. Utley, has stressed that 'the Japanese–American conflict grew out of two mutually exclusive views of world order':

- Japan, regarding herself as a 'have-not' power, attempted to guarantee its access to markets and raw materials by gradually dominating economically and politically not only China but the whole of South-east Asia by creating the 'Greater Asia Co-Prosperity Sphere' (see page 6).
- To the Americans, as was made clear in the **Atlantic Charter**, it was an article of both faith and practical economics that they should be able to trade and invest freely in China and elsewhere.

With Germany having established a self-sufficient siege economy in Europe, it became even more imperative from the US point of view to stop Japan from doing the same in Asia. Washington responded to each fresh extension of Japanese power not only by building up its naval forces in the Pacific, but by restricting more and more tightly the exports of potential war materials to Japan, a measure which in fact only intensified the Japanese drive for economic self-sufficiency.

Both sides seemed therefore to be on a collision course. But history is never that simple. There were sufficiently ambiguous and conflicting signals coming out of Tokyo to encourage Roosevelt and the US State Department sometimes to believe that if sufficient economic pressure were applied, Japan would be forced to pull out of China and the influence of the army would be discredited on its government.

In June 1940 Hitler's victories strengthened the hand of the hawks in Tokyo who advocated the occupation of the European colonies in South-east Asia. A relatively moderate government, which wished to avoid confrontation with the USA, was replaced by a more anti-Western regime under **Fumimaro Konoe**, which

Key question
What did Japan gain from the Anti-Comintern Pact?

Key date
Anti-Comintern Pact signed: November 1936

Key question
Why did US–Japanese relations deteriorate in 1940–1?

Key term
Atlantic Charter
Statement of basic principles issued jointly by Roosevelt and Churchill in 1941.

Key figure
Fumimaro Konoe (1891–1945)
Japanese Prime Minister 1937–40 and from July 1940 to October 1941.

Key dates

Japan occupied southern Indo-China: July 1941

Japan attacked Pearl Harbor: 7 December 1941

USA declared war on Japan: 8 December 1941

Germany declared war on the USA: 11 December 1941

Key question
What were the immediate causes of the Japanese attack on Pearl Harbor?

openly proclaimed its aim of creating a Japanese-dominated Asia. Washington responded by suspending exports of vital aviation fuel and lubricating oil. To neutralise growing US opposition the Japanese then tried to negotiate a Four-Power pact with the Axis states and the USSR. They succeeded in reaching an agreement with Germany and Italy in September (see page 178) and they signed a five-year treaty of neutrality with Stalin the following spring. But the German invasion of the USSR in June 1941 terminated any prospect of a grand four-power alliance against Britain and the USA.

Konoe then urged that Japan should desert the Axis powers and come to an agreement with Britain and the USA, but he was overruled by his Foreign Minister and the armed services, who all believed that Hitler would quickly defeat the Soviets. Thus, Tokyo and Washington remained on a collision course.

Pearl Harbor
In July 1941 the Japanese occupied the southern half of French Indo-China and the Americans responded by imposing a comprehensive oil embargo on Japan. The embargo confronted the Japanese with the alternative of either seeing their war

The USS *Arizona* sinks in Pearl Harbor following the Japanese air attack on 7 December 1941.

machine paralysed through lack of oil or launching, within a few months at the latest, a pre-emptive strike against their enemies.

In early December they received verbal assurances from Ribbentrop that, in the event of a Japanese attack, Germany would also declare war against the USA, even though strictly speaking the Tripartite Pact did not commit Germany to such an action as it was a defensive alliance only. Thus, at dawn on 7 December the Japanese felt sufficiently confident to launch their attack on the US naval base at Pearl Harbor in the Hawaii islands.

Hitler's declaration of war on the USA on 11 December can in retrospect be seen as a major error since one cannot with certainty say that Roosevelt, confronted with war in the Far East, would have been able to persuade Congress to declare war on Germany as well. However, it could be argued that informally the Americans were already at war with Germany, as they were committed to supplying Britain with all it needed to survive. In that sense, Hitler's declaration of war was therefore both a recognition of reality and a politically calculated gesture of solidarity aimed at encouraging the Japanese to tie down the Americans in the Pacific so that they could not assist the British in the Atlantic and Europe.

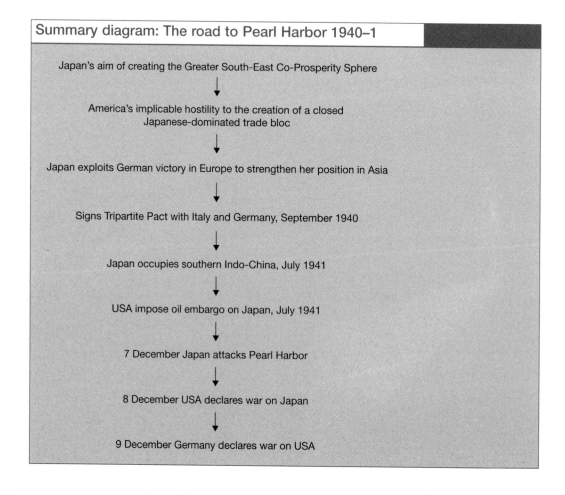

Summary diagram: The road to Pearl Harbor 1940–1

Japan's aim of creating the Greater South-East Co-Prosperity Sphere

↓

America's implacable hostility to the creation of a closed Japanese-dominated trade bloc

↓

Japan exploits German victory in Europe to strengthen her position in Asia

↓

Signs Tripartite Pact with Italy and Germany, September 1940

↓

Japan occupies southern Indo-China, July 1941

↓

USA impose oil embargo on Japan, July 1941

↓

7 December Japan attacks Pearl Harbor

↓

8 December USA declares war on Japan

↓

9 December Germany declares war on USA

5 | The Key Debate

The historian D.C. Watt argued that the Sino-Japanese war had 'little to do with Europe' and was not the start of the Second World War. Certainly the roots of Japanese expansion in China can be traced right back to the 1890s. However, diplomatic and military events in Europe and East Asia inevitably interacted with each other. Japan exploited the absorption of the Western Powers in the First World War to seize Germany's possessions in China and to maximise its own influence there.

In the 1930s Japanese aggression had a direct impact on the policies of Britain and France. The nightmare of a Japanese, German and Italian Triple Alliance, which the Anti-Comintern Pact of 1937 seemed to indicate was in the process of being formed, was one of the driving forces behind appeasement. Similarly, Hitler's victories in 1940 encouraged the hawks in Tokyo to put pressure on the Dutch and French possessions in east Asia. In the end it was the Japanese attack on Pearl Harbor and the subsequent declaration of war by Roosevelt on Japan that prompted Hitler in his turn to declare war on the USA and so fuse both the European and Asian wars.

Study Guide: AS Question

In the style of OCR A

Assess the impact of Japanese foreign policy in the period from 1931 to 1941.

Exam tips

The page references are intended to take you straight to the material that will help you to answer the question.

This question asks you to measure the effects of Japanese diplomatic and political activities and influence during a specific period. You will need to look globally as well as in the Asia–Pacific region because Japanese foreign policy affected the League of Nations and colonial powers such as Britain. Since the end date given is 1941, one effective strategy for your essay plan would be to link developments together to assess how far and in what way(s) each influenced:

- subsequent problems; and
- the build-up to war in the Far East.

So, demonstrate the connections between Japanese policy in Manchuria/China (page 187), their expansionist policies in the Pacific region (page 190) and deteriorating relations with the USA (pages 191–4). Then show why these developments led to the attack on Pearl Harbor.

Keep one focus at the global level and make it clear why the Japanese alliance with Germany affected not just Britain but international politics (page 192). The command 'assess the impact' tells you to weigh it and judge the importance/significance of its various strands. Keep your essay to the topic and you will score well. Tell the story of Japanese foreign policy in 1931–41 and you will score badly.

POINTS TO CONSIDER
This chapter concentrates on the main issues which anybody studying the period 1878–1941 needs to think about. The following key issues are analysed:

- The causes of the First World War
- The peace treaties
- The new global balance of power
- The fragile stabilisation 1924–9
- The road to war in Europe and Asia 1931–41

1 | The Causes of the First World War

Key question
To what extent was Germany the root cause of the First World War?

In retrospect the coming of the First World War dominates the history of the period 1879–1914. The war's causes were complex. Certainly the alliance system, nationalism, militarism, imperialism, economic rivalry and the arms race were all key factors, but at the heart of the problem that led to war was Germany.

Germany after the fall of Bismarck was a clumsy and often aggressive power. The construction of a modern navy, the attempt to destroy the Anglo-French *Entente* during the Moroccan crisis of 1906 and then the humiliation of Russia during the Bosnian crisis of 1908 all helped to isolate it and make it more dependent on Austro-Hungary. On the other hand, Germany was the strongest military and economic power in Europe, and arguably its demands 'for a place in the sun' were, by the nationalist and imperialist standards of the time, justified.

In 1914, Britain, Russia and France went to war to protect their own positions and ensure that Germany did not dominate Europe, and by extension the world, by claiming its 'place in the sun'. Germany too went to war for defensive reasons. The hostile alliance system, which its own power and policies had brought into being, forced it on to the defensive.

Bethmann Hollweg saw the Sarajevo crisis as a window of opportunity. If it could be successfully resolved to Austria's advantage, without the *Entente* backing Russia, then Germany's position in Europe would be greatly strengthened, the Franco-Russian alliance ruptured, and a way opened for future colonial expansion. If the *Entente* stood by Russia 'the war was better sooner than later'. Ironically, if Germany had pursued a more subtle and less aggressive policy, its economic power would in time have secured it peacefully a predominant position in Europe without the need for war.

2 | The Peace Treaties

Key question
How open to criticism are the peace treaties?

After 1945 the peace treaties of 1919–20 were blamed for the rise of Hitler and the Second World War. In its millennium issue a prestigious London weekly, *The Economist*, described the Treaty of Versailles as a major 'crime of the twentieth century ... whose harsh terms would ensure a second world war'. Yet in so many ways Versailles was a compromise peace: the German *Reich*, which had only been created in 1871, was left intact, and with the disintegration of the Austro-Hungarian and Russian Empires in eastern Europe, its position was in fact, in the medium to long term, actually strengthened.

The other peace treaties are arguably even harder to defend. Sèvres had to be revised, under threat of war, with a revived nationalist Turkey led by Kemal. St Germain, Neuilly and Trianon attempted to create a series of states in the Balkans and south-eastern Europe, along the lines suggested in the Fourteen Points. This involved, however, attempting to create nation states where there was no ethnic unity.

3 | The New Global Balance of Power

Key question
How stable was the new balance of power created by the peace treaties?

In 1919 the USA emerged from the First World War as the dominant world financial power. At this stage the USA still lacked the will to play the role of a Great Power. The refusal of the Republican-dominated Senate to ratify the Treaty of Versailles ensured that the USA remained on the sidelines of international politics until 1941. This placed France in a paradoxical position. As a consequence of Germany's defeat and the USA's return to isolation, it had become by default the world's greatest military power, but it was not a role that it could sustain.

In 1919, Russia, like Germany, had been a defeated power. The peace treaties had, in effect, been imposed on it as they were on Germany, Austria, Hungary, Bulgaria and Turkey. Russia had not been consulted about the borders of Turkey or of Poland. After the Bolshevik victory in the civil war, the Soviet Union's greatest priority was to defend the revolution and modernise the economy.

Like France in 1919, Britain still outwardly appeared to be a Great Power, but it was a status that it could not sustain. The British economy, already declining before 1914, had been seriously weakened in the war. Britain's empire too was increasingly being challenged by the rise of nationalism in India and the Middle East.

Japan made considerable gains at Versailles where it was able to increase its influence in China and in the Pacific at Germany's expense, and Japan was also given a permanent seat on the

Council of the League of Nations. However, as the Treaty of Washington showed, Japan was still regarded as an inferior power to the USA and Britain in the Far East.

Apart from benefiting from the destruction of the Austro-Hungarian Empire, which dominated her northern frontiers, Italy gained little from the peace treaties. It could not achieve its territorial ambitions in Africa and the Balkans until it could play off the Western Powers against Germany, a situation which was only possible after Hitler's rise to power.

4 | The Fragile Stabilisation 1924–9

Key question
Why was the period of stabilisation, 1924–9, so short lived?

At the end of the First World War European prosperity could not be rebuilt until the USA partially re-emerged from isolation to assist in restoring European finances after the French occupation of the Ruhr had triggered hyperinflation in Germany and also seriously weakened the franc. The brief stabilisation of the European economy that occurred between 1924 and 1929 had some similarities with the stabilisation of the western European economy after 1948. In 1924 a fragile economic and diplomatic equilibrium was created as a consequence of the Dawes Plan and the Locarno Agreements. As in 1948, US money did flow into Germany and help revive the economy. Confidence was further strengthened by a growing trust between France and Germany symbolised by the Briand–Stresemann relationship and the increasing talk about a European union, which to some extent anticipated the debates of the 1950s.

Are historians, then, correct to see the 1920s as a 'darkening twilight of the liberal era'? One US scholar, Charles S. Maier, points out that this period was in fact a time of new ideas for economic and political co-operation, which could have provided an escape from Great Power conflict. Indeed he argues that if it was a 'twilight decade, the 1920s was one of morning as well as dusk'. The crucial difference, however, between the two post-war periods is that in the 1920s the financing of the European economy was left to private investors, mainly American, while in the late 1940s, through the **Marshall Plan**, investment was guaranteed by the US state itself and was therefore more secure.

Key term
Marshall Plan
Programme of financial support by the US government to western Europe announced in 1948.

5 | The Road to War in Europe and Asia 1931–41

Key question
Why was the impact of the Depression on international politics so disastrous?

The Depression was instrumental in pushing the USA back into isolation just when Europe most needed it. German and Japanese expansion in the 1930s was facilitated by US inactivity in the Far East and the failure of the Anglo-French policy of appeasement in Europe. Only in March 1939, when Hitler occupied Bohemia and Britain guaranteed Poland, did it become quite clear that Britain could not tolerate unlimited German expansion in eastern Europe.

The last chance of deterring Hitler was destroyed when Stalin opted for the Nazi–Soviet Pact, rather than a military alliance with Britain and France, in order to regain some of Russia's former Polish territory. Were the events that led to war in 1938–9 inevitable? What role did miscalculation or just bad luck play in their unfolding? If you are convinced that Hitler was determined on war, then you will clearly be very sceptical of Taylor's argument that there was nothing inevitable about the outbreak of the European war in September 1939. On the other hand, would a crucial difference have been made if Britain and France had managed to keep Italy on their side or to negotiate a successful alliance with the Soviet Union? Is there any truth in the argument that the British feared Stalin more than they did Hitler? An even more important question is the role of appeasement. Was it, as many of the revisionist historians argue, the only rational policy open to Britain and France, given the hostility of Italy and Japan, or could Chamberlain have pursued a different policy, as R.A.C. Parker has indicated, of building up an alliance against Nazi Germany in the name of the League of Nations?

Until 1941 the Second World War consisted of several distinct wars that only gradually merged into one great war. It is arguable that President Roosevelt's determination to supply Britain with all necessary war material and the ever more serious clashes between the US navy and German U-boats in the summer of 1941 would in time have brought the USA into the war, but it was the massive miscalculation of the Japanese at Pearl Harbor, and Hitler's declaration of war on the USA on 11 December, that finally brought about this crucial event.

Summary diagram: International relations 1878–1941

	1914	1919	1941
Germany	The most powerful state in Europe, but felt deprived of colonies and wanted 'a place in the sun'	Defeated in First World War, but position in Europe potentially strengthened through collapse of Austria	Hitler gained power in 1933 and rearmed Germany. In 1940 Germany had conquered Continental Europe, but by December 1941 faced a war she could not win against Britain, the USSR and the USA
Italy	The least powerful of the Great Powers. Entered war on Allied side in 1915	Claimed that it was cheated of its just gains by the Allies in the peace treaties	1940 entered the war on German side. Only saved from defeat by German assistance in 1941. Mussolini overthrown 1943
Japan	August declared war on Germany and seized German territory in China	Kept most of this despite American opposition	1929–31 hard hit by Depression … Embarked on programme of expansion: Manchuria, 1931. Attacked China, 1937. Occupied southern Indo-China, 1941. Attacked Pearl Harbor, December 1941
France	Recovered from defeat of 1871, built up large colonial empire. Through alliance with Russia and *Entente* with Britain escaped from isolation imposed by Bismarck	Severely weakened by war, but emerged victorious, yet lacking an Anglo-American guarantee, was vulnerable to a German revival	Defeated in 1940 by Germany
Britain	Possessed huge colonial empire. Went to war to maintain its position as a world power	Emerged victorious from war, but also weakened by cost of war	After failure to appease Hitler, declared war with France on Nazi Germany in September 1939. By December 1941 junior partner of USA and USSR in Grand Alliance
Russia	Potentially a Great Power but weakened by internal divisions	Revolution of 1917 temporarily eliminated Russia as a major power	Nazi–Soviet Pact of August 1939 brought USSR back as a major player. Nearly destroyed by German invasion of 1941, but USSR emerged in 1945 as victor and superpower
USA	Economically the strongest global power. Only entered the war in 1917	Played key role in peace treaty, but Senate refused to ratify the Treaty of Versailles. Retreated to isolationism	1924–9 played a major part in financial reconstruction of Europe, but driven back into isolation by the Great Depression. Supported Britain economically in 1940–1. Opposed Japanese expansion. Brought into war by Japanese attack on Pearl Harbor in 1941
Austria	Her declaration of war on Serbia led to outbreak of First World War	Austrian Empire dissolved in 1918	1938 rump Austria was absorbed by Germany
Turkey	Joined Central Powers in October. Had lost almost all its Balkan territory by 1913	By the Treaty of Sèvres lost Middle Eastern provinces, but forced revision of Treaty at Lausanne in 1923	Remained neutral during Second World War

Some key books in the debate

V. Berghahn, *Germany and the Approach to War* (Macmillan, 1973).

R. Boyce and E.M. Robertson, *The Paths to War: New Essays on the Origins of the Second World War* (Macmillan, 1989).

J. Charmley, *Chamberlain and the Lost Peace* (Macmillan, 1989).

D. Dutton, *Neville Chamberlain* (Arnold, 2001).

R. Henig, *The Origins of The First World War*, 2nd edn (Routledge, 1993).

J. Joll, *The Origins of the First World War* (Longman, 1992).

J. Lowe, *The Great Powers, Imperialism and the German Problem, 1865–1925* (Routledge, 1994).

M. MacMillan, *Peacemakers* (Murray, 2001).

C. Maier, *Recasting Bourgeois Europe* (Princeton University Press, 1988).

R.A.C. Parker, *Chamberlain and Appeasement* (Macmillan, 1993).

G. Roberts, *The Soviet Union and the Origins of the Second World War* (Macmillan, 1985).

A.J.P. Taylor, *The Origins of the Second World War* (Hamish Hamilton, 1961).

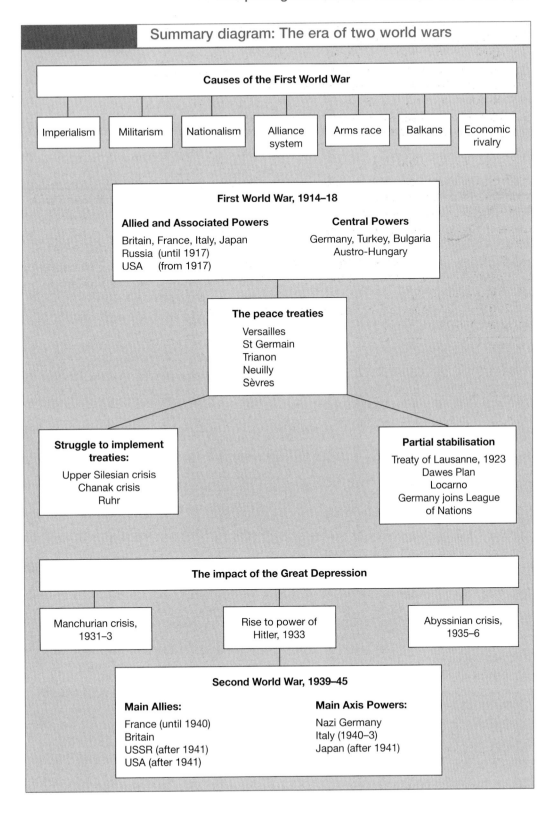

Summary diagram: The era of two world wars

Causes of the First World War

Imperialism | Militarism | Nationalism | Alliance system | Arms race | Balkans | Economic rivalry

First World War, 1914–18

Allied and Associated Powers

Britain, France, Italy, Japan
Russia (until 1917)
USA (from 1917)

Central Powers

Germany, Turkey, Bulgaria
Austro-Hungary

The peace treaties

Versailles
St Germain
Trianon
Neuilly
Sèvres

Struggle to implement treaties:

Upper Silesian crisis
Chanak crisis
Ruhr

Partial stabilisation

Treaty of Lausanne, 1923
Dawes Plan
Locarno
Germany joins League
of Nations

The impact of the Great Depression

Manchurian crisis,
1931–3

Rise to power of
Hitler, 1933

Abyssinian crisis,
1935–6

Second World War, 1939–45

Main Allies:

France (until 1940)
Britain
USSR (after 1941)
USA (after 1941)

Main Axis Powers:

Nazi Germany
Italy (1940–3)
Japan (after 1941)

Glossary

Anatolia   The core territory of the Turkish Empire, covering most of the modern Turkish republic.

Anglo-French colonial *entente*   An understanding reached by Britain and France on colonial issues. Sometimes called the *Entente cordiale* because it led to the restoration of good Anglo-French relations.

Anschluss   The union of Austria with Germany.

Anzac   Australian and New Zealand Army Corps.

Appeasement   The conciliation of a potential enemy by making concessions. The term is particularly applied to Neville Chamberlain's policy towards Nazi Germany.

Associated power   The USA was not bound by any treaties with Britain and France, 1917–19, and was free, if necessary, to pursue its own policies.

Atlantic Charter   Statement of basic principles issued jointly by Roosevelt and Churchill in 1941.

Autarchy   Economic self-sufficiency.

Autocratic   Absolute government by one person.

Balfour Declaration   A communication to the Zionists by A.J. Balfour, the British Foreign Secretary, declaring British support for establishing a national home for the Jews in Palestine.

'Balkan Prussia'   Bulgaria was compared to Prussia, which in the eyes of the Allies had an aggressive and militarist reputation.

Benevolent neutrality   Favouring one side while not officially supporting them.

Bismarckian constitution   Introduced by Bismarck in 1871; kept executive power in the hands of the Kaiser and the ministers he appointed.

Black Hand   This secret terrorist organisation was founded in May 1911 and by 1914 probably had about 2500 members. They included a considerable number of the army officers who had taken part in the Serbian revolution of 1903. Its aim was to work for the union of the Serbs living in the Austrian and Turkish Empires with Serbia.

Blank cheque   A free hand, unconditional support.

Boers   Descendants of Dutch settlers who had originally colonised South Africa.

Bolshevism   The ideology of the Russian Communist (Bolshevik) Party. It was based on the theories of Karl Marx and Lenin, which predicted the overthrow of capitalism and the creation of socialism.

Bonds   Certificates issued by a government or large company promising to repay borrowed money at a fixed rate of interest by a specified date.

Buffer state   Small state positioned between two much larger ones.

Capital ship   A battleship – a ship with heavy armour and powerful guns.

Carnegie Endowment for International Peace   An organisation founded by the industrialist Andrew Carnegie. It describes itself as being dedicated to advancing co-operation between nations.

Central Powers   The wartime alliance of Germany, Austria, Turkey and Bulgaria.

Charismatic   Inspiring great enthusiasm and loyalty.

China Squadron Units of the German navy used for protecting their possessions in the Far East.

Collateral security Bonds or property pledged as a guarantee for the repayment of a loan.

Collective security Security gained through joining an alliance or signing an agreement where the security of each state is guaranteed by the others.

Comintern The Communist international movement set up in 1919 to organise worldwide revolution.

Comity Community.

Condominium Joint control of a territory by two states.

Confederation A grouping of states in which each state retains its sovereignty.

Conference of Ambassadors Standing committee set up to supervise the carrying out of the Treaty of Versailles.

Congress The US parliament.

Congressional elections The elections to the US Senate and House of Representatives took place on 5 November 1918. The Republicans secured an overall majority of two seats in the Senate and 50 in the House.

Conscription Compulsory military service.

Convoy system Group of ships travelling together under escort.

Counter-revolutionary Person who opposes a revolution and wants to reverse its results.

Covenant Rules and constitution of the League of Nations.

Creditor nation A state which lends or invests surplus capital abroad.

Creeping barrage Friendly artillery fire aimed to eliminate opposition in front of advancing troops.

Customs union An economic bloc, the members of which trade freely with each other.

Defensive alliance An agreement between two states whereby each will come to the defence of the other if attacked.

Deliberative chamber An assembly appointed to debate or discuss issues.

Demilitarised Having all military defences removed.

Détente A process of lessened tension or growing relaxation between two states.

Devalue Reduce the value of.

Diplomatic revolution A complete change in alliances and relations between states.

Dominions The British Dominions of Australia, Canada, New Zealand and South Africa were self-governing, but part of the British Empire and Commonwealth, of which to this day they are still members.

Dreadnought A battleship of 17,900 tons compared to the conventional size of 16,000, its speed was 21 knots rather than 16, and it was much better armed than its predecessors.

Dunkirk In May 1940 the British Expeditionary Force in France was forced to retreat to Dunkirk and was only rescued by a risky sea evacuation.

Economic integration Mutual dependence and the coming together of national economies.

Élites The ruling classes.

Entente A friendly understanding between states, rather than a formal alliance.

Executive committee A committee which can take key decisions.

Fascism The Fascist Party was formed in Italy by Mussolini in 1919.

Fatherland's Party The party was founded close to the end of 1917 and represented political circles supporting the war. By the summer of 1918 it had around 1,250,000 members.

Federation   A system of government in which several countries or regions form a unity but still manage to remain self-governing in internal affairs.

Fixed ratio   A scheme whereby Germany would agree not to increase the number of ships beyond a certain percentage of the British fleet.

Formal annexation   Taking over full control of a territory by another power.

Free trade   Trade between nations unimpeded by tariffs.

Free trade zone   An area where countries can trade freely without restrictions.

Fulfilment   A policy aimed by Germany at extracting concessions from Britain and France by attempting to fulfil the Treaty of Versailles.

Furnishing   Provision.

General staff   Military office which plans operations and administrates an army.

German measures to stabilise the mark In November 1924 the devalued German currency was replaced temporarily by the *Rentenmark* and then in August 1924 by the new *Reichsmark*, which was put on the gold standard. Theoretically this meant that paper bank notes could be converted into agreed, fixed quantities of gold.

German satellite   A state completely dominated by Germany.

Gold standard   A system by which the value of a currency is defined in terms of gold. The value of the pound was linked to gold. On 20 September 1931 the pound was forced off the gold standard and its value fell from $4.86 to $3.49.

Great Depression   The world economic slump from 1929 to 1933.

Greater Asia Co-Prosperity Sphere   A bloc of territory dominated and exploited by Japan which embraced Manchuria, China and parts of South-east Asia.

Japan's aim was to create a self-sufficient bloc free of the Western Powers and under its own control.

Honest broker   Impartial mediator.

Howitzer   A gun for firing shells at relatively high trajectories, with a steep angle of descent.

Hyperinflation   Massive daily increases in the prices of goods and in the amount of money being printed.

Ice-free port   A seaport that is free of ice in the winter, so that it can be used throughout the year.

Imperial War Cabinet   A cabinet made up of Prime Ministers of the self-governing Commonwealth countries.

Imperialism   The policy of acquiring and controlling dependent territories carried out by a state.

Inter-Allied commissions   Allied committees set up to deal with particular tasks.

Inter-Allied consensus   Agreement between the Allies.

International civil service   A permanent administration made up of officials from all the member states.

Inviolability   Not to be changed or violated.

Isolationist   Remaining aloof from international politics.

Isolationists   US politicians who were opposed to any US commitments or entanglements in Europe or elsewhere.

Jameson raid   Armed intervention in the Transvaal led by the British politician in Cape Colony, Leander Starr Jameson, over the New Year weekend of 1895–6.

Khedive   The title used by the governor and ruler of Egypt and the Sudan.

Kiaochow   In 1897 the Germans seized Kiachow in revenge for the murder of two missionaries. They also secured mining rights in the neighbouring province of Shantung.

League of Patriots The French far-right league, founded by the nationalist poet Paul Déroulède in 1882.

Lebensraum Literally 'living space' which Hitler hoped to acquire in Russia for German settlement.

Left Term used to denote parties stretching from Social Democrat to Communist.

Liberal ideology Belief in constitutional government and individual and economic freedom.

Locarno spirit The optimistic mood of reconciliation and compromise that swept through Europe after the signing of the Locarno Treaties.

Luftwaffe The German air force.

Maginot line A line of concrete fortifications, which France constructed along its borders with Germany. It was named after André Maginot, the French Minister of Defence.

Magyar Ethnic Hungarians.

Mandates Ex-German or Turkish territories entrusted by the League of Nations to one of the Allied powers to govern in accordance with the interests of the local population.

Marshall Plan Programme of financial support by the US government to western Europe announced in 1948.

Mesopotamia An ancient Greek term literally meaning the land between two rivers: the Tigris and Euphrates. Today this area consists of Iraq, as well as some parts of north-eastern Syria, south-eastern Turkey and south-western Iran.

Militarism Excessive emphasis on military ideals and strength. The supremacy of military values such as discipline, obedience and courage in a society.

Milliard One thousand million; now largely superseded by the term billion.

Mitteleuropa A German-controlled central Europe.

Mobilisation Preparing the armed forces for war.

Moratorium Temporary suspension of payments.

Multilateral commitments Membership of international organisations.

'Mutilated victory' A victory which was scarred by the refusal of the Allies to give Italy what had been promised.

National Service League A British pressure group founded in February 1902 to alert the country to the inability of the army to fight a major war and to propose the solution of national service.

National Socialism German National Socialism had many similarities with Fascism, but its driving force was race, and in particular anti-Semitism.

Nationalism A patriotic belief by a people in the virtues and power of their nation.

Nation-state A state consisting of an ethnically and culturally united population.

Neutral zone A belt of territory which would be occupied by neither German nor Allied troops.

Non-aggression pact An agreement between two or more countries not to resort to force.

Nuremberg trials The trials of German war criminals in Nuremberg.

Official historian A historian appointed by the government to write the history of the war.

Opportunism Seizing the opportunity when it occurs.

Pan Slavs Russian nationalists who believed that the Slavs in central and south-eastern Europe should be liberated by their fellow Slavs in Russia.

Pandemic   An epidemic on a global scale.

Parliamentary government   A government responsible to and elected by parliament.

Passive resistance   Refusal to co-operate, stopping short of actual violence.

Peace bloc   A group of states committed to opposing aggressor powers.

People's war   Popular war fought by the mass of the people.

Permanent Court of International Justice   An institution set up at The Hague, the Netherlands, by Article 14 of the Covenant of the League of Nations in 1920.

Phoney war   The period October 1939 to March 1940 when there was no fighting in western Europe.

Plan 17   The French plan to make a frontal attack on Germany if war broke out.

Plebiscite   A referendum, or vote by the electorate on a single issue.

Power politics   International relations that are based on force rather than moral principles.

Pressure group   An association formed to promote a particular interest by influencing government policy.

Programme school   Historians who believe that Hitler had a specific programme to carry out.

Proletarian nation   A nation that lacked an empire and raw materials. Like the proletariat (workers) it was poor.

Protection   Stopping foreign goods by levying tariffs or taxes on imports.

Protectorate   A territory that is controlled and protected by another state.

Provisional government   A government in power until the holding of elections.

Prussia   The largest federal state in Germany.

Putsch   Takeover of power.

Pyrrhic victory   A victory won at such a high cost that it damages the victor.

Quadruple Alliance   An alliance of four powers.

Ratified   Having received formal approval from parliament.

Red Army   The Soviet army.

Regional power   A state that is powerful only in its own part of the world. It is not a global power.

Reich   Empire.

Reichsbank   The national bank of Germany.

Reichstag   The German parliament.

Reichswehr   The German army 1919–35.

Reparations   Compensation paid by a defeated power to make good the damage it caused in a war.

Republic   A state ruled by a president rather than a monarch.

Rhineland separatism   A movement favouring separation of the Rhineland from Germany.

Right   Term used to denote parties stretching from Conservative to Nazi or Fascist (extreme right).

Rump Bulgaria   What was left of Bulgaria after its partition at the Berlin Congress.

Schlieffen Plan   It envisaged a two-front war against France and Russia. France was to be defeated within a month by a flanking movement through Belgium, Holland and Luxembourg and then the mass of the German army would move eastwards to deal with Russia. The plan was later revised to omit Holland.

Second industrial revolution   The development of electrical, chemical and engineering industries beginning at the end of the nineteenth century.

Secret annex   Secret addition to a treaty.

Secret diplomacy   Diplomatic contacts, meetings and decisions which are not made public.

Self-governing principality   A semi-independent state ruled by a prince.

Senate   The upper house of the US Congress.

Slavs   An ethnic group in central and eastern Europe, of which the Russians are the largest component.

Social cohesion   The social unity of a country.

Social Darwinism   The application of Darwin's theory of the survival of the fittest to international relations, justifying the absorption of smaller, weaker states by more powerful ones.

Social imperialism   A policy aimed at uniting all social classes behind plans for creating and expanding an empire.

Socialism   A belief that the community as a whole rather than individuals should control the economy.

Soviets   Elected councils.

SPD   Social Democratic Party of Germany. Its leaders were hostile to Bolshevism and believed in parliamentary government.

State visit   Ceremonial visit by a head of state.

Status quo   A Latin term to denote the state of affairs as it exists at the moment.

Straits zone   The shores along the Straits of Dardanelles and Bosphorus were occupied by Allied troops.

Strategy   The military planning and management of war.

Stresa Powers   The powers who attended the Stresa Conference in 1935.

Successor states   States that were created after the collapse of Austria-Hungary.

Sudeten Germans   Ethnic Germans who had been settled in the Sudetenland since the thirteenth century.

Superpower   A state much larger in size and possessing much larger armed forces than most of the other powers.

Supreme Economic Council   Allied body with the power to deal with economic issues.

Synthetic materials   Objects imitating a natural product but made chemically.

Tariffs   Taxes placed on imported goods to protect the home economy.

Total war   A war waged by a state in which the whole population is involved and every resource is used to further the war.

Trade monopoly   Exclusive control of trade.

Transvaal   This was an independent state, although by agreement with the British in 1884 it could not conclude treaties with foreign powers without their agreement.

Triad   A group of three.

Triple *Entente*   The name often applied to the co-operation of Britain, France and Russia 1907–17.

Two-front war   A war in which fighting takes place on two geographically separate fronts.

Unrestricted submarine warfare   Sinking by German submarines (called U-boats) of all merchant ships, Allied or neutral, engaged in carrying goods to or from Allied states.

USSR   The Union of Soviet Socialist Republics. The new Bolshevik name for Russia.

Vacuum of power   Territories left undominated by another state after the withdrawal or collapse of the original ruling power.

Volte-face   An about turn; a sudden and complete change of policy.

War guilt   Carrying the blame for starting the war.

War of attrition   A war in which both sides seek to exhaust and wear each other down.

War party   A group of ministers supporting Britain's entry into the war.

Waterloo   In 1815 the British defeated Napoleon in the Battle of Waterloo.

Wehrverein   Literally 'Defence League'. This pressure group was founded in Germany in 1912 to press for an increase in the size of the army.

Weltpolitik   Literally 'world policy' or a policy that attempted to make Germany a global power.

White Russians   The name given to members and supporters of the counter-revolutionary 'White' armies, which fought against the Bolshevik Red Army in the Russian Civil War (1918–21).

Young Turk Movement   The name given to a reform movement in the Turkish Empire. Its members were originally exiles in western Europe.

Zionists   Supporters of Zionism, a movement for re-establishing the Jewish state.

Index

Aaland Islands dispute 124–5
Abyssinia 5, 6, 21, 135, 146–8, 149, 151, 152, 153
Afghanistan 42
Africa, European interests (1897) 21–2
Albania 48–9, 98, 118, 125
   Italian invasion 170
America, see United States of America
Anglo-French entente 41
Anglo-Russian entente 42
Anschluss 97, 18, 163, 164–5, 166
Anti-Comintern Pact 152, 170, 173, 192, 195
Appeasement 8, 162–3, 174, 195, 199–200, see also Munich Agreement
Austria
   attempted Nazi coup 138–9, 144–5
   Italian stance 144–5, 152, 165
   ultimatum to Serbia 51
   see also Anschluss
Austria-Hungary 6, 9, 10, 18, 24, 43, 57, 62, 74, 76, 77, 84, 96, 98
   armistice agreement 77
Austro-German Dual Alliance (1879) 17–18
Axis, Rome–Berlin Pact 148, 152

Balkan crisis 46–9
Beneš, Eduard 167
Berlin Congress 17–18
Bethmann Hollweg, Theobold von 50, 51, 55, 69, 70, 73, 197
Bismarck, Otto von 14, 15–20, 21–2, 24–7, 31, 32, 55
Blum, Léon 150, 151
Boer War 34–5
Bonnet, Georges 174
Boulanger, Georges 22, 24, 25
Briand, Aristide 112–14, 115, 116, 127, 130–1, 139, 180, 199, see also Kellogg–Briand Pact
Britain
   extent of power 7–8
      guaranteeing Poland 8, 169–71
   Hitler's attempts to negiotiate peace 177–8
   Japanese alliance 35, 37, 38, 41, 61, 128

militarism 3
   policy towards Nazi Germany 143, see also Appeasement
   rearmament 160, 161
   refusal to join Triple Alliance 31–2
   relations with Russia 18, 117–18, see also Anglo-Russian entente; War, Russo-Japanese
Brüning, Heinrich 116, 137
Bulgaria 7, 13, 16, 18, 23–6, 48, 49, 53, 66, 77, 87, 92, 96, 98, 127, 170, 178, 198, see also Central Powers

Central Powers 6, 7, 19, 61, 62, 66, 67, 69, 73, 74, 82, 87, 201
Chamberlain, Austen 112, 130–1, 180
Chamberlain, Neville 160, 162–3, 164–5, 166, 167, 170, 171, 173, 191, 200, see also Appeasement; Munich Agreement
Chanak crisis 100, 101
Chautemps, Camille 165
China 35, 192, 195, 198
   former German territories 93
   Japanese attack 190–1, 195
   see also Manchuria
Churchill, Winston 65, 113, 162, 163, 178, 192
Clemenceau, Georges 70, 73, 79, 83–5, 87–8, 89, 91–2, 93, 94
Cologne zone 112, 115
Conferences:
   Geneva (1922) 104
   Geneva Disarmament (1932–4) 129, 137, 138
   Hague (1929) 16, see also Young Plan
   Lausanne (1932) 137
   London (1924) 110–11
   Munich (1938) 168
   Paris (1919) 4, 54, 75, 82–95
Corfu incident 125–6
Czechoslovakia 77, 84, 92, 94, 96–7,
   destruction 164, 168–9
   Hitler's threats 158, 159, 161, 167
   pact with Yugoslavia 118
   Russian support 168
   treaty with France 118, 142, 166
   see also May Crisis; Munich Agreement; Sudeten Crisis

D'Annunzio, Gabriele 98
Daladier, Eduard 167
Dalmatia 6, 62, 83, 88, 97, 98
Danzig 92–3, 103, 114, 122, 170, 171, 174
Dawes Plan 9, 105, 109–11, 112, 117, 130–1
Delcassé, Theophile 40
Depression, Great 4, 5, 7, 9, 116, 129, 135–6,
    140, 141, 145, 146, 180, 187, 199, 201
Disarmament 84, 87, 90–1, 102, 115–16,
    128–9, 137, 138
Dollfuss, Engelbert 145

Entente cordiale, see Anglo-French colonial
    entente

Falkenhayn, Erich von 61, 67, 68
Fascism 4
Fashoda crisis 34
Ferry, Jules 22
First World War, see War, First World
Fiume 87–8, 93, 98,
Foch, Ferdinand 75, 90–1
Fourteen Points 70, 767, 83, 84, 91, 94, 98,
    100, 198
France
    extent of power 7
    Franco-Balkan treaties 118, 164
    Franco-British Agreement 7, 38, 40–1
    Franco-British naval staff talks 45
    Franco-British relations 34
    Franco-German relations 7, 12–13, 21–2,
        25, 27–8, 41–4, 143
    Franco-Italian relations 148, 158, see also
        Rome Agreement
    Franco-Polish Alliance 118
    Franco-Russian Alliance 7, 8, 22, 32, 33, 38
    Franco-Russian naval convention and
        military staff talks 45
    Franco-Russian relations 26, 41
    Franco-Soviet Treaty of Mutual Assistance
        142–3, 145
    rearmament 160, 161
Franco, Francisco (General) 150–1, 175
Franz Ferdinand, assassination 50

Gallipoli landing 65
Geneva Protocol 128, see also Conferences
Germany 28
    armistice agreement (1918) 77
    as 'have-not' power 5
    Austrian coup attempt 138–9, 144–5
    colonies 93
    creation of German Empire 12–15, 22

destruction of Czechoslovakia 164, 168–9
disarmament 84, 87, 90–1, 102, 115–16,
    128–9, 137, 138
expansion into Central Europe (1935–9)
    164–9
invasion of USSR 9, 24, see also Nazi–Soviet
    Pact
Japanese declaration of war 61
militarism 3
nationalism 3
reaction to British guarantee 170–1
reaction to Versailles Treaty 94–5
rearmament 139, 159–60, 161
relations with Russia, see Nazi–Soviet Pact
reparation demands 89–90
responsibility for First World War 54–6
rivalry with Britain 5, 38–40
war guilt 89
see also War, First World; War, Second World
Göring, Hermann 160
Greece 61, 92, 98, 99, 100
    Anglo-French guarantee 169–71
    see also Corfu incident; War, Balkan
Grey, Edward 52

Halifax, Lord 174
Harding, Warren 128, 129
Henlein, Konrad 166, 167
Hitler, Adolf 140–1
    as a cause of Second World War 180–1,
        200
    attempts to negiotiate peace with Britain
        177–9
    declaration of war on the USA 194
    effect of May crisis 166–7
    foreign policy 137–9, 158–9, 164
    hatred of Bolshevism 179
    invasion of Poland 174–5
    on outbreak of Second World War 173–5
    plan to rebuild German power 148–9
    rise to power 5, 61, 137–9
    signing of the Anti-Comintern Pact 152
    view of appeasement 162
    view of Mussolini 126
    view of Stalin 173
    vision for Germany 5, 135, 137
    see also Munich Agreement; Nazi–Soviet
        Pact
Hoare–Laval Pact 146–7
Hossbach memorandum 158–9
Hungary
    seized by communists 129
    territories 92, 96
    see also Austria-Hungary; Treaties, Trianon

Imperialism 2–3
Indo-China 22, 189, 193
Istria 62, 98
Italy 201
    Abyssinia crisis 146–8
    as 'have-not' power 4, 5–6
    effect of Treaty of London 6, 62, 85
    relations with France 148, 158, *see also*
        Rome Agreement
    relations with Nazi Germany 6
    stance on Austria 144–5, 152, 165
    unification 5
    see also Mussolini, Benito; Rome–Berlin Axis

Jameson raid 34–5
Japan 6, 36, 198–9, 201
    aims at Peace Conference (1919) 86, 87, 90,
        93
    American relations 93, 128, 181, 190–4,
        199
    Anglo alliance 35, 37, 38, 41, 61, 128
    Anti-Comintern Pact with Germany 152,
        192
    as 'have-not' power 6
    attack on China 190–1, 195
    attack on Pearl Harbor 9, 181, 192–4, 200
    declaration of war on Germany 61
    effect of Great Depression 135
    Manchurian Crisis 186–9
    Meijii Restoration 36
    membership of League of Nations 120, 198
    reaction to Munich Agreement 168
    relationship with League of Nations 86,
        187, 188, 198–9
    signing of Tripartite Pact 178
    war with Russia 37, 38, 41, 44
Jodl, Alfred 159

Kellogg, Frank B. 129
Kellogg–Briand Pact 129
Kemal, Mustapha 10, 100–1, 198
Keynes, John Maynard 106
Klotz, Louis-Lucien 89
Konoe, Fumimaro 192, 193

Laval, Pierre 146, 147
League of Nations 52, 83, 93, 94, 95, 111,
        113, 119, 130
    attitude to invasion of Abyssinia 146–7
    Covenant 83, 89, 119–20, 122–3
    Germany joins 115
    Germany's withdrawal from 138
    organs 120–1

powers and role in solving international
        disputes (1920–5) 121–3
    role in Upper Silesia frontier 103
    successes 126–7
    US refusal to participate 9, 70, 83, 95
    welfare, medical and economic work 123–4
    see also Mandates
League of the Three Emperors 15, 16, 24
Lebensraum 5, 135, 158, 179, 180
Lenin, V.I. 55, 74, 117, 144
Lloyd George, David 44, 70, 73, 79, 83, 85,
        87, 89, 90, 91–2, 93, 94, 99, 104, 125
Locarno spirit 115, 127, *see also* Treaties
Lodge, Henry Cabot 95
Loucheur, Louis 89
Lytton, Lord 187
Lytton report 187, 188

Manchuria 6, 35–6, 37, 127, 129, 135, 145,
        186–9, 201
Mandates 83, 93, 100, 122–3, 127, 189
May Crisis 166–7
Moltke, Helmut von 49, 60, 61
Moroccan crises 41–2, 43–5, 56
Munich
    Agreement 168, 173, 174
    putsch 140
Mussolini, Benito 126, 201
    and Pact of Steel 173, 174, 175
    declaration of war on Britain and France
        177
    invasion of Albania 170
    involvement with Abyssinia 146–8, 149
    relations with France 148, 158, *see also*
        Rome Agreement
    relations with Nazi Germany 8, 24, 138–9,
        152
    rise to power 4, 6
    role in four-power talks 168, 175
    stance on Austria 144–5, 152, 165
    support of General Franco 150
    see also Corfu incident; Rome–Berlin Axis

National Socialism 4
Nationalism 3, 4, 34–7, 40, 54–5, 72–3, 79,
        129, 135, 166, 197
Nazi–Soviet Pact 9, 145, 151, 171–3, 174, 176,
        179, 200, 201
Nuremberg
    rally 167
    trials 158

Orlando, Vittorio 84, 85, 87–8, 98
Ottoman Empire, *see* Turkish Empire

Papen, Franz von 137
Permanent Court of International Justice 111, 121
Phoney war 176
Plebiscites 91, 93, 94, 97, 102, 103, 124, 125, 165
Poincaré, Raymond 45, 56, 104–5, 110, 131
Poland 8, 74, 76, 117, 129
    Anglo-French guarantee 8, 169–71, 174, 199
    French alliance (1921) 118
    German invasion 172, 174–6
    non-aggression pact with Germany 138, 142
    post-First World War territorial settlement 92–3, 102–3, 112, 114
    Russian relations 142–3, 168
    Vilna dispute 124
    see also Nazi–Soviet Pact

Rathenau, Walter 89, 103–4
Red Army 8, 87, 102–3, 141
Reparations 83, 85, 89–90, 96, 102, 103–4, 109, 110, 116, 123, 137
Rhineland 84, 91–2, 94, 105, 112, 113, 115–16, 142, 148–9, 153, 165, 180
Romania 17, 20, 49, 68, 74, 76, 92, 97–8, 118, 168, 172, 178
    Anglo-French guarantee 169–71
Rome Agreement 142
Rome–Berlin Axis 148, 152
Roosevelt, Franklin 145, 191, 192, 194, 195, 200
Ruhr 15
    occupation 45, 103, 104–5, 109, 110–11, 112, 114, 125, 130–1, 199
Russia
    as a future great power 8–9
    German invasion (1941) 178–9
    in Locarno era 117–18
    intervention in Spanish Civil War 151
    reaction to Nazi Germany 145
    reasons for Nazi–Soviet Pact 8–9, 171–2
    relations with Britain 18, 117–18
        see also Anglo-Russian entente; War, Russo-Japanese
    war with Japan 37, 38, 41, 44
    see also Nazi–Soviet Pact; Treaty of Brest-Litovsk

Saar 91, 92, 98, 115, 122, 165
Schacht, Hjalmar
Schleicher, Kurt von 137
Schlieffen Plan 42, 60

Schuschnigg, Kurt von 164
Second World War, see War, Second World
Silesia 13, 61, see also Upper Silesia
South Africa 34–5, 39, 85, 93
Stalin, Joseph 144
    exploitation of 'phoney war' 176–7
    Hitler's view 173
    implications of opting for Nazi–Soviet Pact 200
    Tripartite Pact membership demand 178
    see also Russia
Stresa Declaration 139, 143, 164
Stresemann, Gustav 5, 105, 111, 112, 114, 115–16, 117, 118, 130, 139, 180, 199
Sudeten crisis 165–7
Sykes–Picot Agreement 99–100

Three Emperors' Alliance 18–19,
    see also League of the Three Emperors
Tirpitz, Alfred von 39–40, 49
Trans-Siberian Railway 35
Treaties
    Anglo-Japanese (1902) 37
    Brest-Litovsk 74
    Lausanne (1923) 101, 126
    Locarno 112–16, 117, 119, 130–1, 139, 142, 158, 164, 180
    London (1913) 49
    London (1915) 6, 62, 85
    London Naval (1929) 128
    Neuilly 98, 198
    Rapallo (1920) 98; (1922) 104, 117, 143
    Reinsurance 24–7, 31
    Riga 103
    St Germain 96–7, 198
    Sèvres 10, 99, 100–1, 198
    Trianon 97–8, 118, 198
    Versailles 5, 7, 88–95, 97, 102–6, 111, 112, 114, 116, 118, 122, 123, 124, 138, 139, 143, 145, 149, 158, 198
    Washington Four Power (1922) 128
Triple Alliance 19–20
Triple Entente 30–45
Turkey 25, 61–2, 76
    armistice agreement 78
    Mosul dispute 126–7
    see also Central Powers; Turkish Empire; Treaties, Sèvres
Turkish Empire 9, 10, 13, 15, 16, 18, 20–1, 23, 28, 47–9, 76, 78

United States of America (USA)
    as a future great power 9–10
    attack on Pearl Harbor 9, 181, 192–4, 200

declaration of war on Germany 9
refusal to participate in League of Nations 9,
70, 83, 95
Upper Silesia 15, 92–3, 94, 103, 114, 125
USSR, *see* Russia

Vilna dispute 124

Wall Street Crash 135
War
  Balkan 47–9
  First World 4, 5, 9, 14, 50–6, 60–79, 85, 119,
    159–60, 180, 195, 197–8, 199, 201
  Second World 9, 10, 106, 140, 173–9, 180–1,
    201
  Sino-Japanese 158, 188, 190–1, 195
  Russian Civil 8, 82, 87, 102–3, 118

Russo-Japanese 37
Russo-Polish 8, 102–3
Spanish Civil 150–1
Wilhelm II 2, 27, 31, 32, 33, 34–5, 39, 41–2,
  49, 50, 51, 55, 76, 77, 85, 89
Wilson, Woodrow 69, 70, 76–7, 82, 83, 89, 91,
  93, 95, 98, 100, 128, *see also* Fourteen
  Points
World Disarmament Conference,
  see Conferences, Geneva Disarmament

Young Plan 9, 116,
Yugoslavia 77, 83, 96, 97, 98, 118, 125, 149,
  170,
  pact with Czechoslovakia 118

Zeligowski, Lucjan 124